IT WAS ALWAYS ABOUT THE WORK: A PHOTOJOURNALIST'S MEMOIR

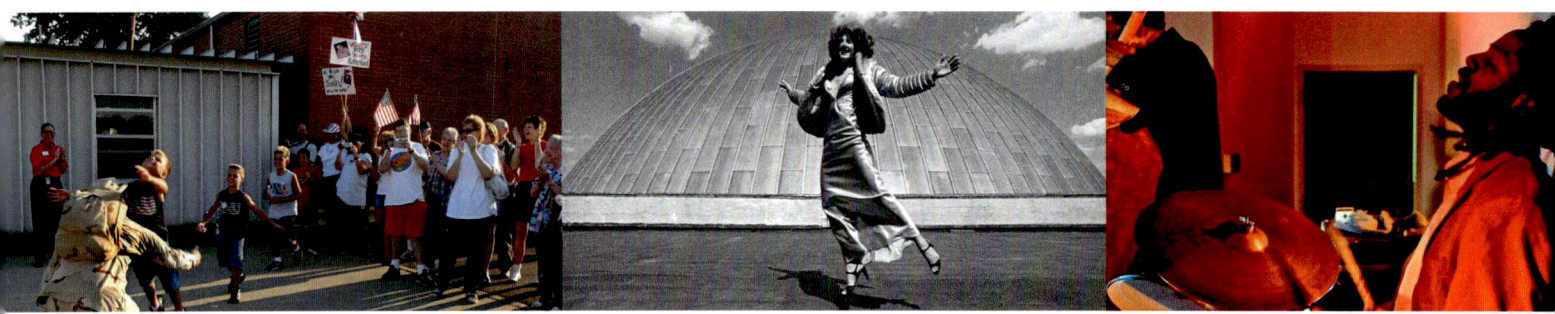

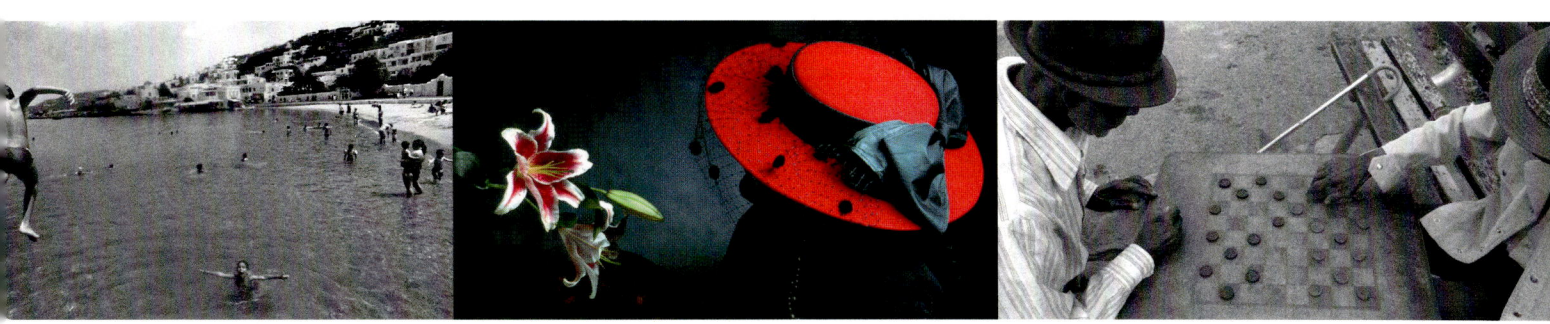

IT WAS ALWAYS ABOUT THE WORK
A PHOTOJOURNALIST'S MEMOIR

BY **MELVIN GRIER**
WITH MOLLY KAVANAUGH

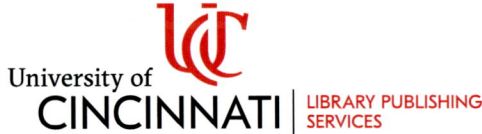

About Cincinnati Library Publishing Services (CLIPS)

CLIPS provides professional publishing services for digital and print publications, conference proceedings, journals, affordable textbooks and open educational resources produced by University of Cincinnati faculty, staff, and organizations with department sponsorship and funding. CLIPS encourages authors to publish in barrier-free open access formats. CLIPS, an imprint of the University of Cincinnati Press, is committed to publishing rigorous, peer-reviewed, leading scholarship in social justice, community engagement, and Cincinnati/Ohio history.

University of Cincinnati Press and Library Publishing Services

Copyright © 2023

Cincinnati, Ohio

All rights reserved. No part of this book may be reproduced or utilized in any form or by any means, electronic or mechanical, or by any information storage and retrieval system, without written permission from the publisher. Permission requests regarding this work should be sent to:

University of Cincinnati Press, Langsam Library, 2911 Woodside Drive, Cincinnati, Ohio 45221

ucincinnatipress.uc.edu

The publisher has deferred to the author's use of language when recalling descriptions of the local history and the daily newspaper business in the Cincinnati, Ohio, and Northern Kentucky area.

ISBN (hardback) 978-1-947603-65-3

ISBN (e-book, PDF) 978-1-947603-66-0

Library of Congress Control Number: 2023938934

Cover and Interior Design: Julie Rushing

Typeset in Mr Eaves San OT

Production Intern: Mars Robinson

Printed in the United States of America

First Printing

Cover images by Melvin Grier

For Brenda then, now and forever

CONTENTS

FOREWORD: Mark Neikirk — ix

INTRODUCTION: Melvin Grier — 1

CHAPTER 1: **WEST END** — 3

CHAPTER 2: **PRE-POST** — 13

CHAPTER 3: **THE POST** — 24

CHAPTER 4: **ART LIFE** — 69

POSTSCRIPT: Molly Kavanaugh — 89

UNFINISHED LIVES: Kathy Y. Wilson — 93

ACKNOWLEDGMENTS — 95

IMAGE LOG — 97

FOREWORD

MARK NEIKIRK
Managing Editor of *The Cincinnati Post* 2001-2007

Melvin Grier wanted to be a jazz musician, and that is what he became. His instrument was his camera.

Though I barely know enough about jazz to applaud at the appropriate time, I do know this. Extraordinary musicians improvise within a structure known to them. Each is given a turn at the forefront as the others fill. Then they rotate. The sax gives way to the piano, which gives way to the upright bass, which gives way to the trumpet, which gives way to the drums. And then they all come in together, harmonized and powerful.

A newsroom is like that. Its whole is the sum of its parts. Reporters. Copy editors. Page designers. Assignment editors. Section editors. Opinion editors. Photographers.

A Nikon camera in the hands of Melvin Grier was like a Martin Committee trumpet in the hands of Miles Davis. Expect music. Not just any music. Something elegant. Something relevant. Maybe a little edgy and with something to say. To provoke. To move. To stir. Something with tones you know, but somehow more beautifully assembled.

Melvin's music was his photographs, and his subject was the city of Cincinnati, its people, its comedies and errors, it triumphs and tragedies. His ensemble, if you will, was *The Cincinnati Post* and its sister newspaper just across the Ohio River, *The Kentucky Post*. *The Post* was my band, too, so I had the good fortune to know him and his work.

Among my favorite Melvin Grier photographs, and there are many, is one of a child playing in a fountain (page 32). The water wets her hair. Her head is upturned toward a sunny day. Were the scene recorded by someone else, it might have turned out as the photographic equivalent of "You Are My Sunshine," three chords and a down strum. Through Melvin Grier's lens, it is more "So What," the Davis composition that opens "Kind of Blue," the album on which the master reinvented jazz.

Melvin's photograph is not something most of us have the imagination to conjure from the reality in front of us. Yet he conjured it from his innate understanding of light and color and exposure time. A smartphone that does all the thinking for us these days will never match this photograph, which is both photojournalism and art.

It is art because, with his instrument, Melvin produced a painting in vibrant streaks of color that, within the framework of his lens, conveys the joy of a summer day. It is photojournalism because it records a moment in Cincinnati. A summer day. The city. A child, as it happens, a Black child. The photograph does not have much news value if news is "if it bleeds, it leads." Murder. Mayhem. Corruption. But if a newspaper is supposed, at times, to just celebrate the community it serves, as I believe a good newspaper should, then the photograph is a masterpiece—which it is.

The book in front of you has some other masterpieces, but just as importantly, it has other photographs that are simply consistently creative, consistently well executed, consistently original, and consistently documentary of some event, or place, or person. They are moments in the life of the city. In the life of America. They also are, when seen together, testimony to what our city lost when *The Post* closed and when our surviving competitors deemphasized photojournalism. Words alone cannot tell a city's story.

Many of the photographs in this book are in black and white because newspapers were in black and white for most of the 33 years of Melvin's career. When color first arrived, the process of reproducing a photograph on a press that turned out newspapers in rapid succession from a machine that sang the song of the Industrial Age was not great at getting the color in register. Consequently, we elected to use color sparingly, until the technology of printing color on newsprint improved, which eventually it did.

The Post was blessed with a fantastic staff of photographers, and Melvin would not want me to say he was the best of them. Nor would I, because some excelled at one thing and others at another. Some played the trumpet. Some the sax. Some were at their best at a fire. Others, in the quiet of the studio taking a portrait. Some could catch the action at a sporting event, which is difficult. No one wants to see a photograph of Pete Rose hitting his 4,191st. Timing is everything.

What was Melvin Grier's strength? It may well have been everyday life. I met him for morning coffee in Newport, Kentucky, a town that gave *The Post* plenty of headlines over the years. Sin City knew how to sin. Today, Newport is sanguine. The gangsters are gone as are the feds. The big, old houses once carved into tenements have now been restored and sell for $1 million.

Before we walked into Roebling Point Books & Coffee, owner Richard Hunt wanted to show us a hand-built, mahogany bookcase. It was a work of art. Each joint was hand cut. I could not see a nail. Richard had it outside, so he could restore it, layering it in tung oil to bring out the wood's beauty. A customer who lived nearby inherited it but couldn't get it up his stairs, so he gave it to Richard. "It was too big to fit on any vehicle we had," Richard told us. So he, his customer, and a companion carried it three-and-half city blocks to the bookstore.

Three men awkwardly carting an unwieldy bookcase down a tree-lined city street. "That," Melvin said, "sounds like a picture." In his mind's eye, the shutter clicked.

That cool, fall morning, Melvin and I spent the better part of two hours talking—something we rarely had time to do when we were both on deadline. We reminisced, telling stories of events but also of colleagues. Any good newsroom has a cast of characters worthy of a Dickens novel. Writ large, they curse like sailors, abide by ethics so strict nuns might rebel if subjected to them, work longer and weirder hours than an obstetrician, and love what they do more than Hades loved Persephone, a story they know because they read almost as much Greek mythology as they read Dashiell Hammett and John McPhee.

We also lamented the state of journalism today. The two of us worked at *The Post* for a combined 61 years, and our time included the final years of *The Post* which closed in 2007 as a revolution commenced that, in time, would neuter local journalism and especially take a toll on photojournalism.

Part of the value of this book is that it documents not just the life of a city and the life of Melvin Grier (there is a photograph of the apartment building in the West End where he was born) but also a now-concluded era of daily metropolitan newspapers. They were once flush with money having cornered the market on hometown advertising. Television took its bite first. By the 1990s, the internet was a nuclear bomb, ticking toward detonation.

Our town's surviving newspaper today is barely worthy of its compound noun of a name. It is made with less news and less paper. Some days, it has so few pages that you could not swat a fly with it, at least not fatally.

I still seek out the work of photojournalists. The Associated Press shooters are, as I write this, doing stunning work in Ukraine. One AP online portfolio by Emilio Morenatti includes a photograph of a woman, who appears from her coat and clothing to have had means. She is fleeing a bombed street. Her anguish is evidenced by her tears. Everything around her speaks of the destruction Putin has unleashed. This one picture of one woman on one street seems to tell the whole story of this painful, unnecessary, and cruel war. It was what photojournalism should be.

I doubt many Americans saw that photograph, because neither newspapers nor their websites bother much any longer with photojournalism. Had I still been managing editor of a daily newspaper, as I was once, I hope I would have had the good sense to put it on page one. Big.

I was the managing editor of *The Post* the day we published Melvin Grier's more-upbeat photograph of that girl in a fountain. I honestly do not recall whether I selected it, or if that recommendation came from a colleague, and I simply had the good sense not to overrule the decision. However it happened, we (forgive my stretched metaphor) jazzed up page one quite nicely that day.

Thank you, Melvin Grier. You have lived your dream, sir, and readers of *The Post*, and of this book, have the great privilege of witnessing the results. We are an appreciative audience. I am applauding now. I hope I am doing so at the right time.

INTRODUCTION

MELVIN GRIER

When I first started out, it was all about the equipment. Throughout my career, I have owned the following:

- Fixed-focus box camera (not a Kodak, an off brand my dad bought in a drug store) that came in a kit with a flash, flashbulbs, and two rolls of film

- Pentax with two lenses (50mm and 200mm) that I bought when I was stationed in England

- Rolleiflex, also bought in England

- Calumet 4x5 view camera with tripod (my dumbest camera purchase)

- Hasselblad

- Nikon F1, F2, F4, F5

- Nikon D1 (my first digital camera)

- Nikon D2H

- Nikon D300, a $1,700 retirement gift to myself that I "loaned" to my daughter Samantha and never got back. I replaced it with a used D300, which I still use today.

- iPhones (currently an iPhone 11)

As for lenses, I routinely carried 50mm, 35mm, 24mm, 105mm, 180mm, and sometimes a 300 and 400mm. I used a spot meter and a Vivitar flash. Listing my photo equipment is easy, but my evolving attitude about being a photographer, well, that's not so easy to explain.

I was a medic in the U.S. Air Force in the early 1960s and stationed in England. This was an exciting time to be in England with magazines like *Queen* and others covering the British pop scene, and beautiful women roaming the city. I also had access to U.S. magazines like *Vogue* and *Harper's Bazaar*. I was struck by the fashion images inside, and the work by photographers such as Helmut Newton, David Bailey, Richard Avedon, and Gordon Parks.

I had time to kill, plus duty-free shipping made purchases like Pentax and Rolleiflex cameras affordable, so I started taking photographs on the base as well as on excursions to London and elsewhere. I decided to enter a few photos in the *Stars and Stripes* photo contest—and won first place.

That was a boost to my confidence, so I started hanging out at the base's photo hobby shop and enrolled in the mail order Famous Photographers School (whose faculty included such notables as Richard Avedon and Alfred Eisenstaedt). When you're young, you want to be famous, and what could be better than to be a famous photographer? I would send the school assorted photographs. They would be returned with detailed critiques.

Back home in Cincinnati, I needed a job and was grateful to get hired by the Austin Bewsey Studios. Not much opportunity to take photos, though I did get to follow around the Revlon Girls when they came to town and appeared on the "Uncle Al Show." Fashion photography was definitely on my radar.

When I got hired by *The Post,* I was excited that I would finally own the latest Nikon and have unlimited rolls of film. Dream on. Boss Jack Klumpe handed me a beat-up Nikon and told me I would have to wind my own film. Thankfully, Klumpe's tenure was relatively brief, and then it was like Christmas—new cameras, "bricks" of film, and a wide assortment of lenses that photographers shared generously. But owning a state-of-the-art camera, like owning a snazzy sports car, doesn't mean you're ready to compete in the Indy 500.

In time, I grew confident at being a *Post* photographer, knowing that whatever assignment came my way—be it sports or spot news—I would be able to produce an image on deadline that was worthy of being published in the newspaper. (I credit my Catholic upbringing, seminary stint, and military service for instilling the discipline needed to do this daily.) And I understood as a journalist that to miss a deadline was frowned upon.

Thus began a gradual transition in my thinking that was really a twofold question. How could an assignment be elevated to a photograph that was exceptional? What else could I shoot that was outside the parameters of an assignment? In other words, how could I expand my vision?

For instance, I took a photograph of a guy standing on a ladder painting a building that was not an assignment and I consider it one of my best (page 25). One colleague I really admired was Alex Burrows, who had a unique way of looking at things through a lens. I tried to emulate him and knew I was onto something when Klumpe complained that my work was challenging, "just like Alex's."

As I traveled to major sporting events like the Super Bowl (twice with the Bengals in 1982 and 1989) and to exotic countries like Cuba, people would often say to me, "That must be fun." My immediate response was, "*The Post* doesn't pay me to go there and have fun, it's about the work."

Even on routine road trips, like going to Cleveland for a Bengals vs. Browns game, I didn't go out on the town. Once there, I'd go out and buy a local newspaper, head back to the hotel room, order room service (burger, fries, two beers), and get to bed early. The next morning, I was on the first team bus to the stadium, and I'd walk around, usually with a headset listening to jazz, and wait for the game to begin. It was all about the work.

And yes, I did cherish the opportunity to cover major events and visit foreign ports. As notorious bank robber Willie Sutton said when asked why he robbed banks, "Because that's where the money is." That's where the photographs are.

Or as we photographers would say, "F8 and be there." In other words, a scene is so rich with photo ops that all that you need is the correct exposure and shutter speed.

In 1990, we were sent to the World Series in Oakland to cover the Cincinnati Reds. I don't remember any memorable photographs from that assignment or much else, except being disappointed that the Reds won in four games and cut our trip short, but I do remember the sign hanging over the parking-lot garage as we exited: Stay Focused.

"Stay focused because it was always about the work," pretty much sums up my career.

CHAPTER 1: WEST END

Every life begins somewhere. Mine began on November 7, 1941, in a three-room-shotgun apartment with a cold-water tap and toilet in Tremont Flats, in the West End neighborhood of Cincinnati, Ohio.

I was the first and only child of Ruby and Leslie Grier, who came to Cincinnati from Locust Grove, Georgia, some 40 miles south of Atlanta. They were part of the Great Migration north to escape segregation and find opportunities to prosper. My mother Ruby was a domestic worker, and my father Leslie, nicknamed Bo, was a factory laborer. They named me Melvin Lamar Grier. I have no idea if I was named for a relative.

My mother died from pulmonary disease just after my second birthday. She was 35. Legend has it

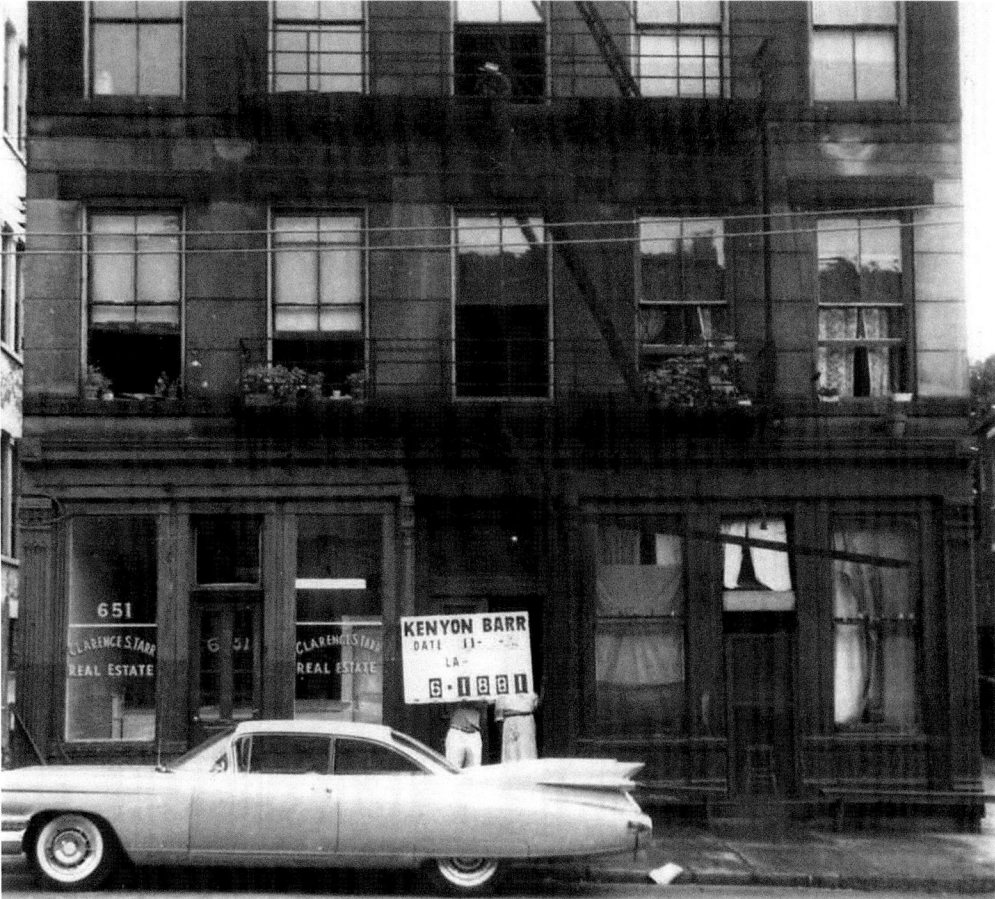

My first home was on the second floor of Tremont Flats at 651 West Fifth Street in Cincinnati's West End.

I don't remember my mother and only have one photograph of the two of us.

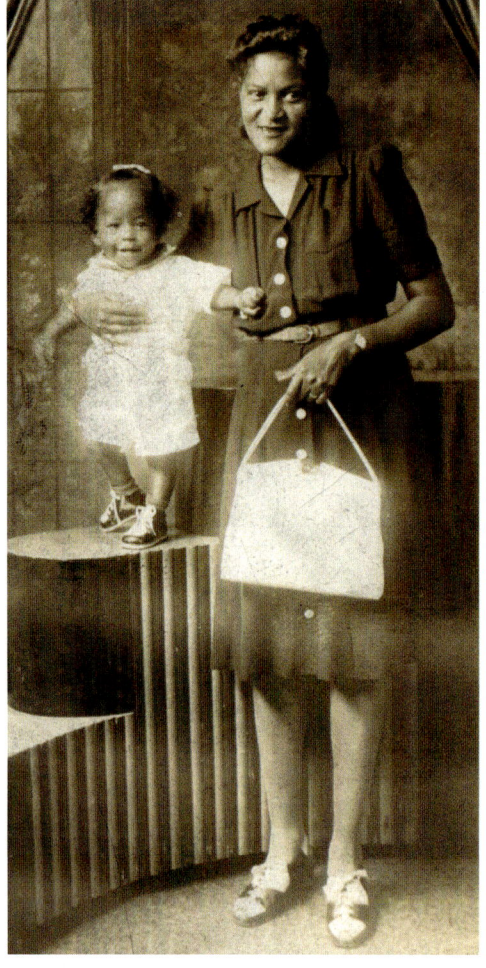

The four-story Tremont Flats was next door to Jackson Public School, which was next door to Holy Trinity Catholic School. Kenyon Barr refers to two West End streets adjacent to downtown Cincinnati that became a term for sites slated for demolition.

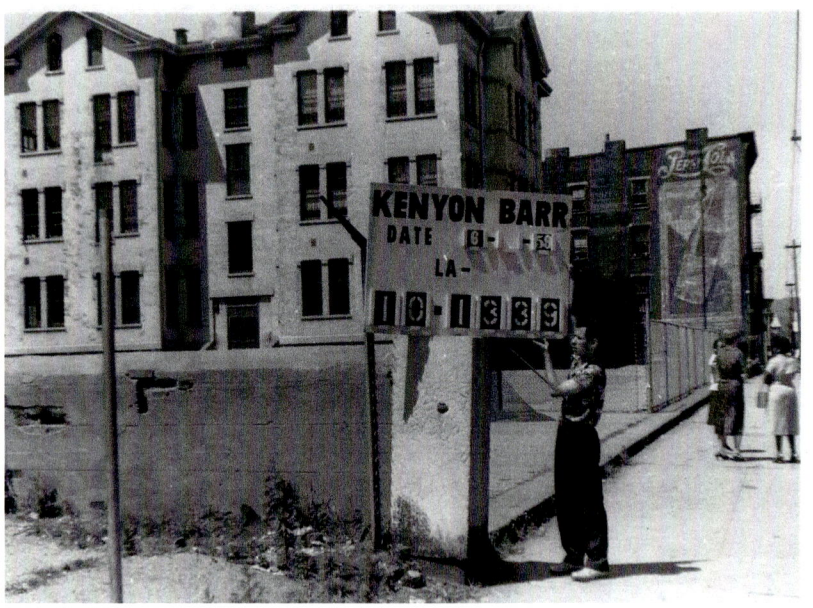

that my mother's dying words were, "Don't send that boy to Jackson School."

My dad told me that when my mother and I returned to our apartment building after neighborhood outings, I would make a lot of noise, and my mother would try to quiet me. I desperately wanted to place this memory in my young mind.

Later in life, I learned that my mother had a relationship prior to my dad and got pregnant. She didn't marry the fella, and the baby died at three months of age. When she and my dad got together, her family was not in favor of their union, because Bo Grier was a bit of a hellion.

But back to the West End. Our neighborhood was almost 100% African American, although at that time, we were classified as "negroes." Our neighborhood had all the services we needed, like the Sixth Street Market, the drug store at Sixth and Mound Streets that had a gas flame where smokers could light their cigarettes.

We had movie theaters—the Pekin, the Lincoln, and the Roosevelt—but negroes were not welcome at the Albee Theater just blocks away in downtown. Of course, we had the everyday necessities of barber shops and pool halls, and, in a time when people still used coal for heating, there were coal yards.

The inside of Tremont Flats was poorly lit and had seen better days. A long entry hallway led to a small atrium with a series of wooden banisters that overlooked the ground floor, where mailboxes were attached to a wall. From the first floor, a series of wooden steps gave residents access to the four floors that were divided into four apartments on the north end of the building and two on the south. The north-end residents shared a toilet, whereas apartments on the south end, where we lived, enjoyed toilets in the apartments. We had only cold water, no shower or tub, and obtained hot water by boiling it on the stove.

At one time, our building had been a hotel, hence the reason each of our three rooms had its own door to the hallway and another door between each room (a total of five doors for a three-room apartment).

Our entrance door led directly to the kitchen with a sink, gas stove, refrigerator, a dining table with four chairs, and a matching storage unit upon which sat our 10-gallon fish tank populated with goldfish. There was also a very small cupboard with shelves that held a few canned goods, and old issues of *The Cincinnati Enquirer* that were delivered to our door. There was also a mousetrap that snapped shut on the unsuspecting rodent from time to time.

The toilet was reached by yet another door off the kitchen. On Saturdays, we'd bring in the tin tub hanging outside on a nail and fill it up with a kettle of boiled hot water for my weekly bath with Lifebuoy soap.

The middle of the three rooms was the bedroom, most of it taken up by a double bed, dresser, a gas stove for heating the three rooms during the winter months, and another small closet. My dad and I shared a double bed that had a light on the headboard. I slept on the inside next to the wall.

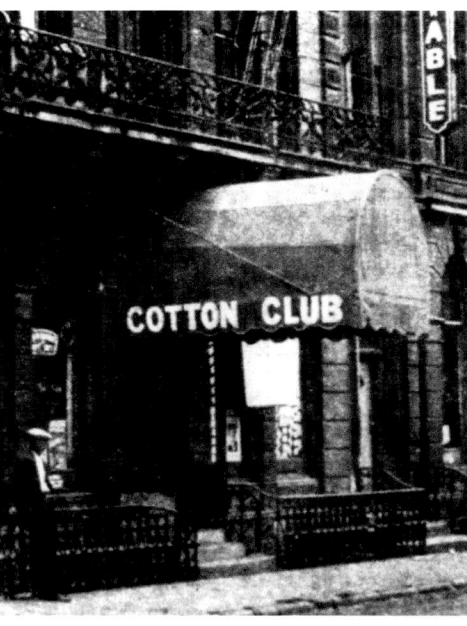

The famous West End Cotton Club in Cincinnati was on the first floor of the Sterling Hotel at Sixth and Mound.

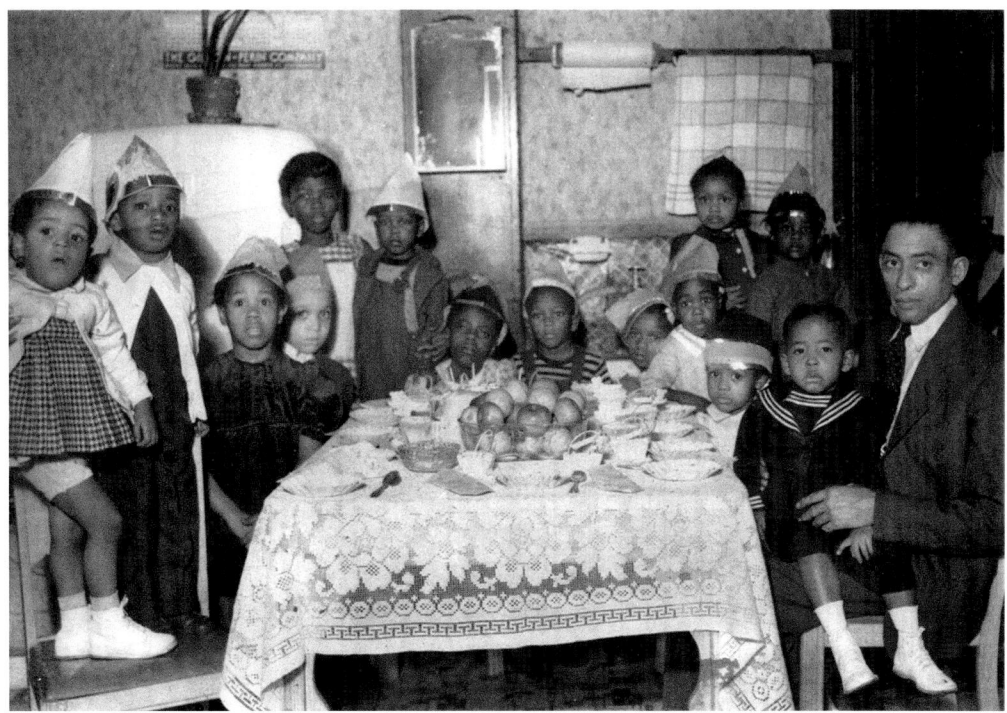

My fifth birthday party was held in our kitchen. The door on the right led to the toilet, the cold-water sink is in the center, and barely visible at the bottom left is the churn where homemade ice cream was made. For a happy occasion, no one seemed to be enjoying themselves.

WEST END | 5

The front room faced south and was our living room. It contained a metal-framed couch with a broken back that was rarely used, a floor model radio with a pullout record player that was close to extinction, and a couple of chairs.

The door opened to the back hallway, where there was a window overlooking a pathway called the "donkey hole," which led to a green patch where homeless men hung out while they drank an alcoholic concoction called "derail." This window was also where my dad would point his pistol, and fire off several rounds welcoming the new year. He wasn't the only resident to do so.

The green patch led to Sweeney Alley. From the back-hallway window, I could see the railroad tracks that carried the Dixie Humming Bird passenger train as it headed toward the bridge over the Ohio River on its way to points south. Of particular interest to me were the Black stewards in their white tunics standing at the openings. I would wave but never get a return recognition.

We had interesting neighbors. One was Mr. Wilson. Each day, he would lower a basket attached to a rope for the paperboy, who put inside the afternoon edition of The Cincinnati Post, an evening newspaper I would come to know intimately.

My childhood neighborhood was eliminated by the so-called urban renewal that started in the late 1950s and wiped out large swaths of the West End so that I-75 could be built. But before that disaster took place, there were times in my young years that found me walking the streets discovering places that shaped my adult life, like the Cotton Club.

I would walk east on Fifth Street past storefront churches where gospel quartets would perform, and past joints where saxophones would sound out the blues. Further on, there was George Shetley's diner serving up hamburgers, daily specials, sweet potato pie, and fountain treats, my favorite being the banana delight. One time, an upstairs resident made the mistake of coming down in his pajamas only to be unceremoniously thrown out by George. That diner also had a jukebox with a great selection of tunes.

My dad, following my mother's wishes, enrolled me in Holy Trinity Catholic School. I have a vague

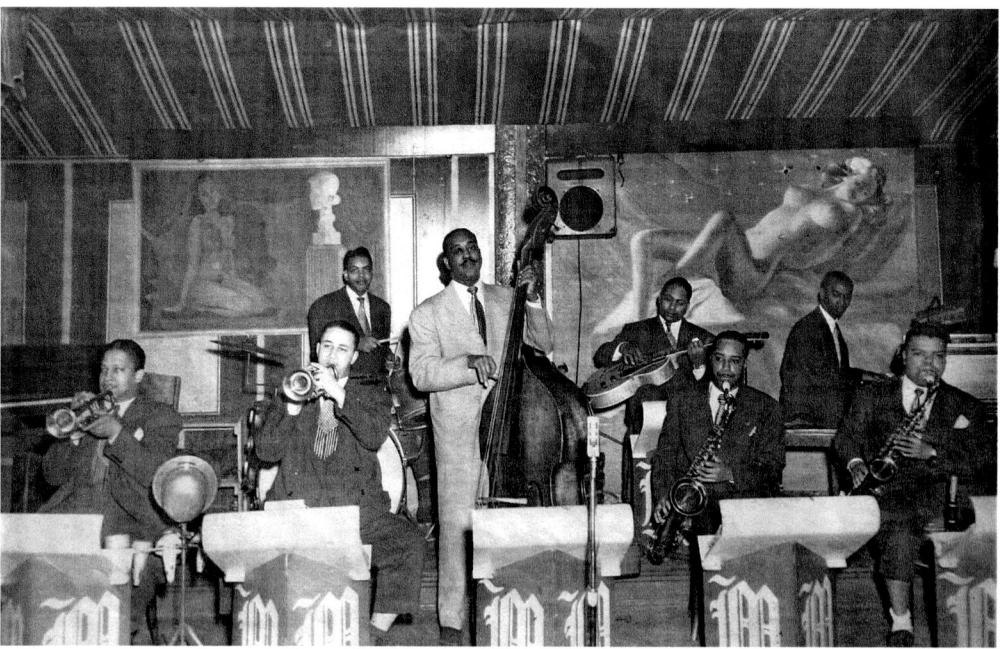

I could hear the big band through the door of the Cotton Club, but I never set foot inside, because I was too young.

recollection of my first day in primer, a grade preceding first grade, because a classmate fell out of his chair, and split his head open, leaving a scar he carried throughout his time at Holy Trinity.

Most students at Holy Trinity were Catholic, but I was not baptized, nor part of the church congregation. It was particularly frustrating, because while I had to attend Mass, I was not allowed to take communion or be an altar boy. Still, I studied Catechism like my peers hoping that one day I might be rewarded. And I was. After I was baptized around the age of 10, I became an altar boy and eventually rose to Master of Ceremonies for solemn high masses on holy days that featured three priests and several other altar boys.

Our school was run by four nuns, of the order of the Sisters of the Blessed Sacrament. Holy Trinity's caretaker, Mr. Carl Bates, would drive the nuns from their Dayton Street convent in his Hudson. We students would be on the playground prior to their arrival, but the nuns' presence brought all play to a halt, and we began to line up by grade.

I remember the principal, Mother Agnita, standing on a stairwell landing. She would give a stern look, say "boy" with a withering tone, and any misbehaving would freeze. Mr. Carl Bates wore many hats—chauffeur, maintenance man, Boy Scout leader of Troop 173. When I think of him, I also remember when I finally got my Scout uniform, which I completed with an Army cartridge belt I bought at the Army Navy store.

Early on, my teacher tried to steer me from writing with my left hand. It didn't work, and I had to suffer the stains of fountain-pen ink as my hand moved across the paper. Getting a new textbook was big but came with the responsibility of covering it with a precut book cover in order to protect it. We were taught a full range of subjects. Religion, English, and reading were my favorites (arithmetic not so much).

During recess, we were pretty much left to our own devices. There was a set of swings (not enough to accommodate all the kids wanting a turn), hopscotch, and pickup baseball played with a rubber ball.

Sometimes, our school day started with Mass in a very large church that had been built by Germans. Prior to Mass, one of the altar boys would have the task of going to the vestibule to ring the bell, and he would let its weight pull him up off the floor. Oh, how I envied him. Mass was in Latin, girls had to cover their heads (scarfs tied at the throat being

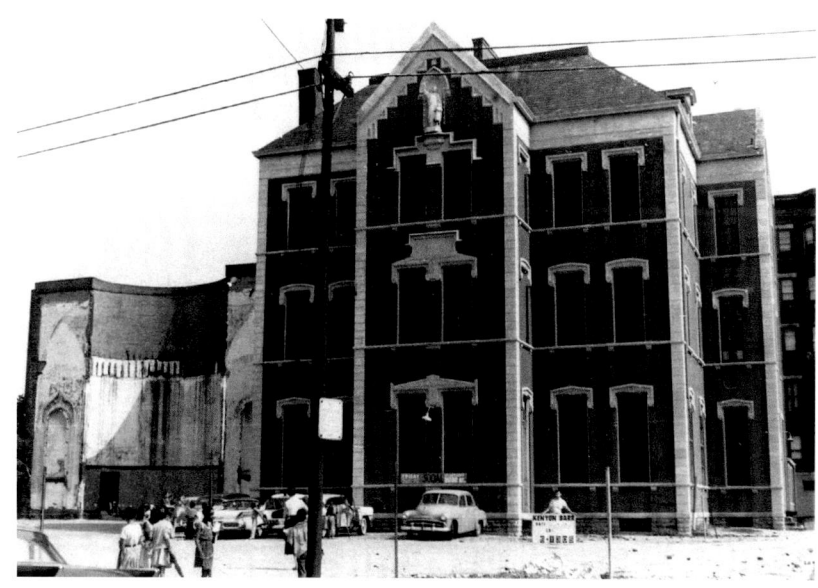

I attended Holy Trinity Catholic School in Cincinnati's West End.

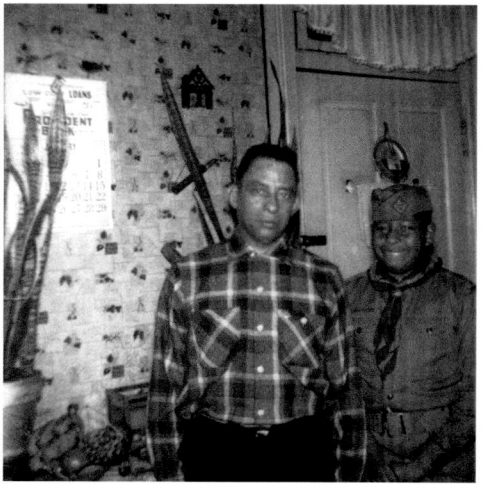

My father, Leslie Grier, with one proud 13-year-old Boy Scout in our Tremont Flats apartment. I still have a cutting from the plant in the background of this photograph.

favored), and for the boys, it was collared shirts and ties. Early on, Father Nardi was the celebrant. Eventually, he was replaced by Father Branchesi. Both were from the Verona Fathers, a missionary order based in Italy that I would come to know even better.

Around fifth grade, my daily school routine was disrupted when it was announced that our church would be demolished. This became official for us students when the bells were lowered and hauled away. I recall some of the girls crying. One last school day, while we were in class, there was a tremendous roar that sent everyone in our room running away from the sound. It was the west wall of the church tumbling down. Soon, many buildings in the West End became piles of bricks and assorted debris. The village it takes to raise a child was being razed.

However, the Holy Trinity school building remained intact, and a large sliding door served as the barrier between our makeshift church and fundraising bingo. I was recruited to do my bit in service to the parish by working as a "pop boy" carrying a galvanized bucket with ice and a selection of bottled soft drinks. I worked my way up to manager of the pop boys and eventually the plum job of rotating the basket that held the little bingo balls. This action was done in a private office, and the numbers were broadcast over a sound system, complete with the rattling sound of twirling balls, until someone shouted out "Bingo!"

Meanwhile, at Tremont Flats, I was learning how to play the piano, thanks to my neighbor Mrs. Leatha Brown, who had a piano and paid for my lessons. She also looked after me when my dad worked the second shift at GH&R Foundry in Dayton. In return, I accompanied her to Sixth Street Market and helped carry her grocery bags.

Mrs. Brown also came to my rescue during a rather desperate situation. I was a latchkey kid, so I let myself in the door leading into our kitchen one afternoon after shopping with Mrs. Brown. Because my dad worked second shift, the apartment was kept as dark as possible which necessitated me turning on lights to chase the semi-darkness. When I did, I saw a bloody mess on the bed and the wall adjacent to it, but no dad.

I panicked and ran to Mrs. Brown's door. She already knew what had happened and arranged for us to be driven to Cincinnati General Hospital (now University of Cincinnati Medical Center) to find my dad. Eventually he was discharged, bandaged, and still wearing the bloody shirt. I was relieved but distressed by my vulnerability. Without him, I would become an orphan and probably shipped south to live with relatives in Georgia.

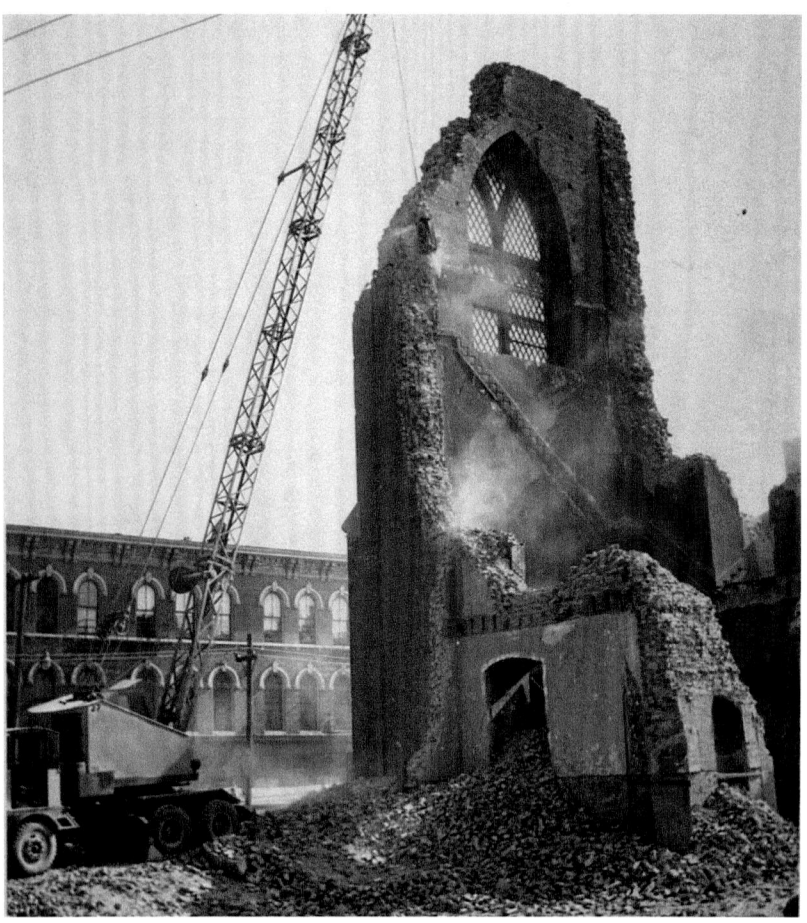

The destruction of Holy Trinity Catholic Church. Soon other buildings on West Fifth would be gone.

Mrs. Brown had a folding rollaway bed that I slept on that night, while my dad rested in our bed. My dad and I never talked about it, but I learned that one of his female friends had stabbed him and only missed killing him by a few inches.

Summer officially began after my piano recital, a nerve-wracking event for me that was held at a nearby music school. After that, Mrs. Brown would put together a boxed lunch of fried chicken and pound cake (which I can still taste), and one of my dad's buddies would drive us to Union Terminal for my solo 13-hour train ride to Locust Grove, in Henry County, Georgia, to visit my parents' relatives. (My father didn't own an automobile; he said he could drive, but I never saw him do so.) Somewhere in Tennessee, a friend of my dad's, who worked as a porter, would climb aboard, and keep an eye on me during his breaks.

Getting off the air-conditioned train, the heat hit like a backhand slap. My uncle Jack Grier, my aunt Zelma, and cousin Wymond would all pick me up, because the passenger train stopping in Locust Grove was a big deal. They'd take me along a dusty red-clay road to their house. There was no air conditioning, no TV, and no running water. We drew cold water from a well.

On my first day, I would walk into town with Wymond, who was about my age, and buy a straw hat for the hot summer days. When I visited with my mother's family, they had a swimming hole, and I spent some afternoons there, though I didn't know how to swim (and still don't).

At the Grier's, we'd hang out on the front porch of my great uncle and aunt's house and count how many Fords and Chevys came down the country road. On Saturdays, we'd drive 40 minutes to Griffin, where my aunt Zelma shopped at Piggly Wiggly, and then we'd go to the theater to see second-run movies. The theater that featured first-run movies made Blacks sit in the balcony, which was a humiliation, so we went to the other theater where we could sit anywhere.

Water fountains were the same. My cousin pointed it out when I tried to take a drink from a fountain that said "White." There was discrimination in Cincinnati, but in the South, it was blatant. Plus, I was a child of the West End, which was a Black community, and we stuck close to home, because there was no reason to go elsewhere. For instance, I didn't realize Coney Island in Cincinnati kept Blacks from swimming, because we never ventured that far.

Uncle Jack worked in a factory, and he also farmed an acre of cotton. My aunt Zelma sewed plush animals at her day job and then prepared marvelous dinners from produce she grew, as well as chickens she raised, killed, and plucked. Sunday afternoons brought homemade peach ice cream after hot church services—me squirming in a wool suit—at Shoal Creek Baptist.

My time at "the Grove" would end after the multiple-night church revival at Shoal Creek just before Labor Day. Sometimes, my dad came down late in the summer, and we'd travel home together on the train. If not, I headed north alone. This was my summer for at least three years.

Summers spent in Cincinnati meant playing street games like post square, baseball, and marbles. Every once in a while, we'd have a picnic at Burnet Woods, and my dad would take me to a Reds game at Crosley Field. We had no green space; everything was blacktop and cement.

I was pretty much left by myself those summers, because my dad was at work. On more than one occasion, when I'd come home late in the afternoon or early evening, the apartment was dark and empty,

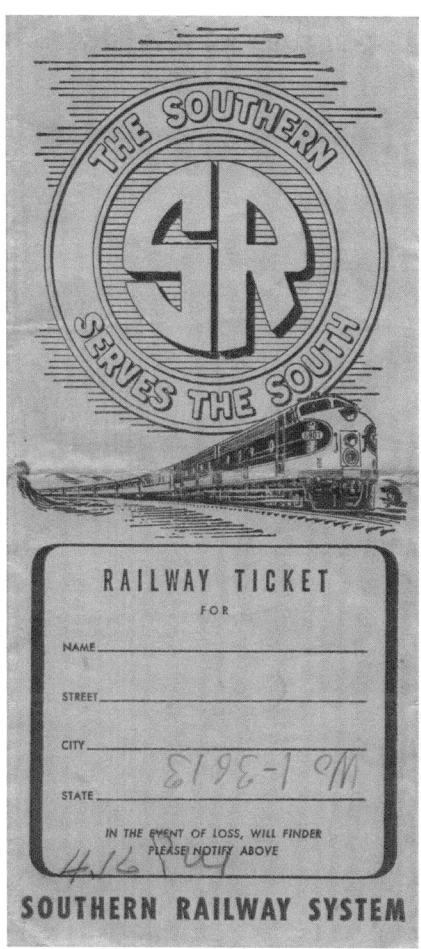

Cars on the train were segregated. "The Grove" was such a small Georgia town that my dad had to make special arrangements for the train to stop.

and I would just put myself to bed. I still have dreams about that.

When I was in seventh grade, the powers that be announced that the Holy Trinity school would be demolished. My best option was St. Henry, located on Flint and Cortlandt at least a dozen blocks away. The new school was in the West End, but many of the streets were unfamiliar to me because of the vastness of the surrounding area.

At St. Henry, I became convinced, with the urging of the eighth-grade nuns, to pursue the priesthood.

I also aspired to be the next Art Blakey. I figured I could do both.

During grade school, my dad had bought me a set of drums, a hideous yellow-and-black design, which I stored in an old classroom at Holy Trinity. I packed up the drums and took them to Sacred Heart Seminary in Anderson Township. By the way, he had also bought me a camera that I just had to have. It came with a kit—film, flash, and a case. I soon lost interest. I had no desire to be a photographer.

The seminary on Beechmont Avenue was a world away from the West End. Where I had been just another Black face among many, I was now surrounded by white boys from various cities. Among the hundred or so students, I was one of just two Black students.

The seminary was run by the Verona Brothers, from the Italian city of the same name, and I quickly realized I had chosen a very challenging scholastic environment. We studied algebra, Latin, and eventually geometry. And to make matters worse, I learned that I was in dire need of glasses. Fortunately, there was a two-week break at Christmas, and my dad, with his small paycheck, spent part of it on my first pair of glasses.

I got rides home from Sacred Heart Seminary with a couple of classmates who lived on the West Side but in very different homes. I was shocked to see carpet instead of linoleum, and cloth drapes instead of plastic—all things I had seen on TV but never experienced firsthand. When it came time to drop me off, I was not going to invite them up to our Tremont Flats apartment to see how my dad and I lived. With good reason, because one day, soon after I got home, a rat ran across the floor.

While I was back in my old neighborhood, I could see that the wrecking ball had started its work. Some of my friends had moved to the Lincoln Courts, better known as "the projects."

I owned a camera but was not interested in joining the seminary's camera club.

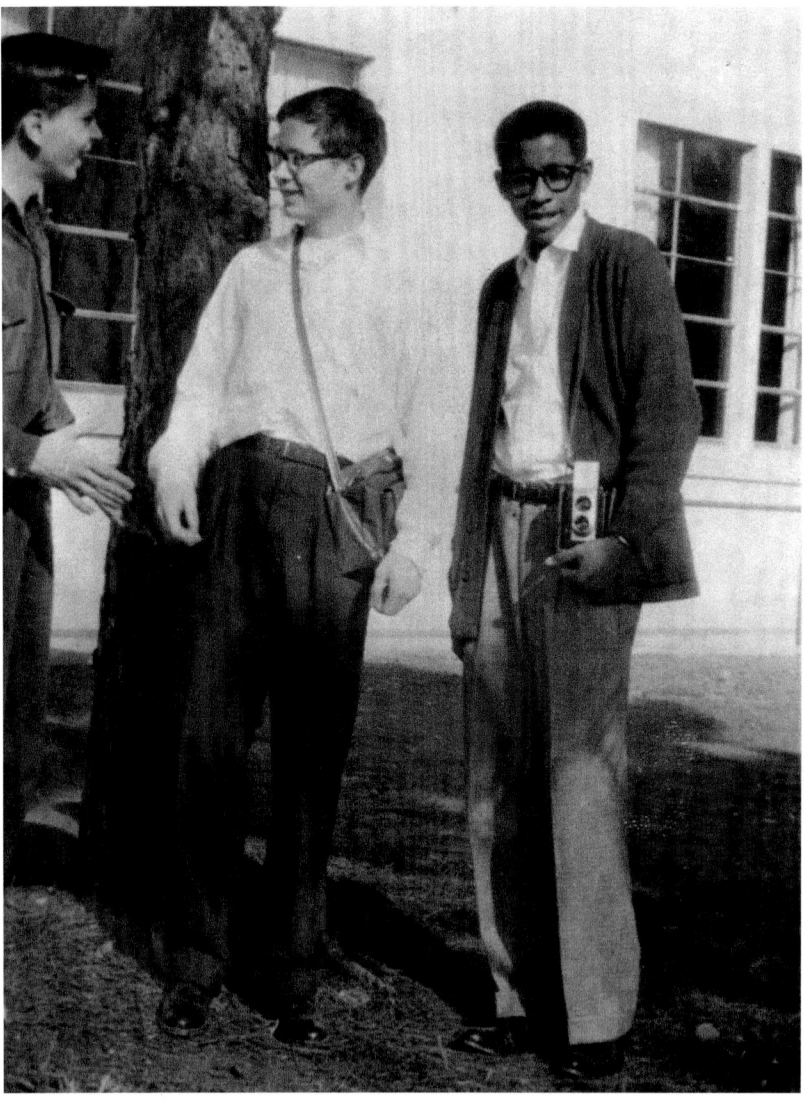

When we visited, we were amazed at the grass lawns and amenities like hot running water.

At the end of my Christmas break, now wearing glasses, I opened my suitcase to pack, and there was the rat I had seen earlier, now dead and stiff. I screamed for my dad. He picked it up and threw it out a back-hallway window. End of story, but not the end of seeing rats inside.

Our daily lives at Sacred Heart were very structured, but we seminarians found ways to amuse ourselves. A particular favorite was irritating an easily excitable teacher. We would quietly pass the word that when the wall clock hit, say, 1:30, we would all stretch, yawn, and cross our legs left over right. It really got a rise out of him.

Once in a while, with little advance notice, the student body would be sent out to hike the countryside. There was very little development near our school, so the hike was up and down rural roads with no destination other than getting back to the seminary at some point. On one particularly freezing winter day, we cut our hike short because of the weather and returned to find a group of young girls visiting the seminary. The priests were not happy that our paths crossed.

The first Sunday of each month was visiting day at Sacred Heart. My father would enlist a friend to drive him there; I guess he paid them for the ride. In addition to seeing my dad, I also looked forward to him bringing me a Frisch's Big Boy double-decker hamburger with two all-beef patties, lettuce, cheese, and tartar sauce; and strawberry pie in a gelatin-like mixture topped with whipped cream (still one of my favorite meals).

Once, during my junior year, he brought two double-deckers. I ate one and put the other in the locker next to my bed in the dormitory. One night, about a week later, I was hungry and remembered that extra sandwich in my locker. I quietly retrieved it and counted this blessing as I gobbled it down. As

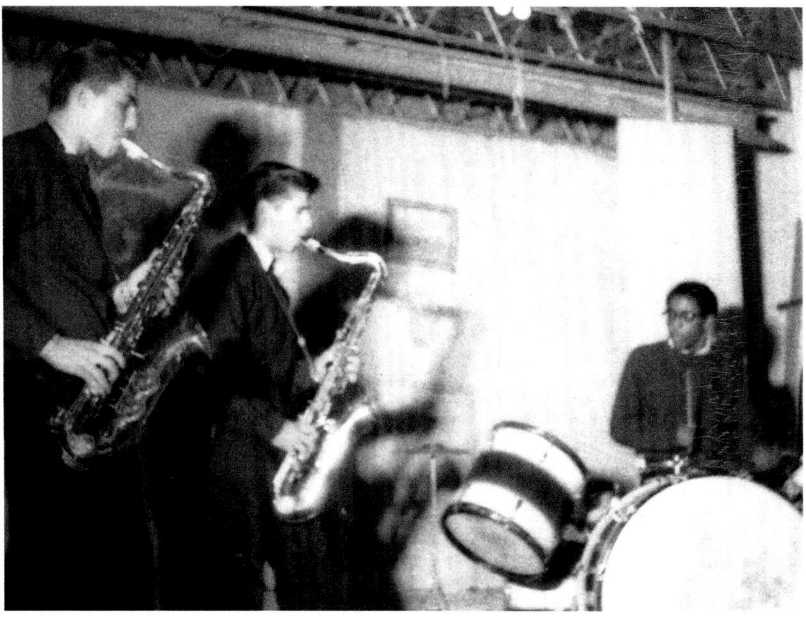

Herb Bill and John Caravella on tenor saxes, and me on drums during our concert (prematurely halted by the priest) at Sacred Heart Seminary in Anderson Township.

I settled in to sleep, I realized it was Friday and a sin for Catholics to eat meat. Confessions were weekly, and when it was my turn, I said, "Bless me Father, it has been one week since my last confession, I ate meat on Friday." There was a long silence followed by, "You did what?" (Even to this day, I take a bit of pride that I ate meat on a Friday while in the seminary.)

Another distinction I managed during my time in the seminary was to help convince the good fathers to let our trio play a concert for the student body. I was the pitcher for the softball team and drummer for the student band. Our big rival was St. Gregory Seminary who it was rumored referred to us as the "little girls from up Beechmont Ave." Their seminary was in a much larger building on Beechmont (it still stands as the Athenaeum of Ohio—Mount St. Mary's Seminary, and Sacred Heart Seminary is now Comboni Missionaries.)

We defeated St. Gregory in softball at our field and had a second game coming up at their field. Coincidentally, there was also a big Sunday event for parents and families, when the band was to perform.

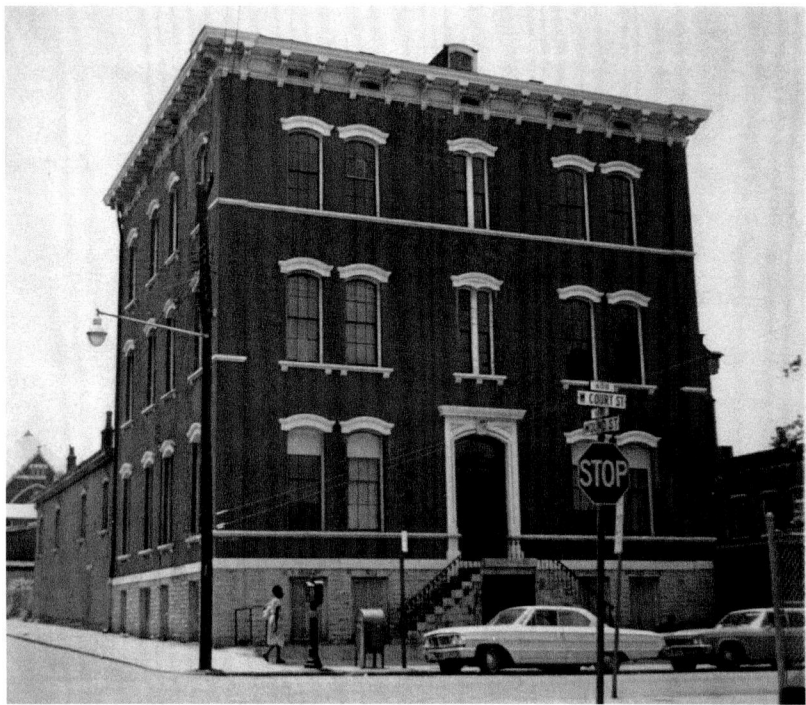

I finished high school at DePorres, an all-boys, entirely African American school in a West End I hardly recognized from my childhood.

Since at least two of us were both in the band and on the baseball team, we asked if we could use the time at the end of daily classes to first participate in band practice, and then be excused for baseball. The agreed upon time was 4:00 p.m.

As the hands of my wristwatch moved past 4:00, I gestured to the band director, who replied with a vigorous shake of his head a refusal to let us leave. After a few more minutes, I tried again only to be told "no" by another shake of his head. At this point, I got up from my drums and walked out followed by the catcher.

During study hall that evening, I was summoned to the rector's office where I was told that my presence would not be welcomed next year. "In my opinion, this is not your vocation," he said. Maybe he had found out that I spent time in the laundry room listening to jazz on WNOP. Still, we managed to win the game against St. Gregory, and give a mostly flawless band recital. I left the seminary on a high note, with my drums.

By then, my father had remarried, and we had moved to Avondale after being displaced by the West End demolition. I got a job at the Shubert Theater as a janitor and an occasional doorman for Wednesday and Saturday matinees, and I played drums with the Four Winds at Snook's Nook on Eastern Avenue. But I was not very happy with my job at the theater. After a few months, that problem was solved, because I was let go. The Snook's Nook gig also came to an end. Fortunately, I could file for unemployment compensation, and each Wednesday, a check would arrive. A lackluster routine developed with my friends, hanging out at Big Louie burger joint and bowling at the lanes on Reading Road.

It was 1960, and my future was very unclear. I had no interest in or prospect of attending college, and a career playing drums in a band was on the skids, so I decided to stop by the Air Force recruiting office. Among other things, the recruiter told me, "Oh yeah," I could play drums if I signed up.

I boarded my first airplane headed for Lackland AFB in San Antonio, Texas. I was dressed pretty snazzy in plaid pants and a yellow sweater but stood out once again. The drill sergeant assumed that since I was Black, I must be a gang member and rode me pretty hard. "Hey, you, yeah you with the glasses on, I'm going to stomp your ass," he yelled. I looked around and saw I was the only one wearing glasses.

About a week into basic training, I heard a band playing and volunteered to join the drum and bugle corps (affectionately called "dumb & bungle"). When it came time to try out for the Air Force band, I was handed a piece of music I couldn't read, and that marked the end of trying to take drumming to a higher level.

But not the end of my military service.

CHAPTER 2: PRE-POST

The Air Force introduced me to Montgomery, Alabama, where a Black man was treated like dirt. Many incidents, but the first slap in the face says it all. My three white buddies and I arrived by train and needed a ride to get to the medic tech school. "I can't take a colored boy in my cab," the driver told us, so I had to sit on the floor so no one would see me.

At Gunter Air Force Station, we were shown an instructional movie about delivering a baby. "But don't worry, you won't have to do this," the instructor said. Famous last words.

From Montgomery, I headed across the ocean to England. My first evening, we went to Cambridge, where I saw my first red double-decker bus and a British bobby. Soon after I arrived at the base in Lakenheath, England, I went into a nearby shop and was greeted by the owner who called me a Yank. I was no longer a colored person; I was a Yank. Unlike in Alabama, in England I encountered someone who treated me with respect and considered me just like all the other airmen, a Yank. That was so important to me, and a welcome change.

There were signs everywhere that told colored people what door not to enter, where not to sit, and so on.

I was assigned to the 48th Tactical Hospital located at Lakenheath, where there was a squadron of U.S. fighter aircraft. We were assigned to provide health-care services to this squadron and their families. The enlisted men's barracks appeared to be holdovers from World War II. The quarters had the smell of paraffin, or kerosene as we Yanks called it. The smelly stuff was used in heaters that warmed the barracks. Since the living quarters was an "open bay," that meant personnel were coming and going depending on the hospital shift they worked, and

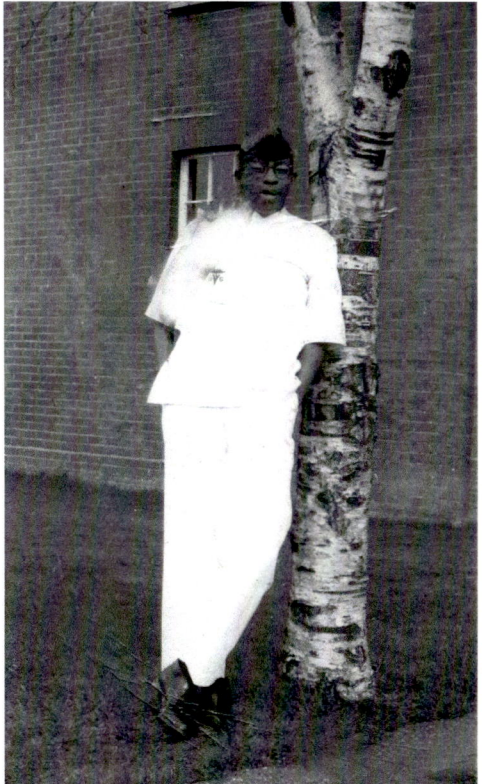

Airman Grier in my "whites" outside the RAF Mildenhall barracks in England, where I spent two years.

noise was a problem. Eventually, I learned that there was another Air Force medical facility about five miles away. It was located at Royal Air Force (RAF) Mildenhall, but it wasn't popular, because it was an obstetrical hospital. When I asked about the living quarters, I learned the barracks were brick, so I put in for a transfer.

My Air Force hospital duties were to work a five-day shift in the delivery room and one shift in the nursery. Our hospital served the spouses of Air Force personnel, both officers and enlistees. I was a member of a three-person medical team. Along with helping to deliver dozens of healthy babies, I was also present for 11 deaths.

During my first shift in the delivery room, four sets of twins were born, something so unusual the BBC showed up to report on the births. A shift in the nursery meant changing diapers (cloth), mixing formula, and feeding babies at the nurse's discretion.

When I had worked long enough, I took my first leave by train to London. I had brought my drugstore camera with me from home, but beyond typical tourist snaps, I had little interest in photography. I was very disappointed when I got to Buckingham Palace for the first time to find the guards wearing long gray overcoats (because it was cold) that covered their iconic scarlet tunics.

I had shot film, and since there was no corner drug store, I went to the photo hobby shop on the base. There I met Victor Creswell, who managed the photo facility and was key to my early days of being a photographer, teaching me the basics of darkroom work. I needed a better camera and eventually saved enough money to buy a Pentax with two lenses (I wish I had held onto that camera). I ordered the equipment from Japan to get the military discount, and it took a long time to arrive. But once it did? Now I could be arty.

I took a photograph of a guy playing an upright acoustic bass, his reflection in a door painted in a high-gloss enamel. I was proud of that portrait and submitted it to a photo contest sponsored by *Stars*

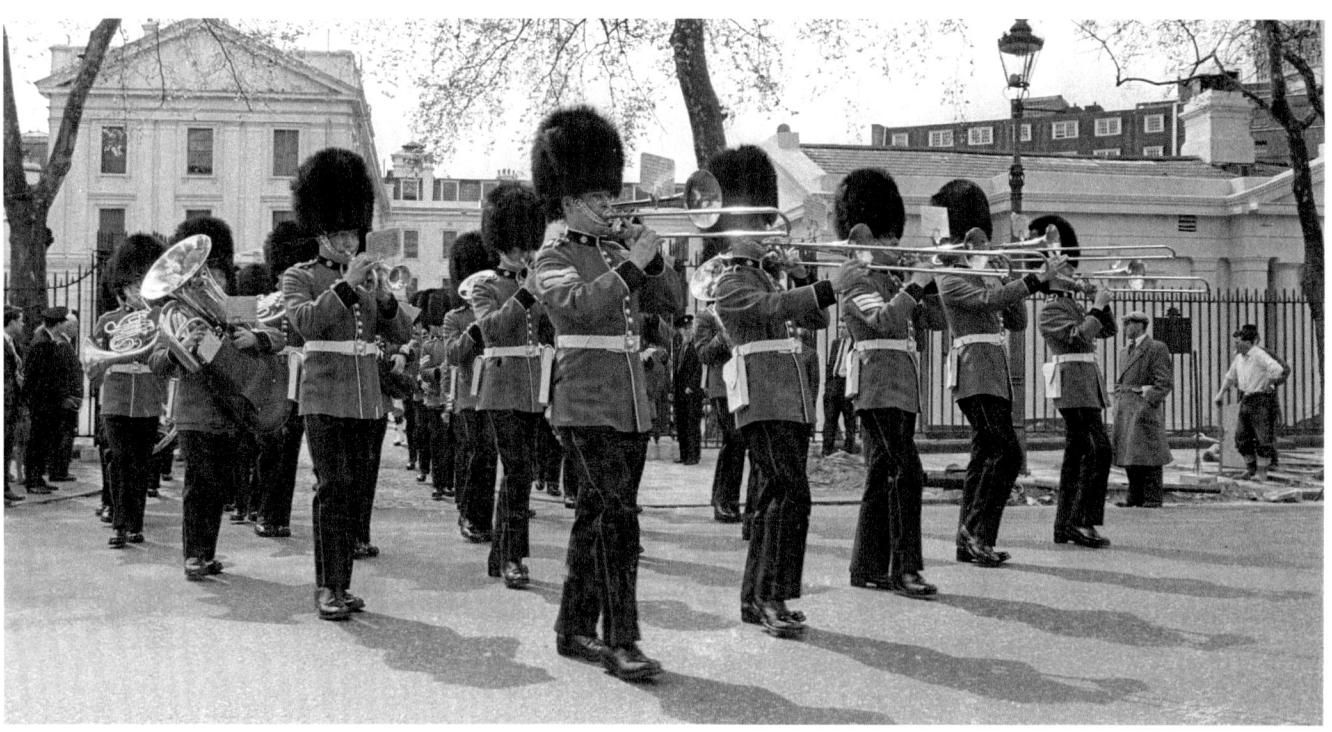

A Guards band leaves Wellington Barracks on their way to Buckingham Palace, this time with scarlet tunics in view.

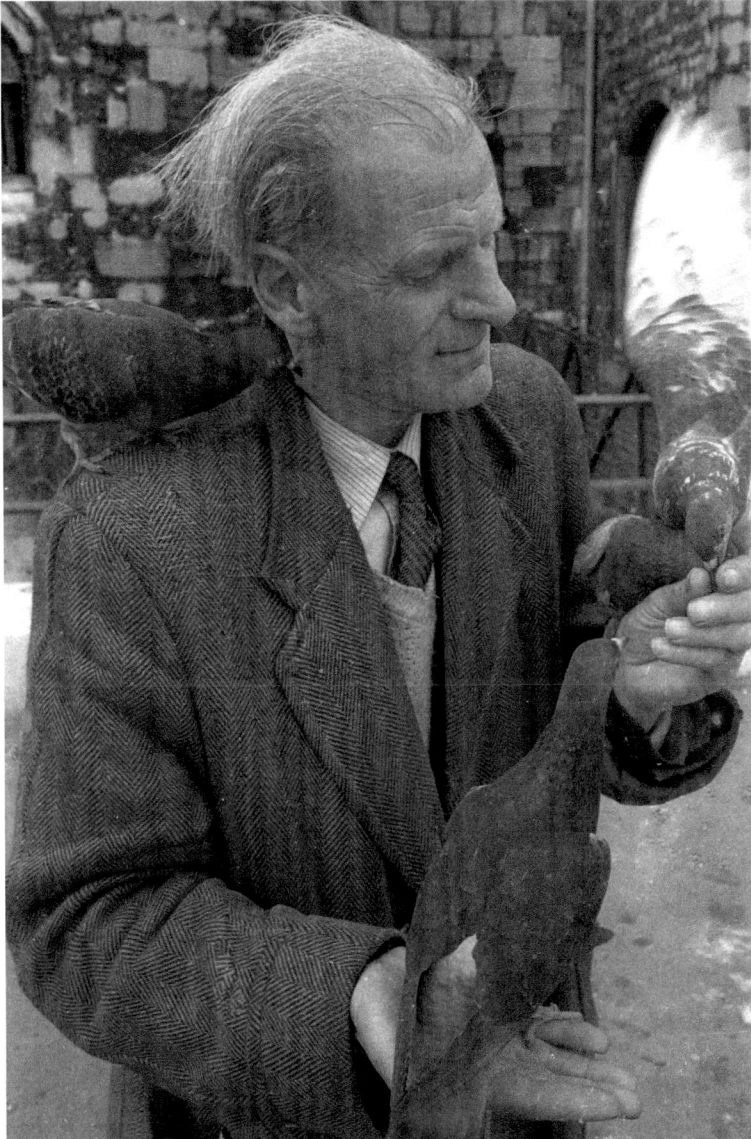

On a trip to London, I approached a man who was feeding pigeons at the Tower of London and asked if I could photograph him.

and Stripes, the newspaper that served the military. I had forgotten about the contest when, several months later, after a trip to the hospital mess hall for coffee, I tucked a Stars and Stripes under my arm and headed to the nursery to begin my day shift.

"Hey, somebody took a picture just like mine," I said to myself. Then I saw the name—Melvin Grier, First Prize. I also won second place in the experimental category.

At the photo hobby shop, there were a couple of regulars who found one of my questions about photography cause for ridicule and pretty much ignored me after that. I took the Stars and Stripes into the hobby shop and showed them my award-winning photo. They hadn't won jack, and it gave me so much pleasure to shove it in their faces. I continued working on my photography, even trying to shoot fashion. I never had much of a problem going after a photo opportunity.

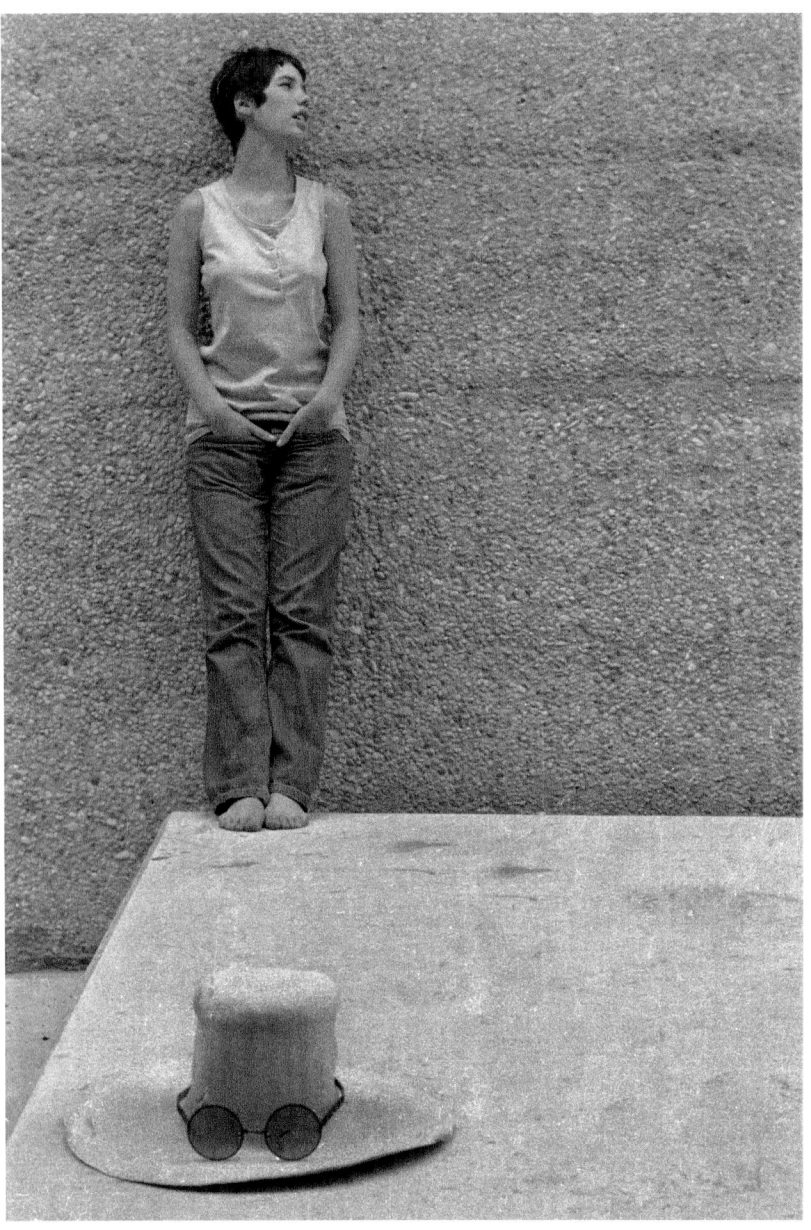

One of my early attempts to shoot a fashion photo. I think this young woman was the girlfriend of a fellow airman at Mildenhall.

I spent time in the base library and started to associate certain photographers with images that impressed me. I was attracted to fashion photography and really liked the work of David Bailey, a famous British photographer who took cutting-edge photographs of beautiful women.

I had decided upon my discharge in late 1965 that I wanted to be a professional photographer. I was drawn to both street photography and fashion but went in search of any position that involved photography.

When I got back to Cincinnati, I went to see my father and found him dutifully sweeping the sidewalk in front of the four-family apartment in South Avondale where he lived with my stepmother Corine. His first words were, "You need a haircut," followed by, "Now you can get a job at the post office." I told him I didn't want to work at the post office (one of the few reasonably well-paying steady careers open to Blacks). I told him I wanted to be a photographer. He asked, "What kind of old devilish photographer?" At that point, I couldn't give him an answer.

Despite my father's advice to work for the U.S. Postal Service, I put on one of my two suits and got an appointment to interview at a commercial photo studio in downtown Cincinnati. When the owner laid his eyes on me and my Afro, it was immediately apparent he had no interest in further discussion. Disappointed, I decided on a different tactic. I began flipping through the yellow pages.

When I got to the "Bs," there was Austin Bewsey Studios on West Fourth Street. I called. To my surprise, a woman answered with a British accent. I told Olga Bewsey, Austin's wife, that I was looking for work, and she said they needed help with the Christmas rush.

I had only worked with Austin for a matter of months when I made an appointment to meet Daniel Ransohoff, a social worker and photographer. I was impressed with Danny's photographs of the inner city that had been published in the *Enquirer Sunday Magazine*. That was the kind of photography I wanted to do.

When I arrived at my appointment, Danny looked through my meager portfolio of pictures, pointed to himself and said, "Now I'm a whore but you are an underachiever."

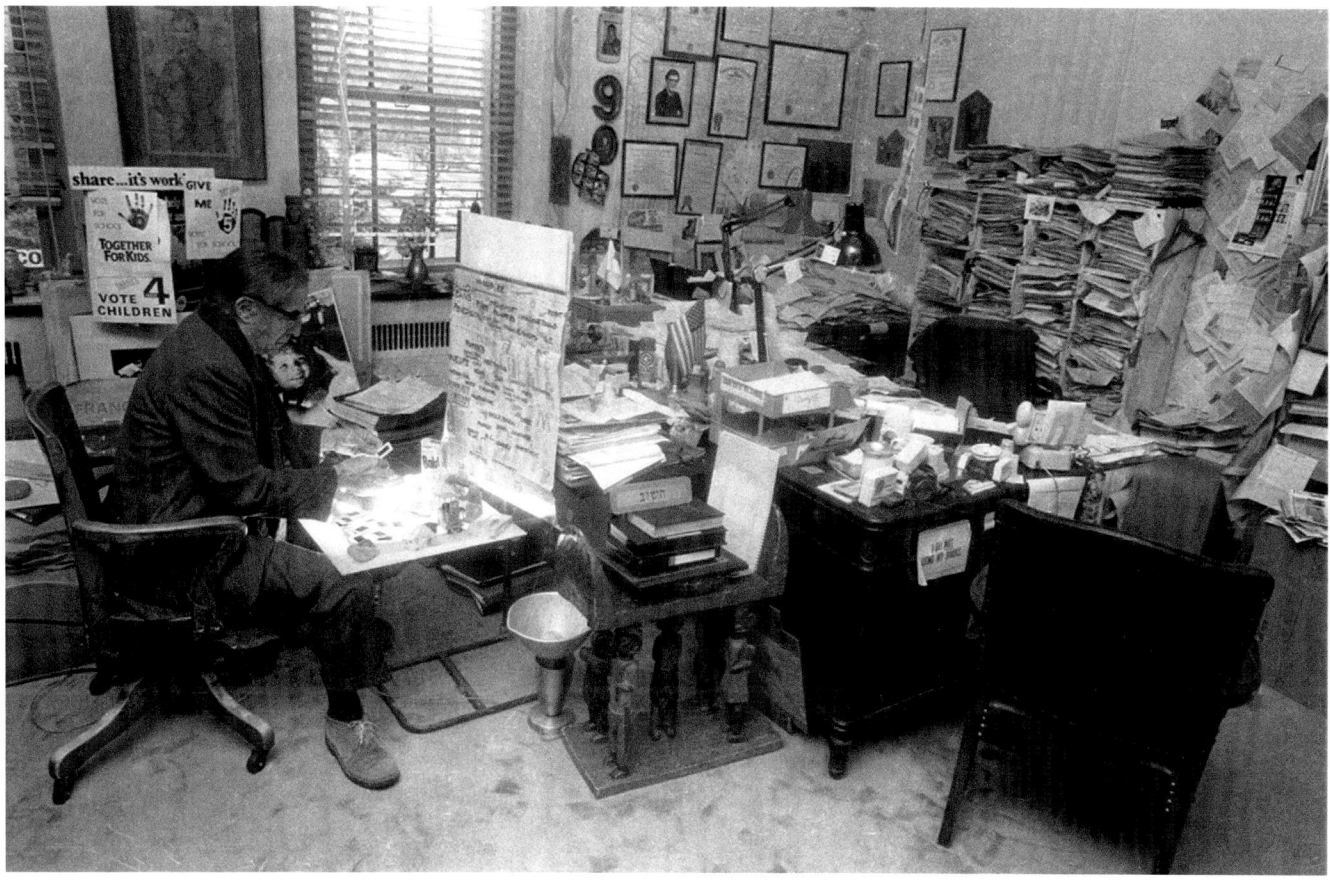

Danny Ransohoff in his office on Reading Road in Mount Auburn. Our first meeting led to a longtime professional relationship.

That stung a bit, but I replied that I needed a job, as Austin had told me I would not be needed after the holidays. Luckily for me, Ransohoff had a working relationship with Young and Klein lithographers, a printing company in Northside, a middle-class Cincinnati neighborhood that still had farms. The company was run by Benjamin Klein and Ed Young. I was hired as a casual laborer at $75 a week, meaning no benefits but the opportunity to work my way into an apprenticeship, journeyman status, and union membership.

The following Monday, when I walked into Young and Klein for my first day of work, I experienced what made it a unique place of employment. Ben Klein was in rare form, spewing a string of profanity to whoever had not measured up to the high production standard demanded at Young and Klein. His eruptions were equal to the worst I had heard from my training sergeant during basic training in the Air Force. There was one standard at Young and Klein—excellence. Woe unto him that didn't meet this requirement.

Their clients included leading Cincinnati institutions, both art and commercial. The company had about two-dozen employees trained to do precision camera and press work. A man named Johnny Rodgers guided me through my struggles to learn shooting halftones using various line screens that gave 150-200 dots to the inch.

With time, I attained journeyman status with all its privileges. I felt a sense of accomplishment in the fact that I had hung in there and was a full member of Young and Klein's workforce. Still, this job did

In 1969, I married Brenda Turner, the woman that has been by my side for more than 50 years. Fairly soon after being hired by The Post, Brenda and I used my G.I. Bill benefits to purchase a house in Cincinnati's South Avondale. Our family included Calhoun, an old English sheepdog, and Rufus the cat.

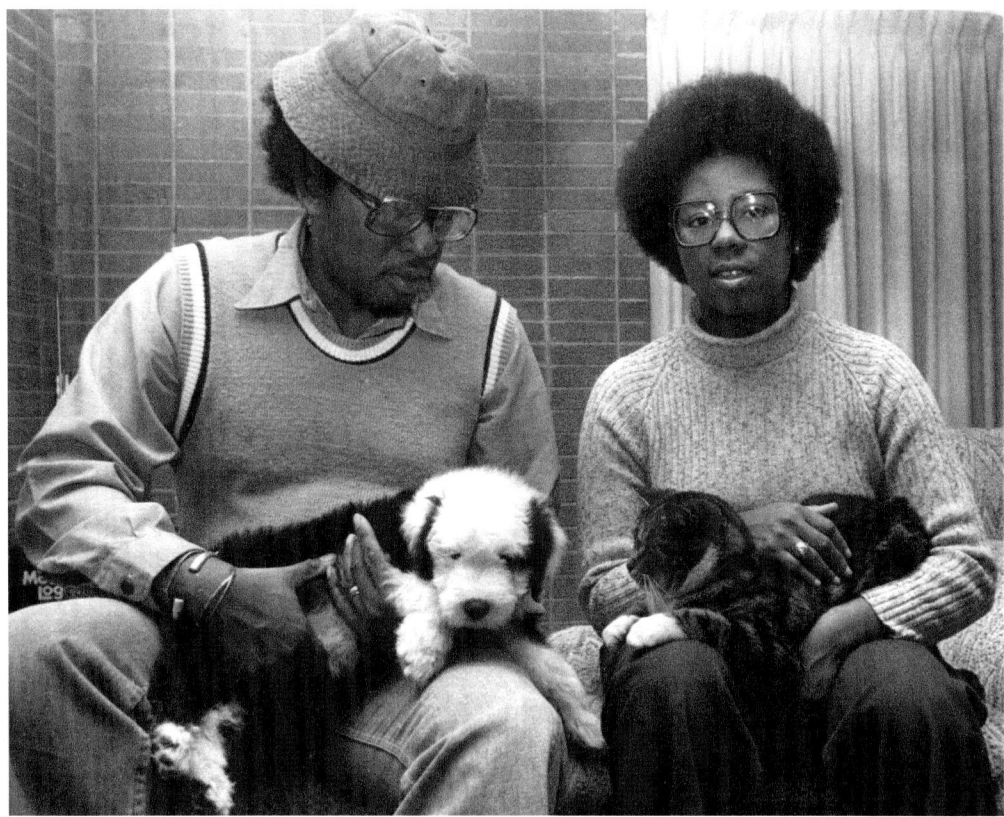

not fulfill my passion for my own photography, and I devoted my off time to its pursuit.

I began teaching photography during this time and met my future wife Brenda Turner at the old DePorres school building in the West End, where I was teaching in exchange for darkroom space. She and a few of her friends signed up for the class, and I sensed almost immediately there was a feistiness about Brenda that I liked. We dated less than a year and were married in 1969.

After we were married, Brenda and I lived in an apartment in South Avondale, not far from where we live today, and her sister came to live with us. I wanted to develop my own prints, which was a lot cheaper than going to a lab, plus it gave me more control over the images, so I set up a temporary darkroom in the bathroom, which consisted of a large sheet of plywood over the bathtub and a small piece that covered the sink. When I needed to use the darkroom, I would announce to Brenda and her sister that if they needed the bathroom it would be best to act promptly, because I had work to do. This system worked quite well. Several years later, when we bought our first and only house, the first thing I did was put in a darkroom, which is still in operation today.

On two occasions, I had several of my photographs published in the *Enquirer Sunday Magazine*. This was thanks to a man named Jack Cannon, who was the editor. One was a spread of Findlay Market, and the other featured various local African Americans. This satisfied my appetite, but the satisfaction was short-lived.

Among other magazines, Young and Klein printed *Cincinnati Magazine*. When I came across photographers that to me lacked soul, I became frustrated, because I was confident I could do a better job. A plan began to form in my mind.

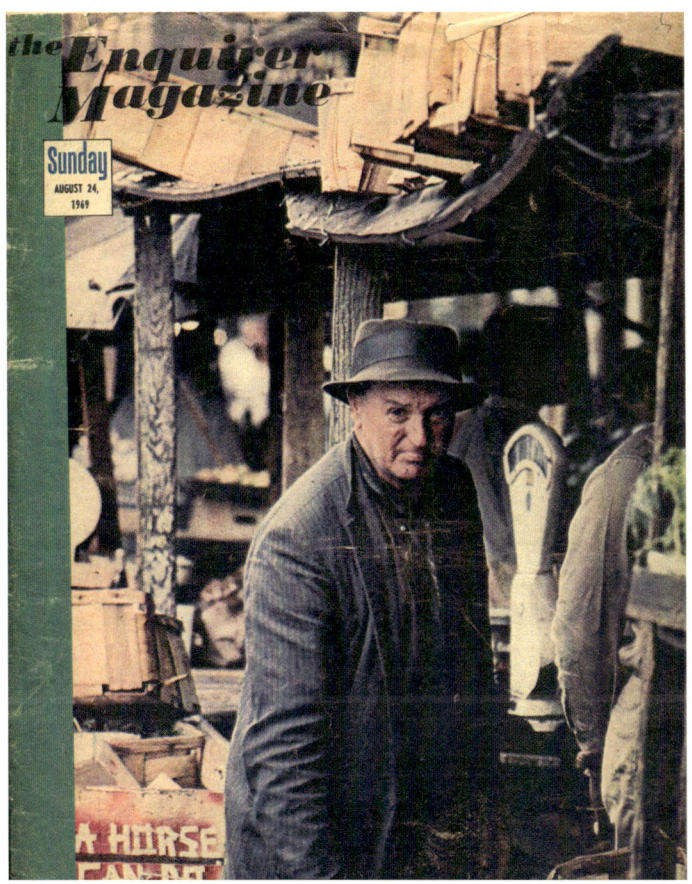

Cincinnati Enquirer Sunday Magazine, August 24, 1969, featuring my Findlay Market photographs.

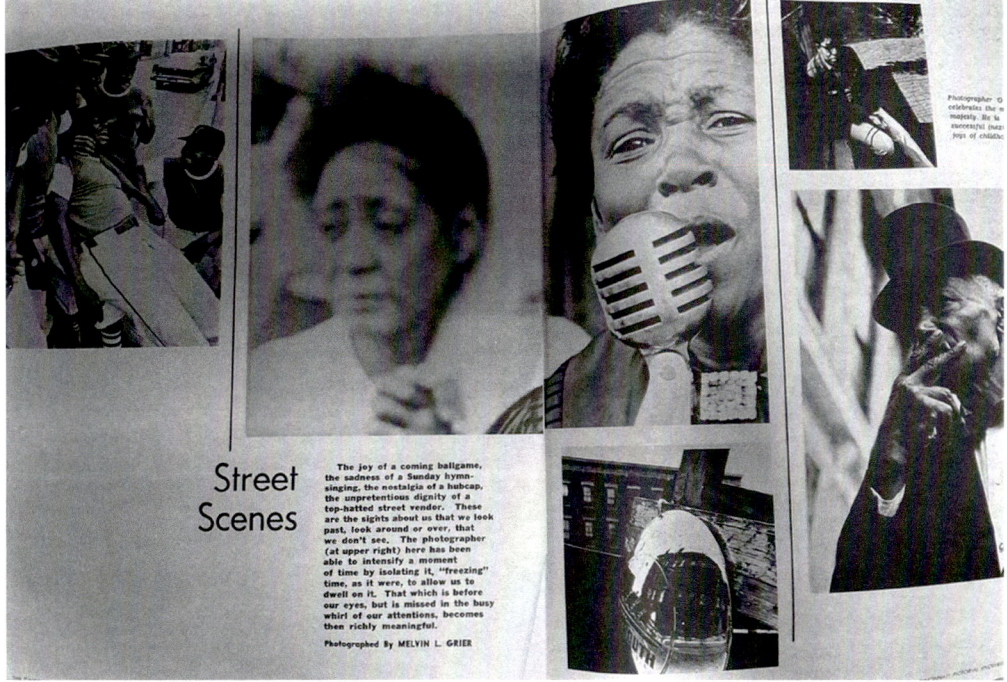

Cincinnati Enquirer Sunday Magazine, October 29, 1967, that included a series of my street-scene photographs of African Americans.

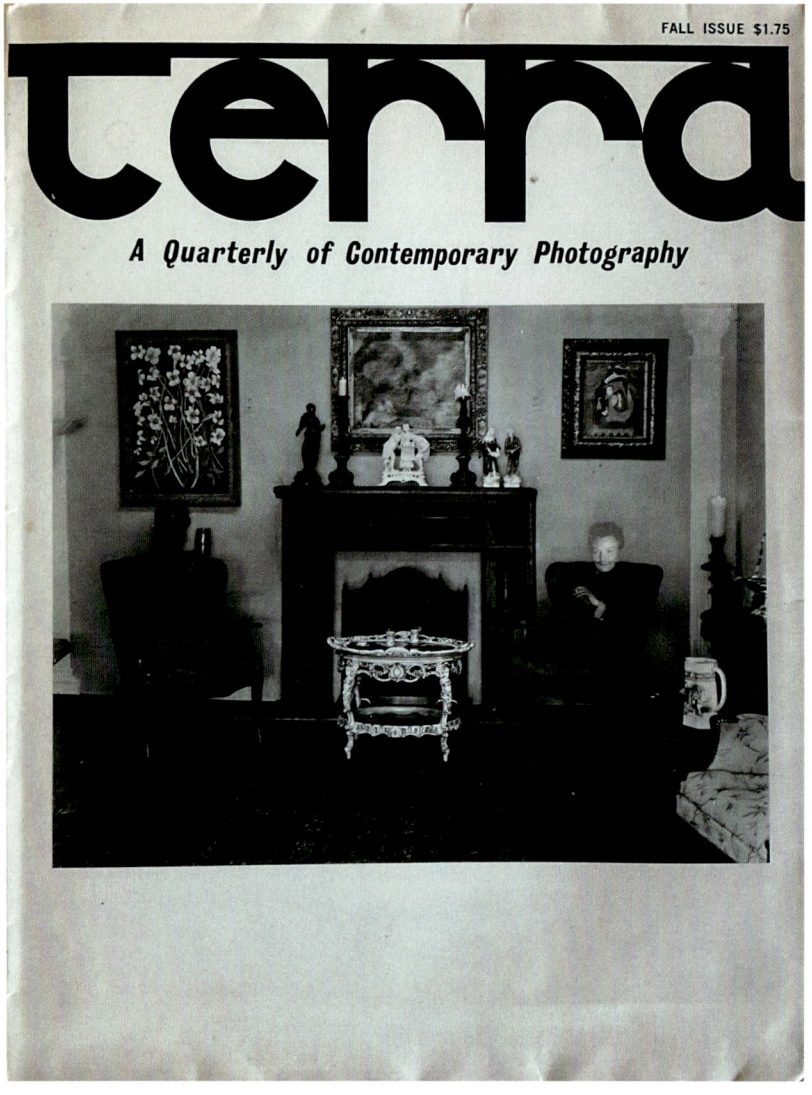

This artistic endeavor became TERRA, Latin for earth, a publication that had a brief but critical existence in my career. The cover photograph was made by Jan Lipicky.

TERRA was a one-of-a-kind publication, not a magazine or journal, but a collection of frameable, loose, 8½ x 11 inches, black-and-white photographs in a die-cut folder. It was an artistic success but a business disaster. I was the editor, while Gordon Baer and a couple of other photographers were on the staff. The limited promotion budget was one obstacle, and my lack of enthusiasm for pounding the pavement to sell the magazine was the other.

I did manage to get copies in a few downtown camera stores, but TERRA was expensive (it cost $2.75 to ship, and we only charged $1.75). It was also difficult to peruse because of its portfolio format. We managed to publish three issues over a period of about six months before financial considerations told us it was time to move on.

About the same time, more change was in the air. My wife was finishing up her studies at the University of Cincinnati which meant she would find employment as a social worker. Our financial responsibilities were few, and I decided that it was time for me to get serious about professional photography. After discussing it with Brenda, I gave my two-week notice at Young and Klein. The last day came, and as I packed up, a coworker gave me a small bottle of Mateus wine. I vowed to myself I would only drink it if I failed. It's still sitting on the shelf unopened.

My mind was full of happiness and excitement. I felt confident, and Brenda's support was unwavering, as it would be throughout my career. Heading home with my dream and my bottle of wine, I caught the 17 Metro bus downtown, then transferred to a bus that would take me to my stop.

First thing on my to-do list was to learn how to drive. We had just bought a new Volkswagen Super Beetle, and Brenda offered to teach me

One of my workplace friends was Bob Salt. Bob was a very talented guy both with photography and graphic design. I shared with Bob my idea for an ambitious photography publication, and to his credit, he hesitated not one second. Together, we produced a prototype designed like a Christmas card. The die-cut envelope was printed on heavy paper that opened to reveal a collection of black-and-white photographs submitted by photographers, local and national. We designed a protective box to ship the publication.

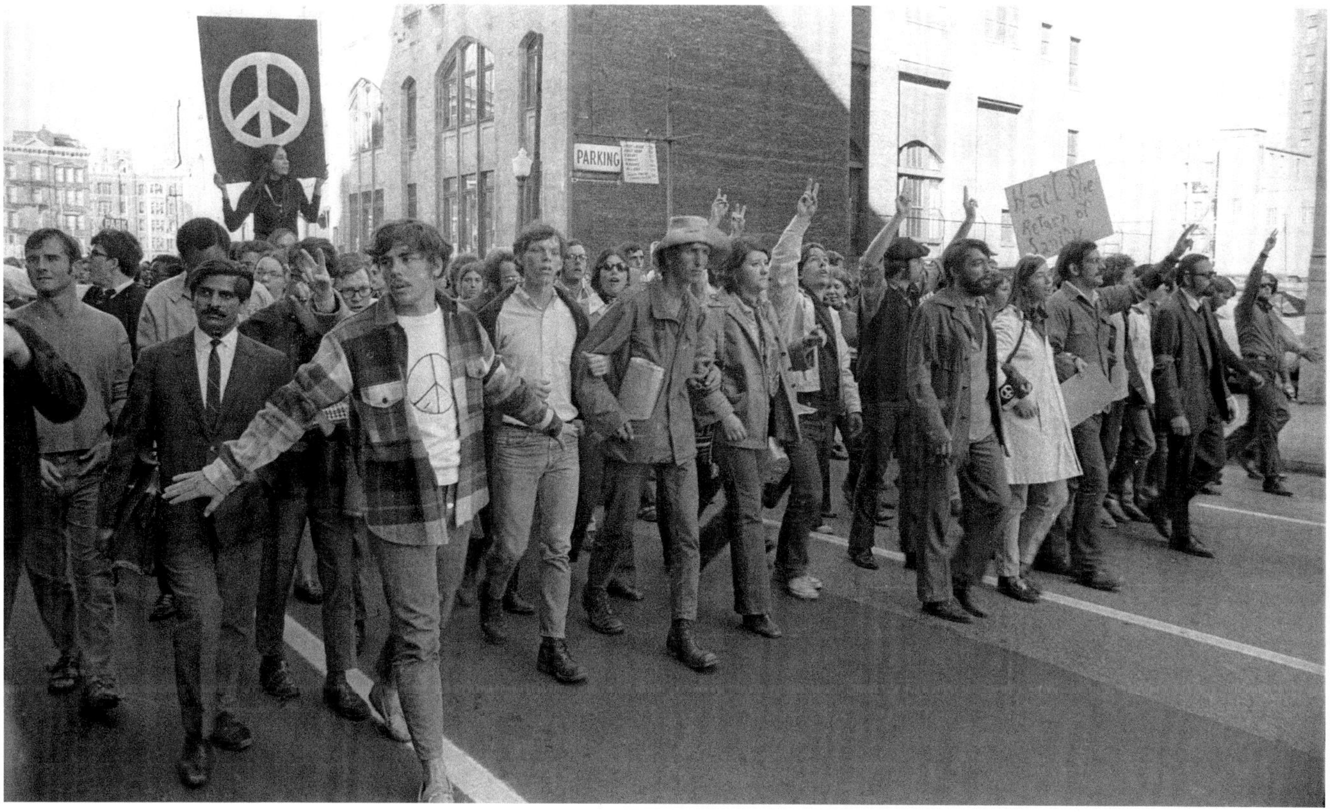

to drive. Next up, success as a photographer, not as a wedding photographer but as a street photographer. Although I did have one source for earning a bit of money. Doris Rankin Sells, one of the founders of the Robert S. Duncanson Society (a group I would one day become very familiar with), was a civic leader and major figure in local politics. She would hire me on occasion to photograph a conference or portraits of individuals for publicity purposes.

I had also done occasional work for *The Independent Eye*, an underground newspaper which focused on opposition to the Vietnam War and other social justice issues of the day (I use the word "work," but I was never paid). I did both writing and photography for *The Independent Eye* and met some interesting characters along the way. We had our editorial meetings at a large house in Clifton

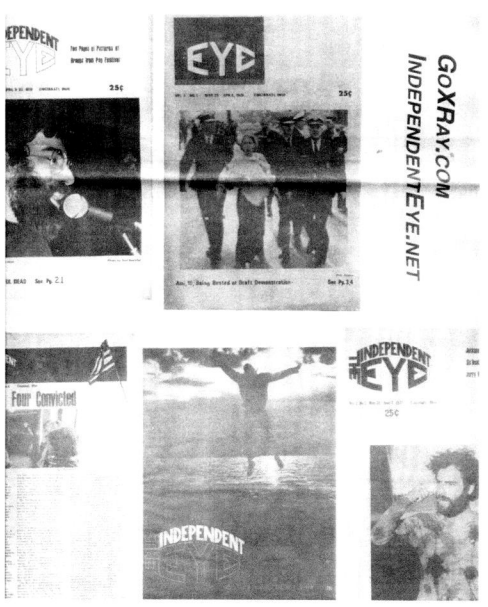

During a peace march, protestors head up Walnut Street in downtown Cincinnati.

This is a compilation page celebrating the now defunct Independent Eye. The photo at bottom center I made while stationed in Maine the last year of my enlistment, which I called "Gruber Jumping."

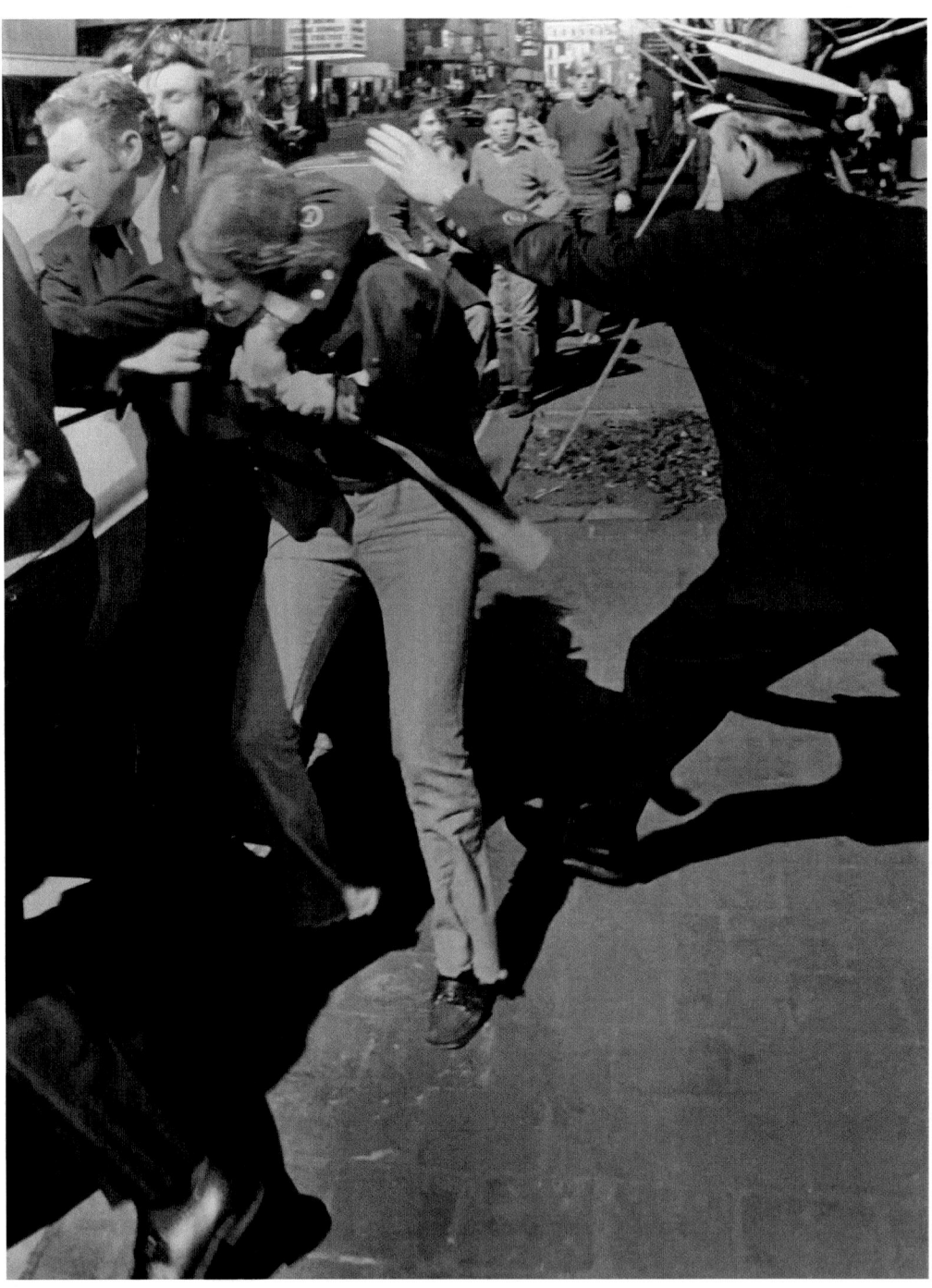

Cincinnati police arrest a protester after a U.S. flag on a pole in Fountain Square was taken down by people protesting the Vietnam War.

owned by Ellen and Monty Sher. On one occasion, a staffer got overly excited, and jumped barefoot on top of the dining room table, leaving black footprints up and down the white tablecloth. There was a rotating cast of characters working to get the *Eye* published, and at least I saw my work on the printed page.

It was at this point that a chance encounter happened that changed the trajectory of my life. During the brief life of *TERRA*, I had published a photo by Kay Brookshire, who had introduced me to her roommate Mimi Fuller, a staff photographer at *The Post*. One day, while waiting for the walk light at Fifth and Elm, Mimi happened to drive up and quickly informed me that there was an opening at *The Post* for photo staff, and I should apply. I was at the right place at the right time. It was safe to say, I was living off of Brenda and needed a real job ASAP.

I gathered my meager portfolio of prints from the *Eye* and elsewhere and headed to *The Post* for my interview with chief photographer Jack Klumpe, who had a plaque on his desk saying he was a "Nikon Expert." My wardrobe was very limited. I came to the interview wearing blue jeans and a denim jacket, with the excuse that I had just come from shooting on a project. It worked, because soon I was a probationary employee of *The Cincinnati Post*.

CHAPTER 3: THE POST

EARLY YEARS AT THE POST

I arrived for my first day of work in December 1974 excited and nervous. I had always followed *The Post* photographers, and now I was going to meet them. I was already acquainted with Mimi Fuller, but Ken Stewart, Terry Armor, and Alex Burrows were only names to me. Now I was one of them, but unproven. Also, like most everywhere else I went, I was the only Black face in the newsroom, so that was on my mind too.

The Cincinnati Post had its offices, newsroom, and printing presses in the iconic art deco building at Eighth and Broadway. When you walked in the first-floor lobby, the smell of ink was strong. The photo department was on the fourth floor up a short flight of steps. I checked in with my boss Jack Klumpe, and he walked me down the corridor that had individual darkrooms for each photographer. He returned to his desk and left me alone in my darkroom. It was outfitted with a wet area for developing and printing, and opposite was a dry area with the enlarger and paper safe for the light-sensitive printing paper.

At approximately 10:00 a.m., I could feel a slight vibration coming from the floor below. A press run was underway. Standing in the darkroom and feeling the power of the presses, I began to feel both joy and a slight panic that I might screw this opportunity up. (That sentiment stayed with me for a long time as I progressed in my *Post* career. "Don't screw this up," I'd tell myself when faced with an important photo opportunity.)

My first assignment was to sign out one of *The Post* blue staff cars with the help of Terry Armor, a veteran staff photographer, who rode along with me so I could take a picture of a No Parking or No Entry sign. I can't recall the exact wording. It was not exactly great photojournalism, and I'm pretty sure it never saw the light of day. Some of my early assignments were what we photographers dubbed "WMB" or water main breaks. My first WMB was on the approach to the Eighth Street Viaduct.

Jack Klumpe was—to put it kindly—a challenging boss. Like the other staff photographers, I ended each day with Jack critiquing all my photos, and he was brutal.

Many of my assignments were pointless other than keeping me employed. A couple of these stick out. I was assigned to take a photo of a kid playing trombone in a high-school marching band because the kid's father was a friend of Jack's (of this, Jack said, "We take care of our friends," which I found somewhat laughable). The high-school band was performing at a game on the West Side of Cincinnati, which might as well have been in Istanbul, because the West Side was that foreign to me. Adding to that, I had another assignment before the game, which made me late and very anxious about the sacred deadline. I managed to shoot a little game action before halftime and was looking for the trombone player, when I heard "psst psst." It was the kid's dad pointing out his son. Fortunately, I had a passable game-action photograph and one of the trombone player.

On another occasion, and late on a Friday afternoon, Jack handed me a pile of negatives to make prints for yet another "friend." After I was finished, and since Brenda was out of town, I went to a steakhouse and treated myself to prime rib and a couple of vodka and tonics. My job was safe for the time being.

Klumpe always said, if you needed a prop or idea for a photo, you could have the subject give the OK sign (thumb and forefinger coming together, and the other three fingers extended). I'm pretty sure I avoided that gesture, but it became a tradition that whenever staff photographers had reason to shoot each other, we would give Jack's OK gesture.

At this point in my career, I wasn't exactly brimming with confidence in my photographic ability but being in the right place at the right time could ease that empty feeling. One day, as I walked to a downtown assignment, I came upon a man painting the entrance to a building on Broadway a block or so from *The Post* building. He was contouring his body in order to reach a portion of the structure. I shot a few fast frames, got his name, and hurried on to the assignment.

Right place at the right time proved fortuitous more than a few times. I had an assignment to drive north on I-75 to Lincoln Heights, an African American suburb of Cincinnati. The story was that by an unfortunate placement of I-75, the General Electric jet-engine manufacturing facility was in the neighboring village of Evendale, so Evendale got the tax benefits instead of Lincoln Heights. On my way to the assignment, I thought I might get elementary school students at recess with a General Electric water tower complete with a logo as a background. To this end, I brought along a 400mm telephoto lens to compress the scene. However, when I arrived, recess was over. The youngsters were beginning to line up to go back to class. I hurriedly attached the lens, approached one class, and shot a few frames.

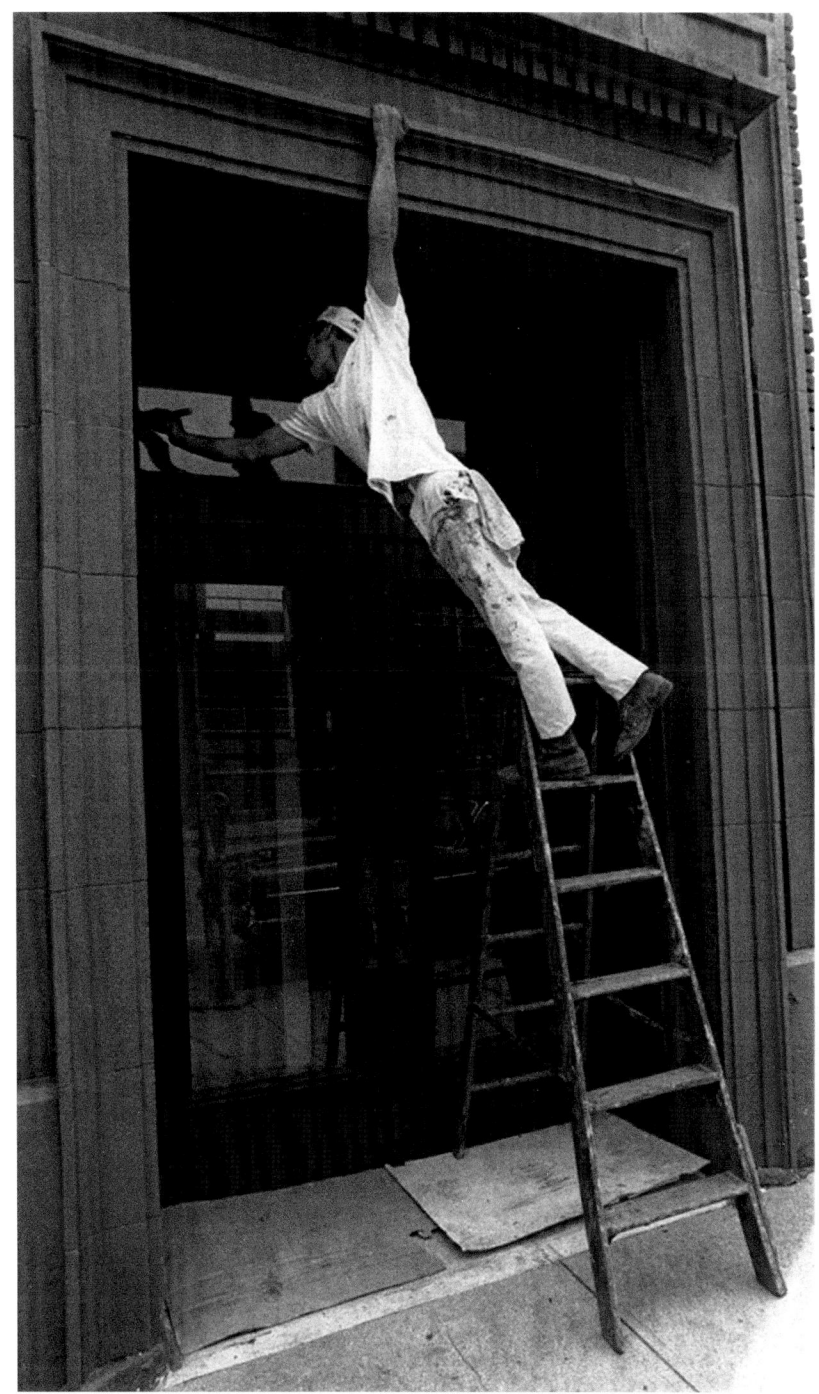

Once back at The Post, I hurriedly processed the film and was very pleased with what I saw from those few frames. Not quite Gordon Parks or Henri Cartier-Bresson quality but close enough to ease my anxiety.

This photo, taken at Lincoln Heights Elementary School, became one of my most popular photographs for The Cincinnati Post. *A friend dubbed it "One by One."*

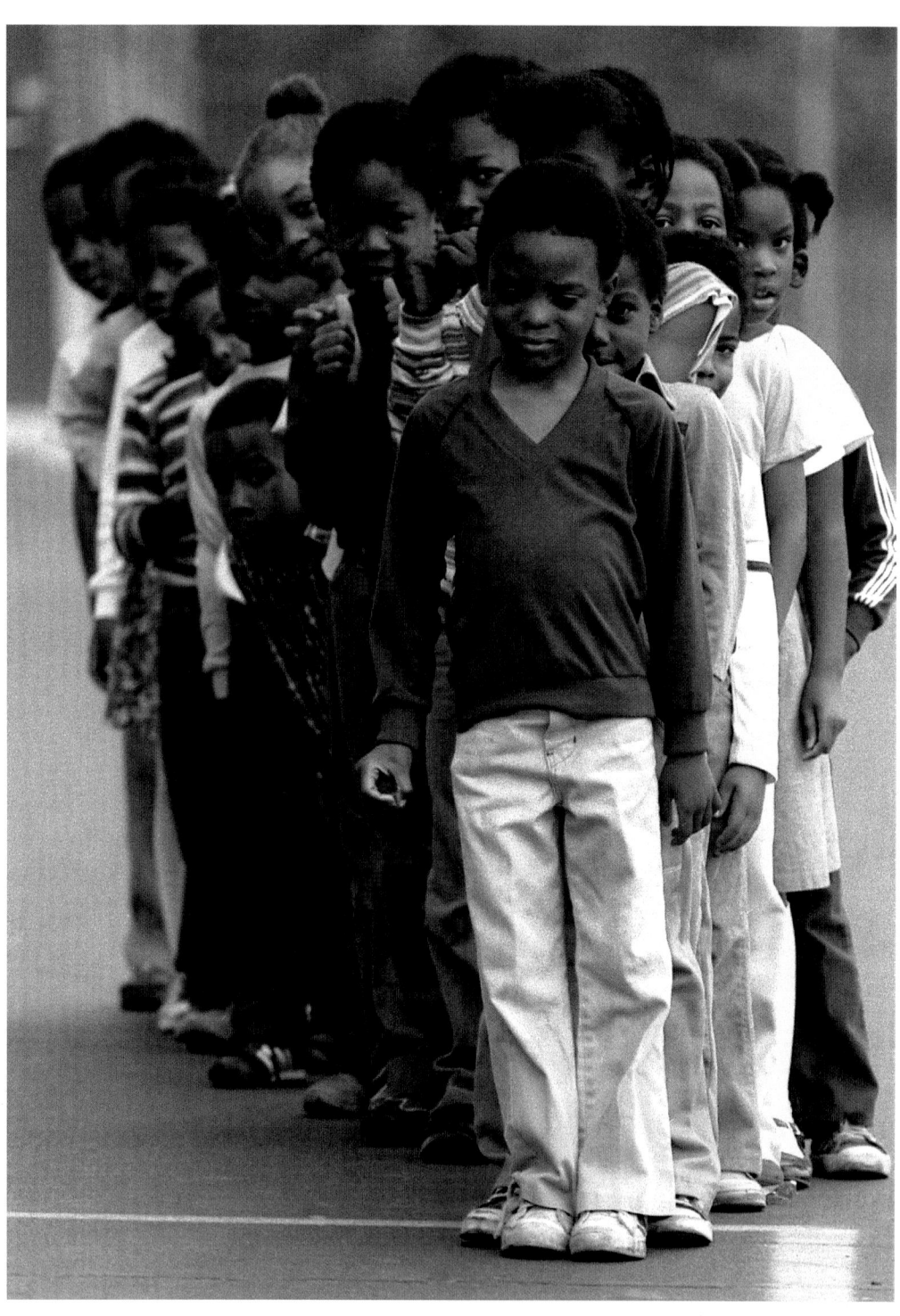

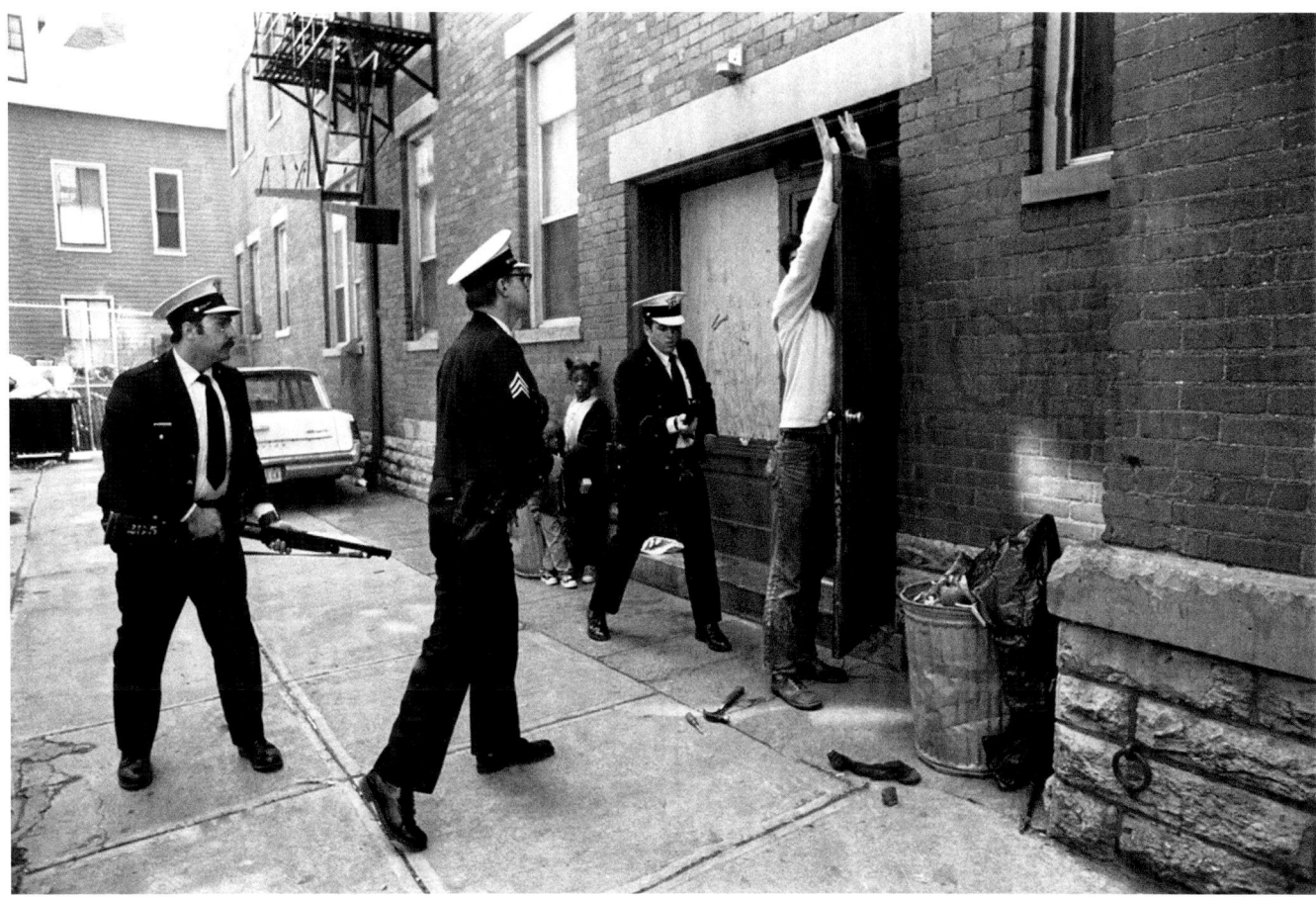

Boss Jack Klumpe said he was impressed with this photograph. Maybe I did belong at The Post after all.

I was not enthused. When I processed the film, however, I became a lot more enthusiastic because I could see that I had nailed something.

Another time, a reporter named Gary Grace and I were told to head to Walnut Hills because a pharmacy had been robbed, and the cops were in pursuit of the criminals. We happened to follow a particular cop car. As we drove down Woodburn Avenue, the officers jumped out of the car and moved at a fast pace into a courtyard. We were not far behind and arrived in time to see the two officers, one with a shotgun drawn and aimed at a man who had his hands up leaning against a door. You couldn't see the man's face. I thought "If I don't screw this up, it's going to be a good photo." After I printed it, I saw two little kids, unidentified, standing in the background. The photo was even better than I first thought. The suspect was a workman with a tool clearly visible on the ground at his feet. He wasn't arrested, and since his identity was hidden. the photo could run in the paper in the next edition.

The Post was an interesting place to work because in the early days, it was like what I had seen in the movies with reporters working at typewriters, some of them smoking cigarettes and calling out "Copy!" Ed Halloran, one of the editors, comes to mind as a newspaper guy from central casting with his starched white shirt, crusty demeanor, and quick wit. When I had a morning shift, sometimes the phone in the photo department would ring, and it would be Ed barking

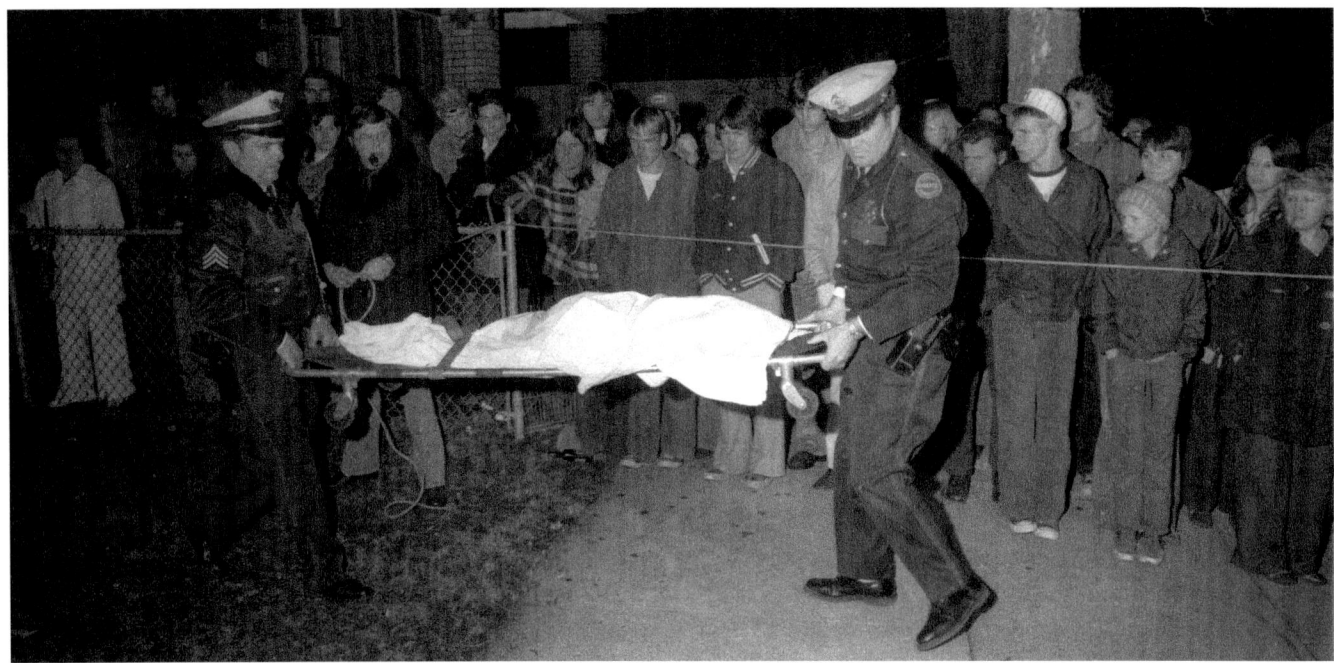

Police carry out the body of one of the 11 victims from the Easter Sunday 1975 massacre.

that I had to "Move out and move out fast" to the scene of an accident. The accident might have happened five or six hours earlier, and there'd be nothing to shoot. Because of the travel time, and because I was a newbie, I thought it was my fault that there was no sign of an accident, but slowly and surely, I got over that.

My first big spot news assignment came three months after I was hired. Late afternoon on Easter Sunday, 1975, an editor called me at home and told me to drive as quickly as possible to Hamilton, Ohio, where James Ruppert had shot 11 family members dead at the grandmother's house. Being a newbie, I was quite nervous as I arrived at the small home on Minor Avenue. I worked my way through the crowd to get as close as I could. At this point, I still did not own a reliable flash. That, coupled with not being sure what f-stop worked best at what distance, added up to a real case of the jitters.

Eventually, police started to remove the bodies, and I had multiple opportunities to get a storytelling photograph before I hurried back to Cincinnati to make the early deadline for the first edition. On my way in, via two-way radio, Jack instructed me to put a photo on the wire first. That meant making a print, typing a caption using the United Press International (UPI) format, putting it on the UPI transmitter, and calling to let UPI know it was available. In a few minutes, a very angry managing editor was banging on the door wanting to know why UPI had the photo before *The Post*. I simply said Jack told me to do it, he stormed off, and I avoided him for a pretty good while.

Legend has it that one newspaper had a headline saying "Easter at Grandma's" regarding the 11 people murdered. I always thought of the perpetrator as "Little Jimmy Ruppert" because of his slight build (he died in 2022 in prison at the age of 88).

Looking back on that Easter Sunday assignment, I was a very inexperienced staff photographer. As I grew more comfortable in my own skin and in my photo techniques, I came to realize that I was just lucky to have made something usable for the first

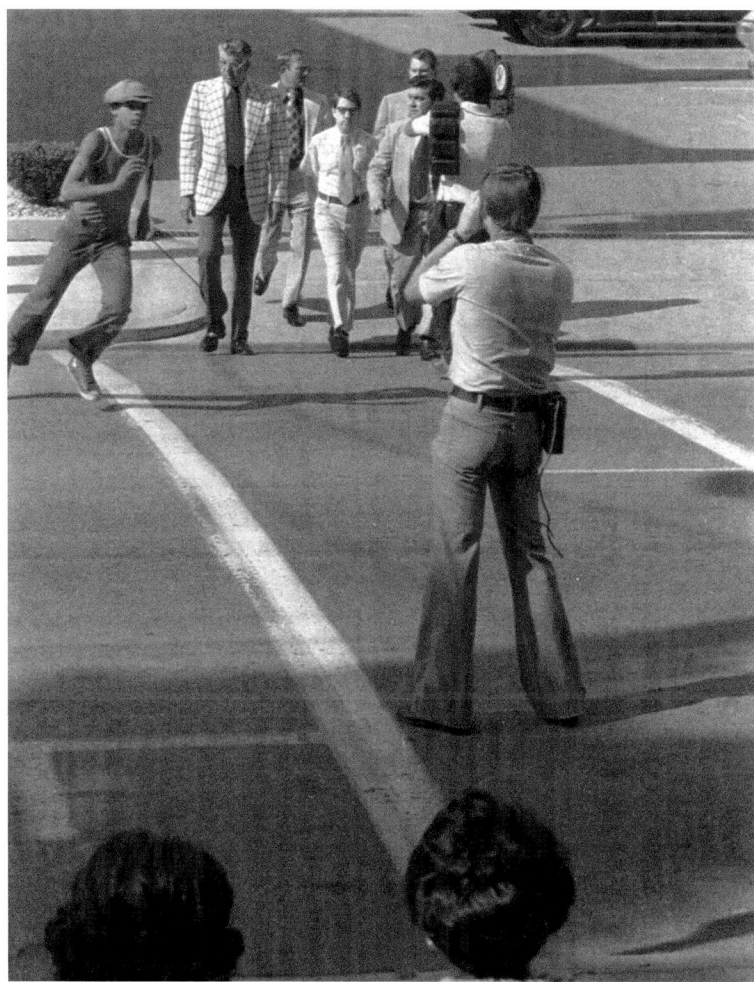

Jimmy Ruppert (center) is escorted to his trial at the Butler County Courthouse in Hamilton, Ohio.

edition. After so many years, and looking at what I managed to capture, I can say I did a fairly decent job.

I had no formal education in photojournalism. I was self-taught, which meant I was learning on the job. Along with *The Post* photographers whose work I admired and learned a great deal from, I was also a fan of such excellent photographers as Gordon Parks, Henri Cartier-Bresson, Richard Avedon, and W. Eugene Smith. I read a lot, and the lessons came hard when I failed at something, which became apparent once I had processed the film. I was striving to emulate these great photographers, and when I did not produce a photograph I felt was up to their standards, I felt like a failure.

Since I was the only Black person on *The Post* photography staff, I felt that I could not fail, because that might make it harder for Blacks who followed me. I was often the only Black still photographer at an assignment such as a press conference. Also, I stuck out like a sore thumb, because I was this large guy with two cameras, assorted photo gear, dressed in jeans, with a serious Afro, atop which sat a little blue bucket hat (later, I wore either a baseball cap or a Kufi, the traditional West African hat for men). Whatever impression I made, however, I was usually respectfully welcomed, managed to get the photos I needed and went on my way.

When Jack extended my probationary status for six more months, for no good reason, I walked into my colleague Alex Burrows' darkroom threatening to quit. "Don't let him get to you," Alex said. I impatiently hung on, and eventually, William Burleigh became editor of *The Post*. It didn't take me long to knock on Mr. Burleigh's door to see if the leadership of the photo department would be changing. He asked for six months to put changes in place.

After bringing in Tom Dunning as managing editor, Randy Cochran came from *The Kentucky Post* to serve as *The Cincinnati Post* graphics director and photo's new boss. At one of our first meetings, Randy said, "You have a bad attitude." I pulled out some of my better photos and asked him if he knew what my attitude was when I shot those photos. From that day on, we got along just fine. Jack Klumpe was demoted back to staff photographer.

Randy's motto was, "You make the best photo you can make, you run it as big as you can, and then you do it again the next day." It was a simple formula, but it gave me focus. The joy was back.

THE NUTS AND BOLTS

When I started in 1974, *The Post* staff had a newsroom of approximately 130 employees, with reporters assigned to the various desks or departments: Metro, Business, Sports, Accent (the former women's section). Along with photographers, the staff included graphic artists, editorial cartoonists, and hardworking copy editors.

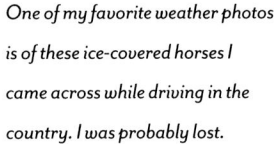

One of my favorite weather photos is of these ice-covered horses I came across while driving in the country. I was probably lost.

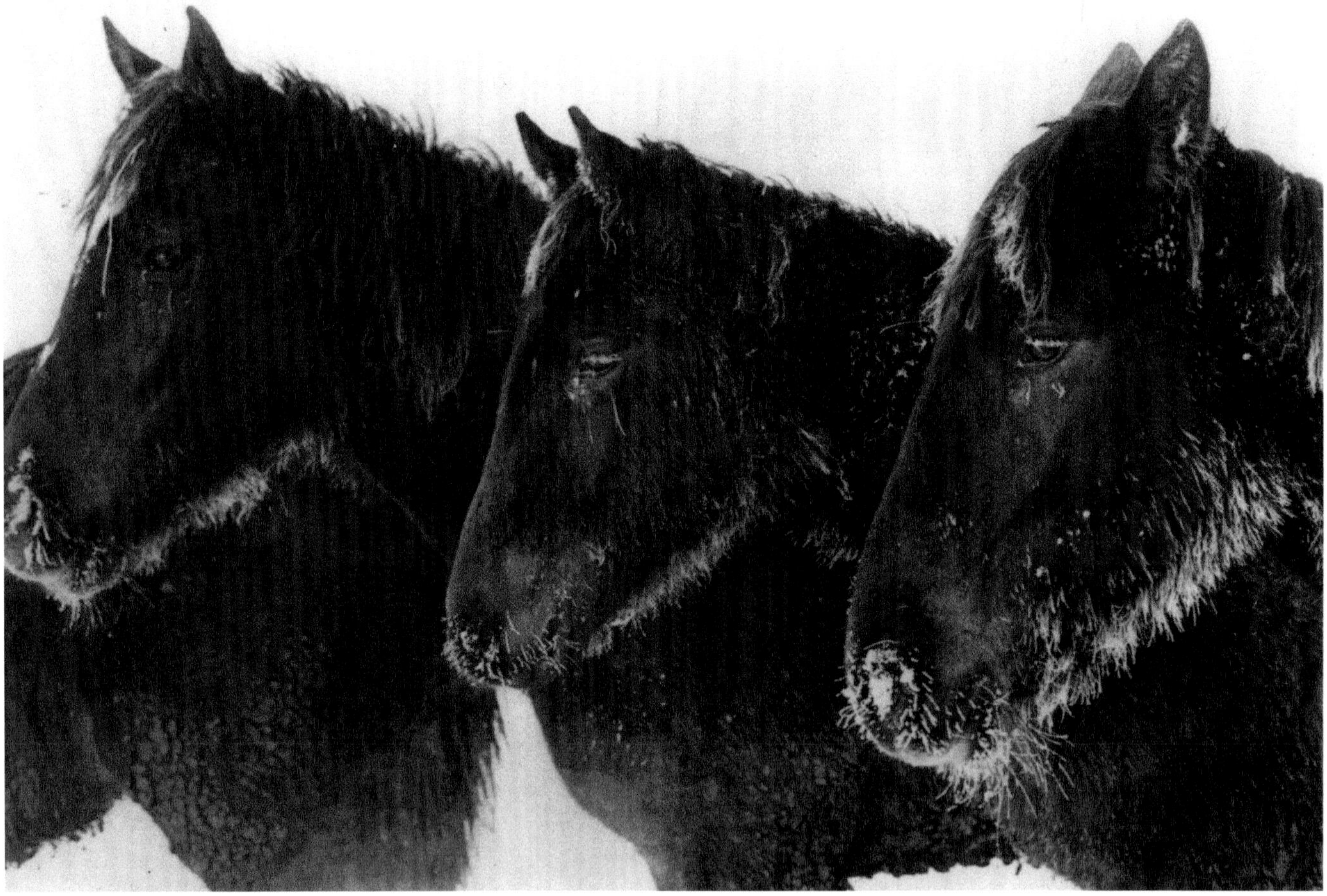

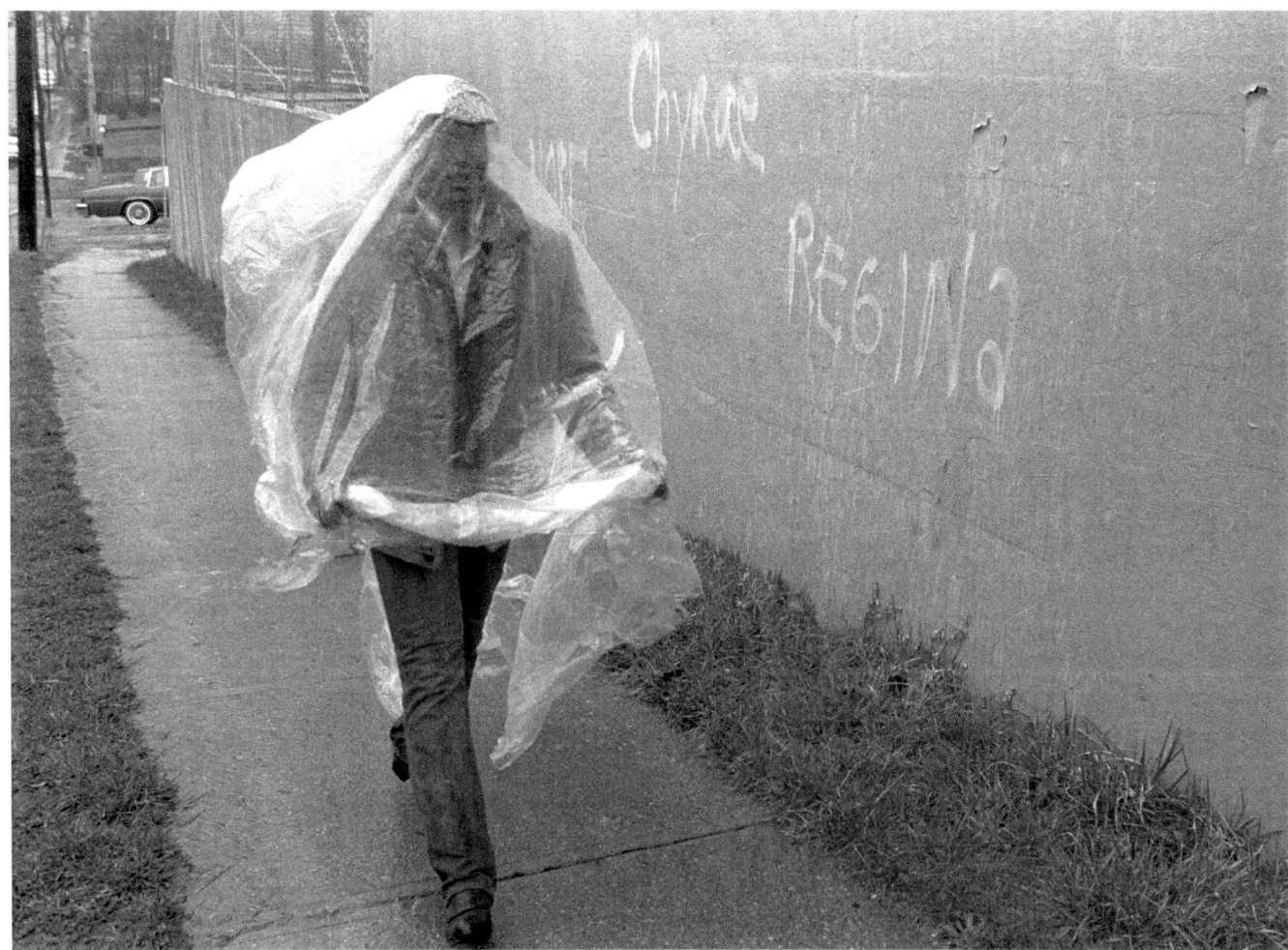

This is the type of weather picture I looked for—this man's creative attempt to stay dry.

Photographers worked for all the departments. Every day was different. You walked in the door, picked up three or four assignments and headed out, driving all over the tri-state depending on the assignments. Sometimes, you shot a portrait in The Post's small in-house studio.

Most every day, it seemed one of The Post photographers had to take a photo that said, "It's beastly hot," "It's snowing like the Arctic," or "It's just another pleasant day with people out and about." One year, The Post published a portfolio of staff photographers' cold-weather photos. Even now, one of those photos, unattributed, will appear on Facebook.

Like other Post photographers, I had my favorite weather route. I left my Avondale home, drove through Over-the-Rhine, then the West End, swung back through OTR, up to Walnut Hills through Eden Park, and hopefully by then had found something to photograph. I always tried to find a little offbeat opportunity like this improvised rain coverup.

As silly as it may seem, weather photographs usually ended up on page one. A go-to story for extremely cold weather was to find homeless people living off the grid. If a reporter was with me, we would head out to find their camps. During daylight hours, it was fairly simple—follow the trail of trash. In the dark, you listened for voices and possibly saw smoke

Hot weather was a prime subject for a storytelling photo. One Friday, I was on feature patrol looking for something, anything to use for the Saturday paper. I headed to the West End and came across a pool that had been replaced by an installation of water features. Just before the kids took a break, I got this shot.

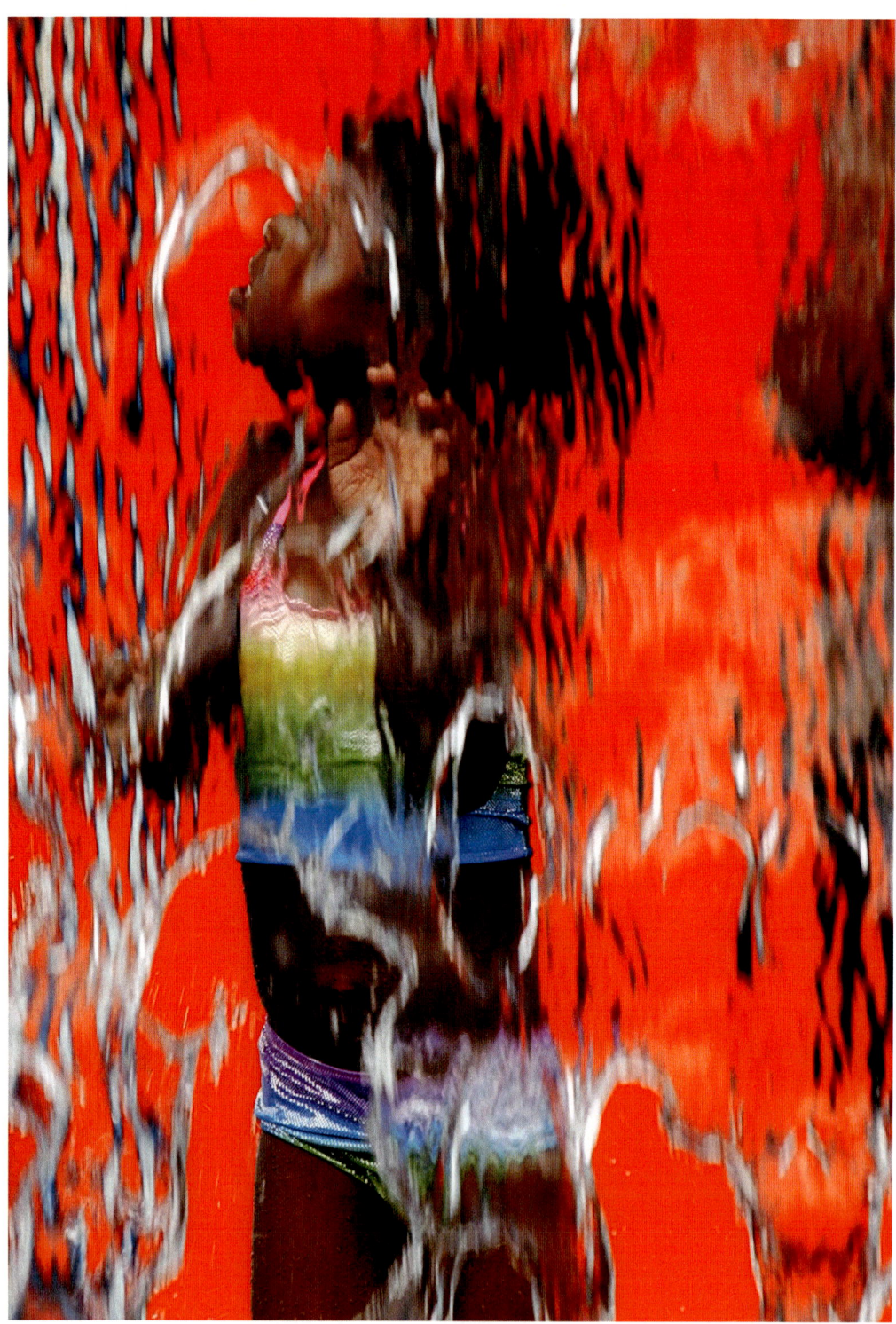

from a campfire, usually on the riverbank. When we did find the camp, sometimes we could sense that our intrusion was unwelcome and resented. It was difficult to make a photograph in the dark; flash was a last resort. I was happy to leave the campers to their evening. (By the way, I use the term "make" a photo when I feel I have succeeded in creating something that has a visual impact. When I "take" a photograph, I have just done the job.)

Traffic accidents were another staple. TV crews had a much easier time getting to the scene, because they drove easily identifiable news cars. Print photographers drove their own cars, so we had to talk our way onto the berm or whatever stood between us and the accident, and not every police officer was eager to accommodate our requests (though I have to say Northern Kentucky cops were more agreeable than most.)

We lived by deadlines, which at *The Post* involved three different editions—early or bulldog, downtown boxes, and home delivery. I made every deadline, though at times I pushed right up against it. When the time came that we no longer had our own presses but shared with *The Cincinnati Enquirer* on Western Avenue, a photographer or clerk would have to drive the photos to Western. In a tight spot, two of us would go—one driving while the other held the print out the window to dry.

I was very sensitive when it came to photographing my fellow Black people. Too often, I had seen photos where there was not enough light on Black faces, rendering them unidentifiable. It was a big deal to have

This driver wrecked his car in Norwood, Ohio during a police chase.

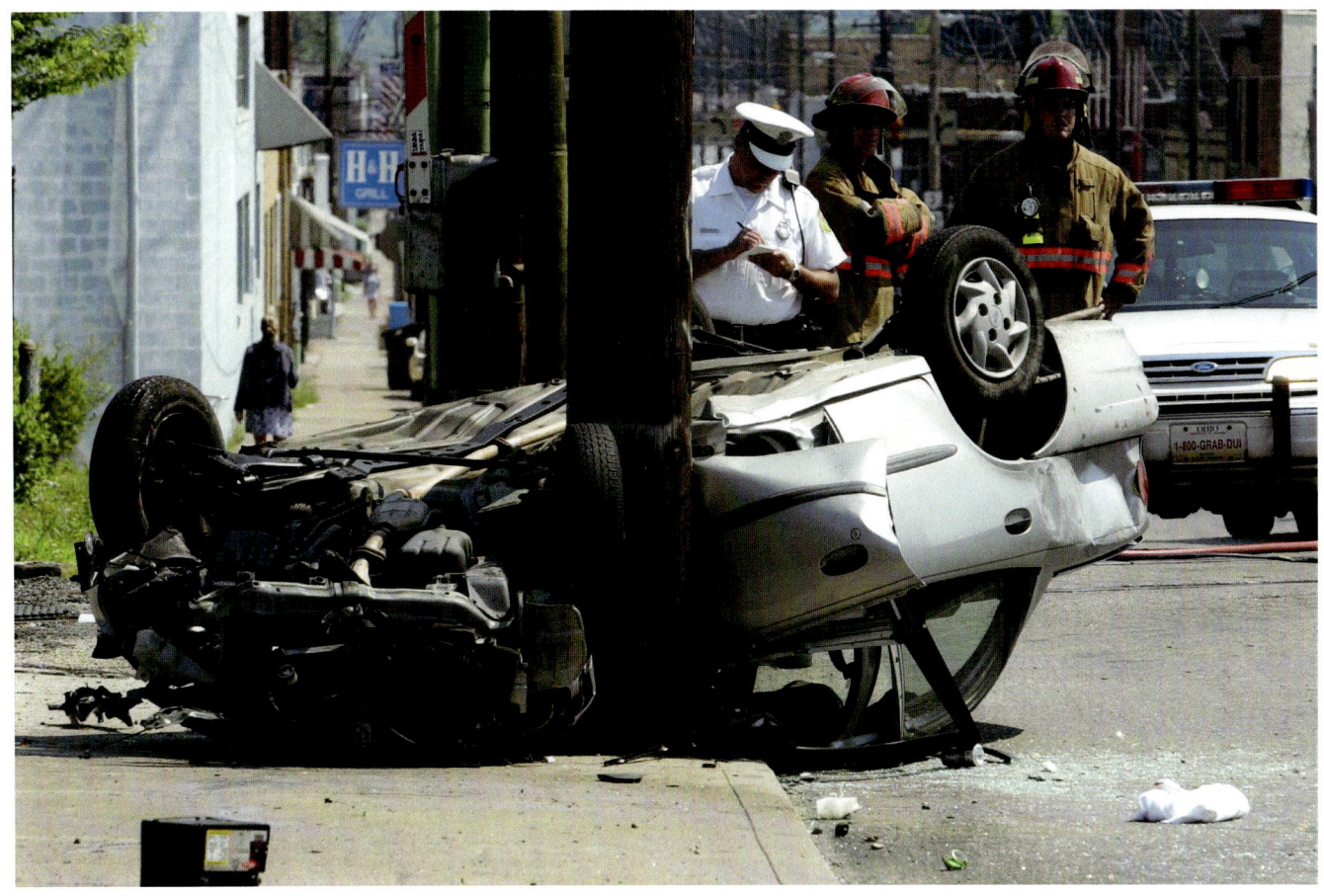

I used late afternoon sunshine for this portrait of Jymi Bolden, director of Art Beyond Boundaries, a gallery in downtown Cincinnati.

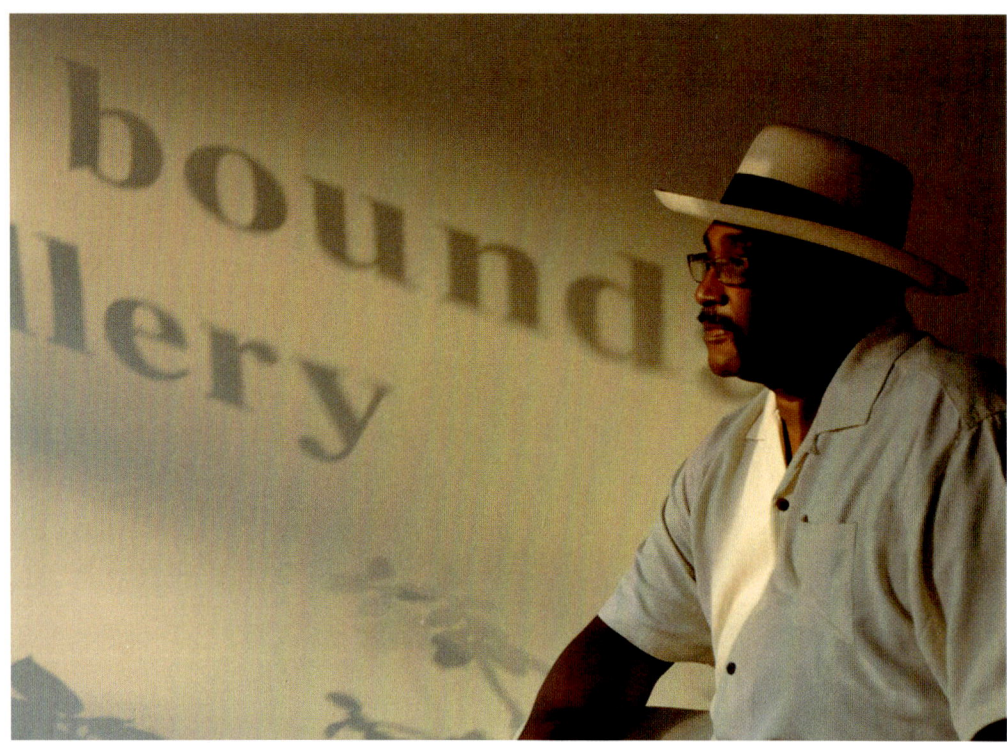

your photograph in the newspaper, and to lose your identity because of a lack of light was unforgivable to me.

One of the most important relationships at a newspaper was that between a reporter and photographer. Most assignments came to "photo" because of a request put in by a reporter who had been assigned a particular story. All stories were not equal in interest or as likely to lead to good "art" as photos were called. On a daily basis, I could not pick and choose my assignments. I took them as they came and did the best I could. On most assignments, I headed out alone, sometimes hooking up later with a reporter. We would touch base during the assignment to make sure we were telling an accurate story in words and photographs.

There were times, however, when a reporter was working on something special and approached me about working with them. As a photographer, I had my assignments for the day, and any extra work, even a request from a reporter, had to be approved by the head of "photo." I often was able to convince the boss and got permission and time to work on the assignment. Time was important, because often, I had other assignments that had to be done in and around the time I could devote to the special assignment.

Molly Kavanaugh came to *The Post* in 1982, and early on, we found common ground being productive colleagues and as a result became good friends. We began a long spell of working together on some very special assignments. One of my favorites was a trip to Parris Island, South Carolina, where young Marine Corp recruits were welcomed and went through basic training. Molly is a tenacious reporter. I recall sitting in a van with one of the sergeants. I felt almost exhausted after many hours of work, and this tough Marine turned to me and asked, "Does she always ask so many questions?" Without hesitation, I answered, "Yes she does."

In 1987, Molly and I accompanied Army reservists to Honduras, where they were undertaking an

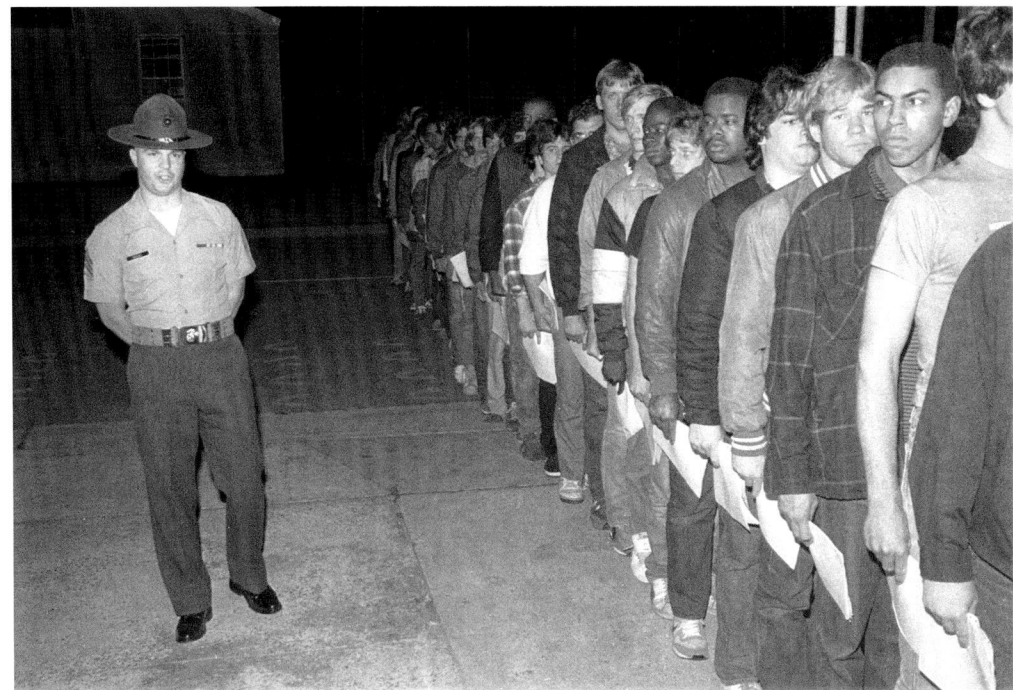

Welcome to Parris Island, Marine Corps Recruit Depot in Port Royal, South Carolina at about 1:00 a.m.

A drill instructor sets a recruit straight.

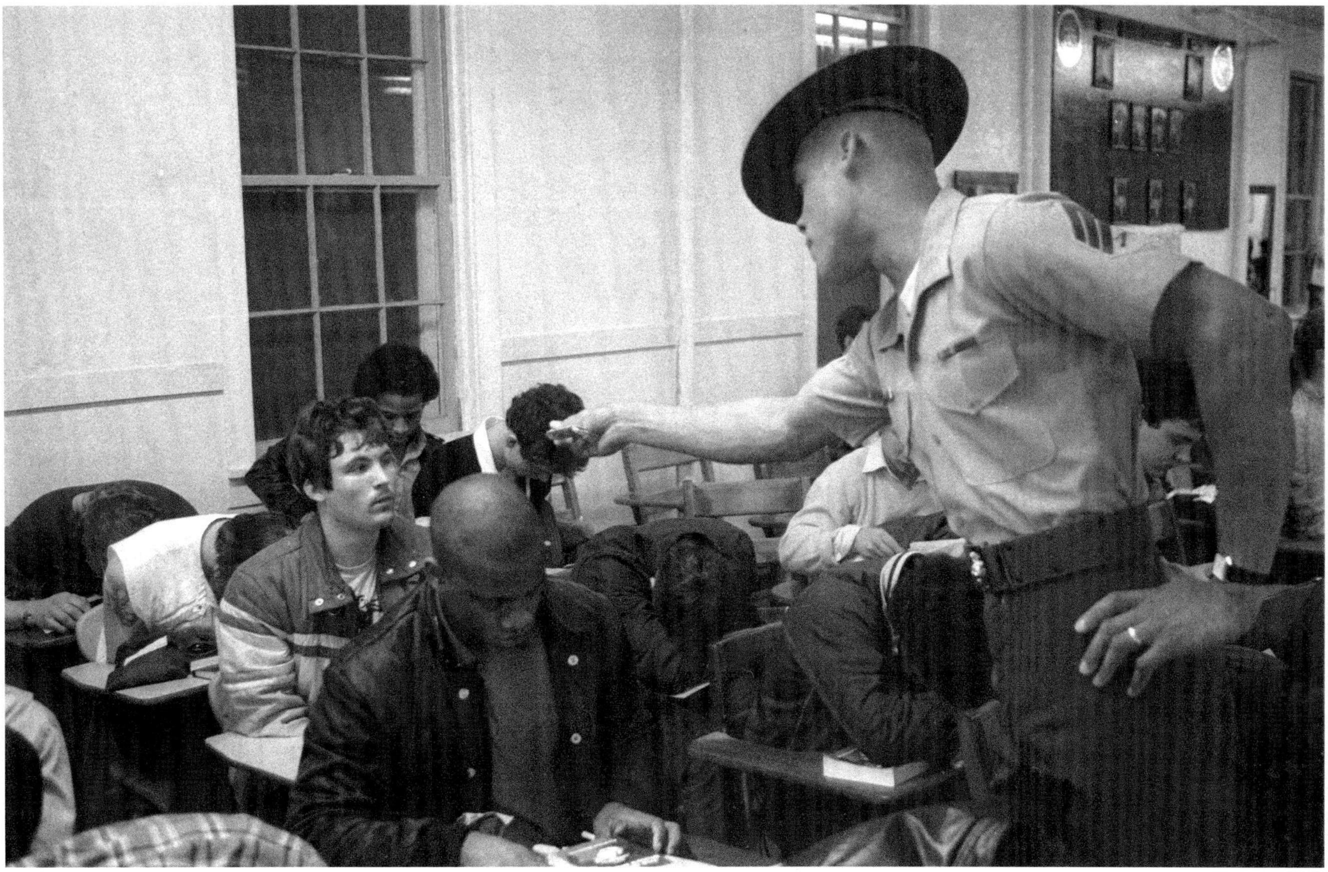

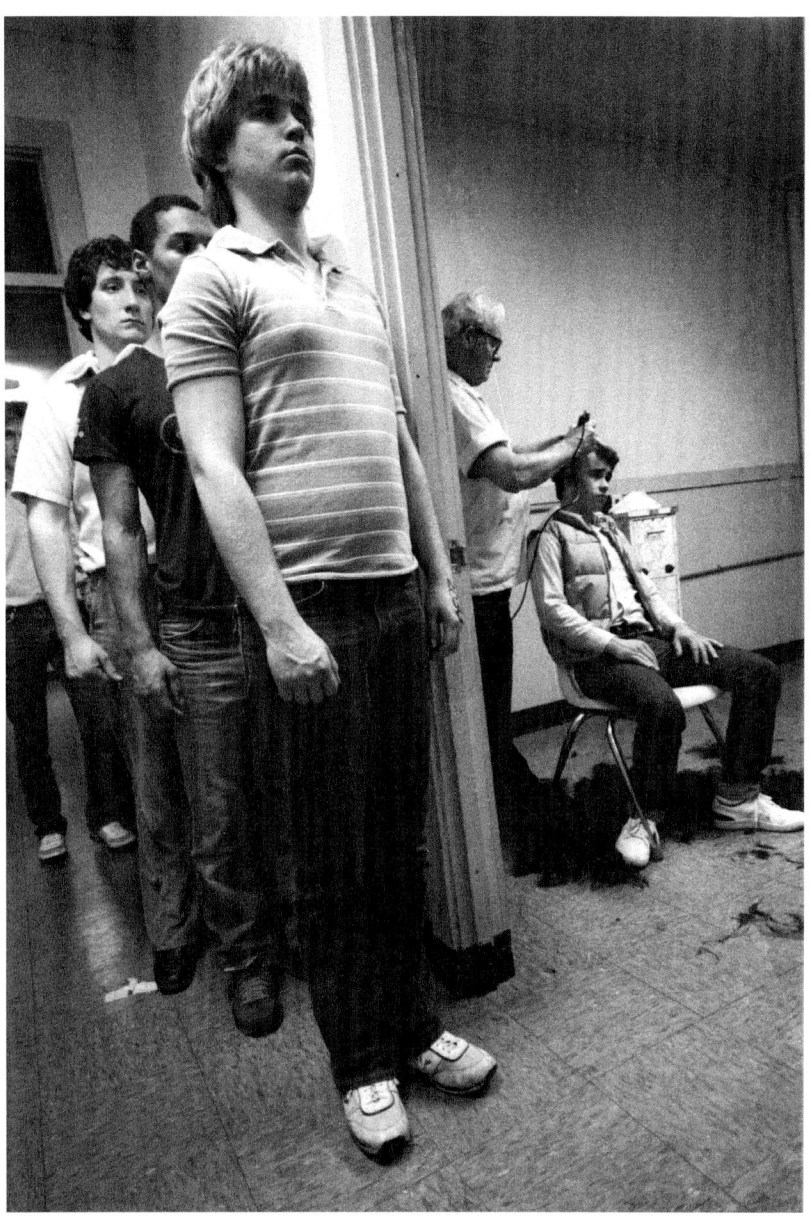

Next in line to get those golden locks cut off, courtesy of U.S.M.C.

operation called "Blazing Trails." We flew there in a cargo plane and took a long bus ride to their camp at Oso Grande, dubbed "not so grande" by the troops. It was hot and dusty, and soldiers were working to improve the rather primitive local infrastructure. We slept on cots in tents and spent time waiting on something, anything, to happen. One eventful morning, the latrine deposits were burned, making for a quick exit from the tents. For one outing, we boarded a Huey helicopter. Molly was belted in a seat near the open door, and I quietly signaled to the pilot to bank the chopper over to give her a better view of the countryside.

After a week in-country, we were homeward bound from the airport in Tegucigalpa, where we encountered a long line. As we pondered our next move, a young boy approached, and suggested we follow him, which we did, and found ourselves at the head of the line. He found some money in his hand from two grateful travelers. Our airline was TACA, also known as "take a casket along." But they served free drinks, and we got to watch the movie "Top Gun." It was a great trip and flight back to the states, but there was work to be done.

Back in the newsroom, we were thrown into daily assignments, and it took us a couple of weeks of collaboration to compose a series of stories with words and photographs. The time lag was due to two things—the Honduras story was not breaking news and finding space in the newspaper to tell a lengthy story was always an issue at the ad-scarce *Post*.

Once in a while, I would suggest a story about something that I thought would make for interesting photographs. I have always had an abiding interest in the so-called inner city, because I was a child of the inner city and now, I had the opportunity to document various everyday scenes from the lives of those who lived there. Sometimes it wasn't pretty, because poverty is not pleasant, but sometimes it was joyful because of the warmth and striving of the inhabitants.

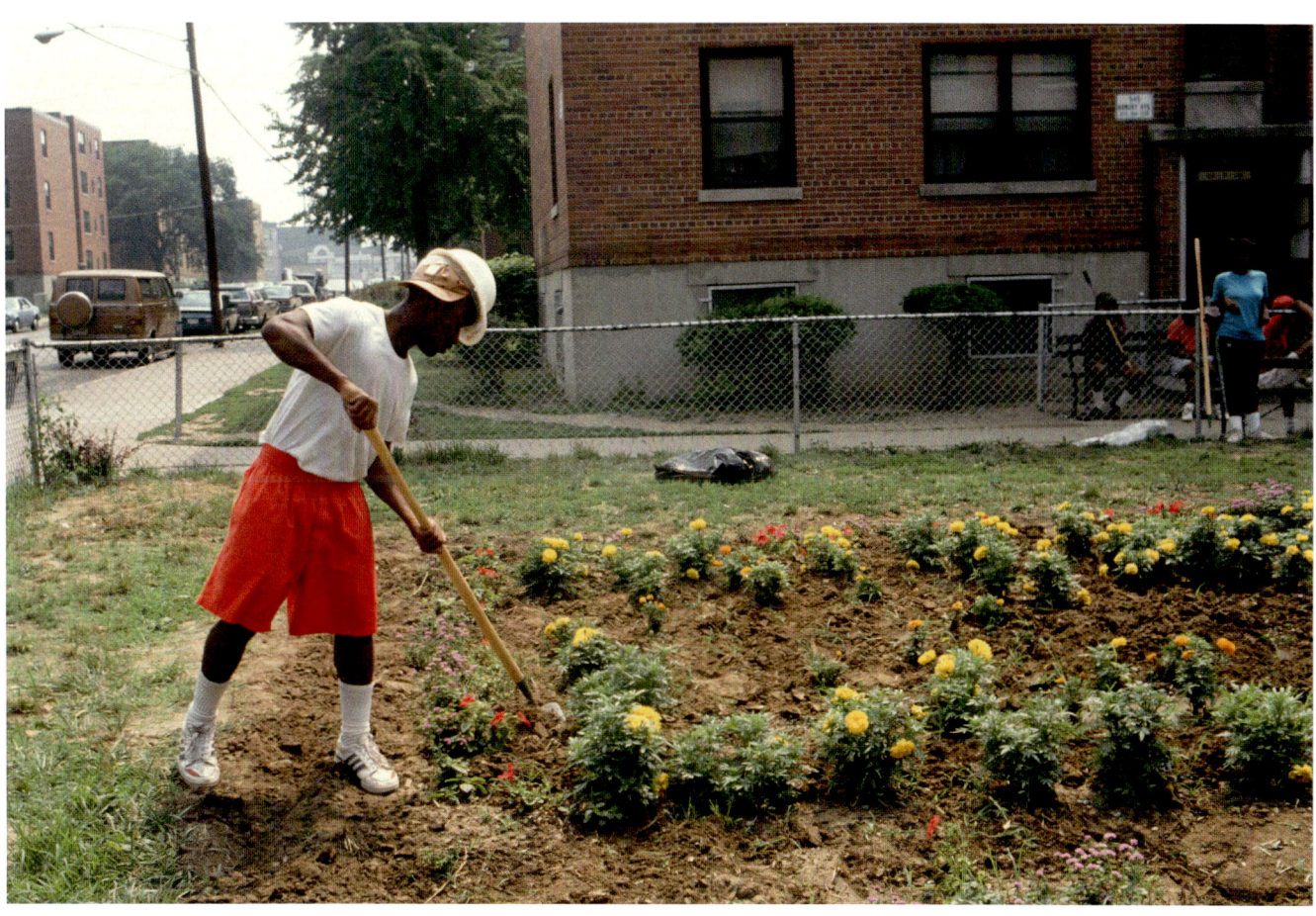

This man tends a garden in the Laurel Homes projects. Consisting of 29 buildings, it was the first housing project built by the Public Works Administration (PWA), and the second-largest housing project in the U.S. It was listed on the National Register of Historic Places.

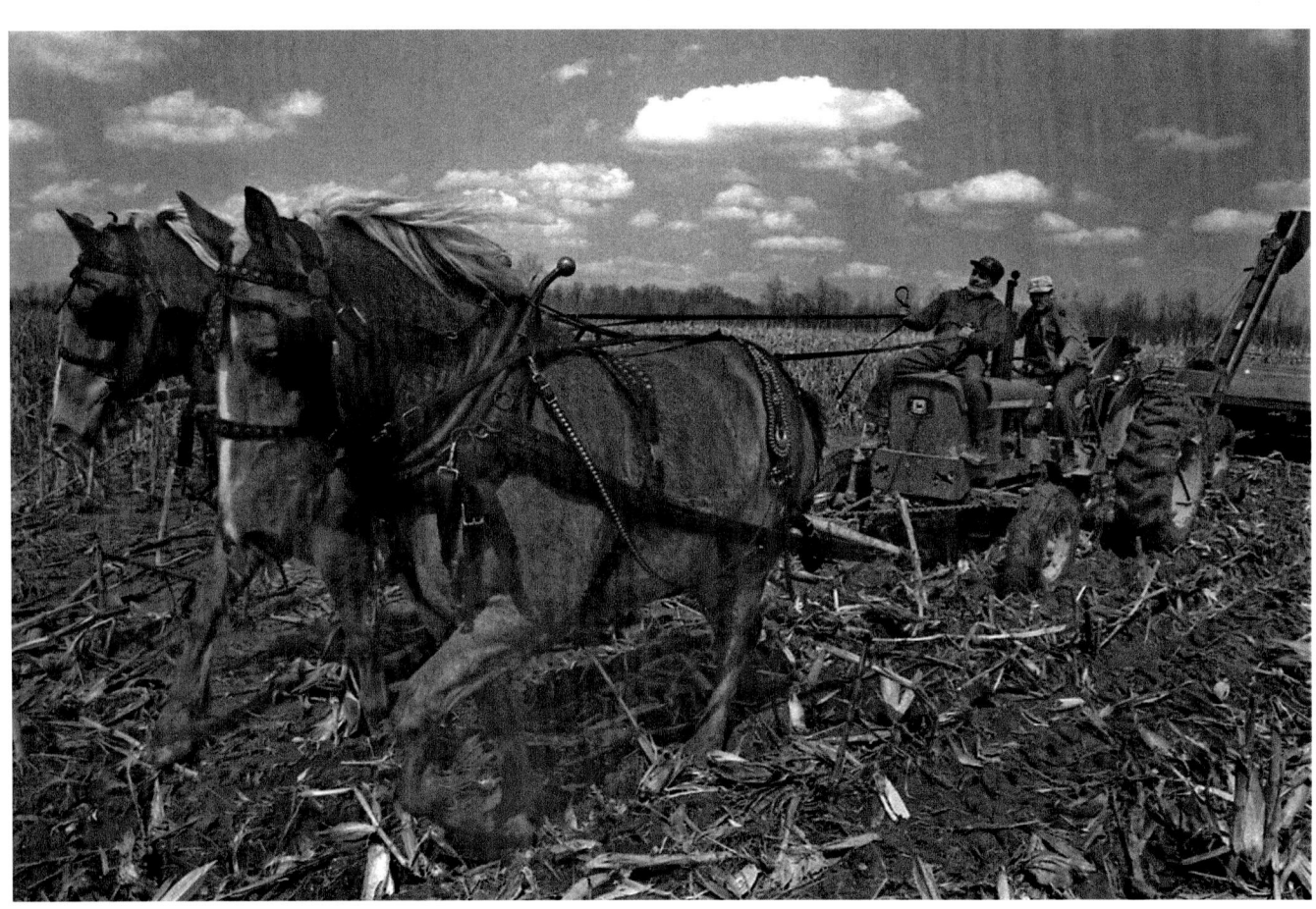

This fortuitous photo op gave me and Post readers what I considered one of my best-ever photographs because of what it says about the spirit of humans to get a job done. A farmer uses a team of horses to pull his stuck tractor out of a muddy field in Clermont County, Ohio.

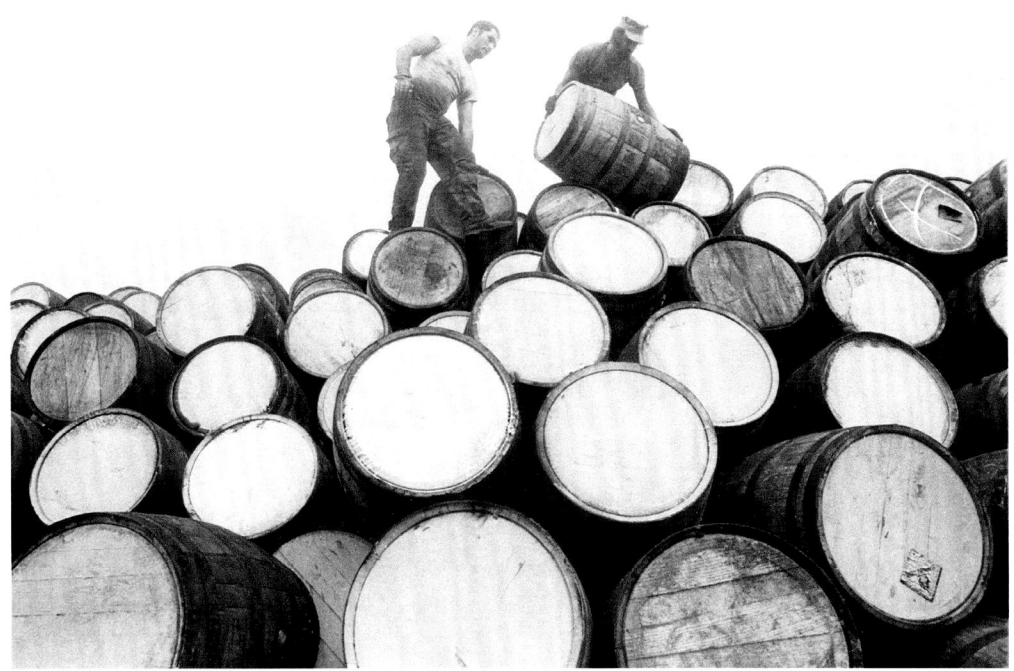

Post photographers also had assignments in Indiana. I was sent to the Schenley Industries distillery in Lawrenceburg, and fortunately for me, workers were stacking more whiskey barrels in a storage area.

In order to convince a reporter of the normalcy that could be found even in the projects, I took them to the Laurel Homes where my wife Brenda grew up. Since her mother and brothers still lived there, I was very familiar with what would be found, including gardens that some residents cultivated. I often saw that a reporter's idea of what life was like in the projects changed for the better.

There was a never-ending search for feature pictures, which was art that could fill a hole on a page in the Metro section. We called it "feature patrol," and because of this necessity, I got to know the city and its outskirts very well.

One day, while out in Clermont County with reporter Tom Fortney, we happened upon a farmer who was pulling his stuck tractor out of a muddy field using a team of horses. He sat on the engine compartment, while a friend guided the John Deere using the steering wheel.

Sometimes, a routine, boring assignment led to something quite different. Oftentimes, what I covered had a lasting impact on me, or at least gave me something to think about, be grateful for, or ponder. I was driving my Isuzu Trooper with Dan Horn, now a reporter at *The Enquirer*, and we stopped on Race Street in OTR. We were to pick up a landlord for a story on housing. I waited, sitting in the driver's seat. Soon, Dan came back saying that there was a fire about a block and a half away. I grabbed my gear, and we hurried to the fire scene (in newspaper parlance, this is "spot news," in other words, live news reported in real time).

On another occasion, I was out cruising, accompanied by a high-school student on a ride-along, when I was sent to an address in South Avondale not far from my home. A fire had occurred in an apartment, and three children died. It was particularly painful to see the firefighters carrying out the little bodies wrapped in blankets. To see the tragedies that occurred to other people had the effect of making me more aware of how important my loved ones were to me.

My interactions with police officers were a mixed bag. For the most part, it was cordial despite the

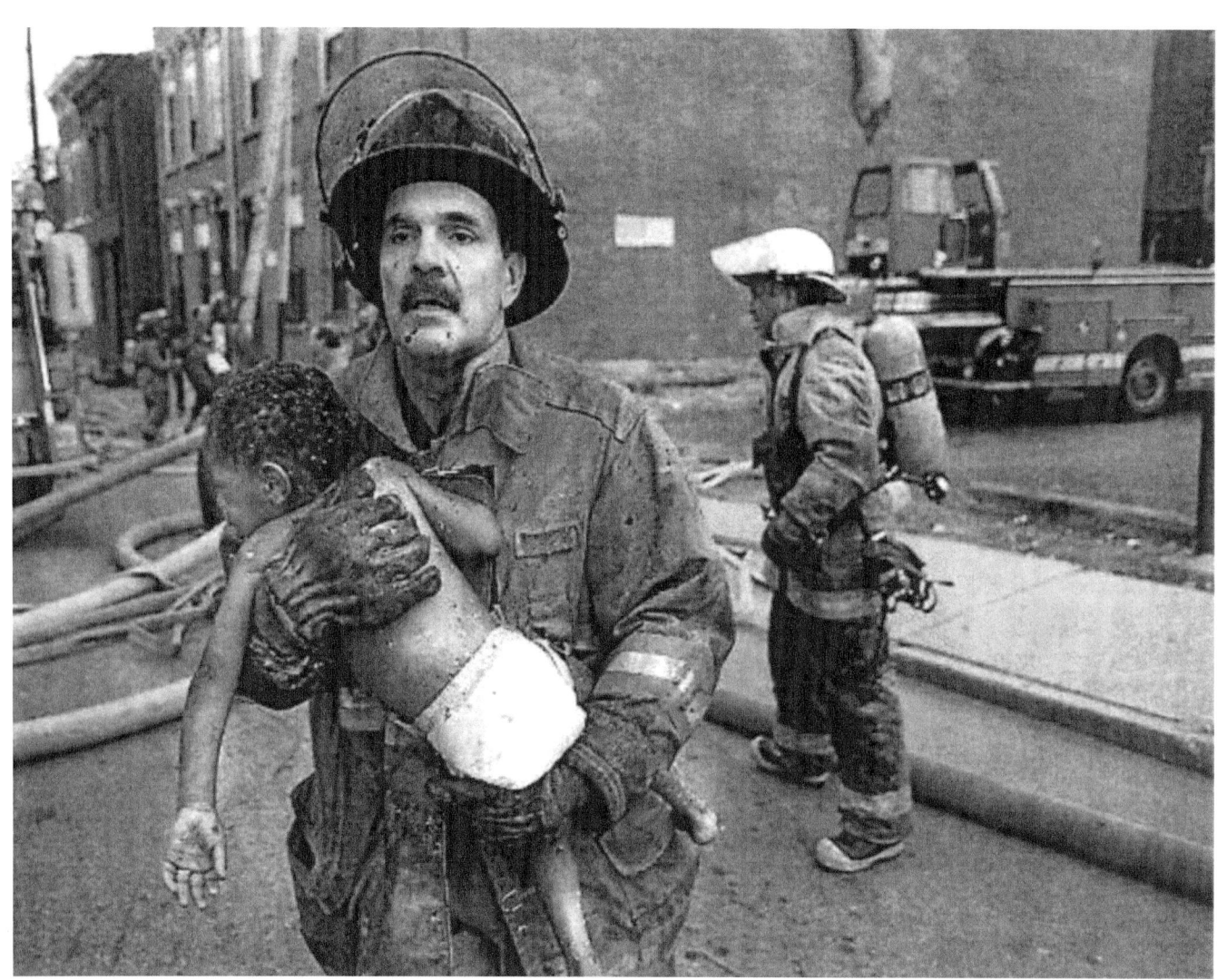

When we got to the scene, firefighters were helping a man exit the building via a ladder. Another firefighter ran out carrying a small child. All in all, it was a productive day.

sometimes-unreasonable rules. Arriving at the scene of an automobile accident or fire, I would be stopped from getting closer to the incident. When I asked the officer why I couldn't move closer he (I seldom encountered female cops) would say, "Because I'll arrest you." Officers (not all of them) acted this way because they could, and often said it was for our "safety." This was particularly maddening when I saw a group of civilian gawkers standing much closer.

In 1979, Cincinnati police officer Melvin Henze had been shot multiple times, killed in an alley, and his fellow officers were fed up. One day, the officers drove their cruisers to city hall and left their neckties and car keys in a pile.

I arrived late to city hall and saw a procession of officers going into the building as anti-police protestors gathered on the sidewalk. As I was shooting, a police officer ripped the camera from my hands and threw it to the ground. I picked it up and remarkably, it still worked! Looking around, I saw Fraternal Order of Police (FOP) President Elmer Dunaway and angrily told him that he should get his officers under control. There was no reply as he walked away to join his fellow officers.

Now *The Post* had two stories to run in its May 9, 1979 edition—one about the police protest and one about me being harassed by a police officer.

Some assignments were really fun. When we needed aerials, the lucky photographer would meet the helicopter pilot at the heliport located atop a

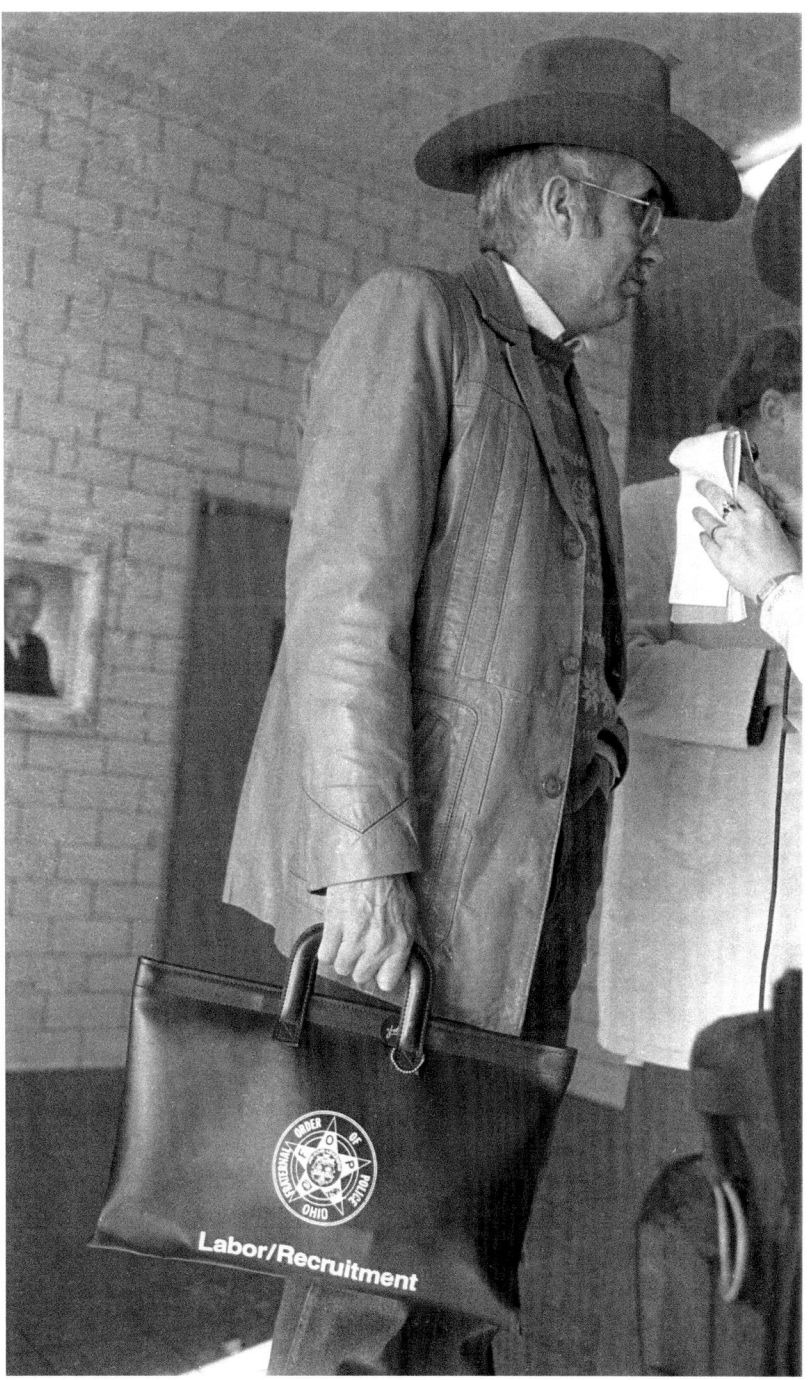

A regularly scheduled Cincinnati City Council meeting was disrupted by an onslaught of police officers and families led by Fraternal Order of Police (FOP) president Elmer Dunaway, a somewhat flamboyant president fond of wearing a cowboy hat and boots.

downtown parking garage. It was beyond exciting taking off and watching the buildings get smaller as we obtained altitude. We sometimes flew with the passenger door off, so we could get a better shot. That said, I quickly learned it was about the work and not the fun of the experience. I was paid by *The Post* to take photographs. That became my mantra.

By the way, my last chopper ride was to shoot boats on the Ohio River gathered outside the Riverbend Music Center to hear Jimmy Buffet. When the pilot walked out, he looked to be 15 years old and flew with the abandon of a teenager. I was done.

Being from the so-called inner city, some assignments gave me entry into lifestyles I had only seen on television. Fundraisers in sprawling private homes were such occasions. Many times, I was sent to these upscale residences in advance of the actual event, what we called getting-ready assignments. This worked for all concerned, because they got publicity in our paper, and we got the opportunity to do a story that was more accommodating to our deadline, though the photograph was less than exciting.

Cincinnati has two well-known rich neighborhoods—Hyde Park and Indian Hill. Hyde Park abuts poorer, racially diverse neighborhoods, whereas predominantly white, affluent Indian Hill is approximately eight miles away from downtown Cincinnati, featuring hilly roads and large estates. Indian Hill is patrolled by the Indian Hill Rangers Police Department, and it was possibly just a coincidence, but it seemed whenever I was driving down a road in Indian Hill, a Rangers cruiser was behind me. Once it became apparent that I was driving to an actual destination and not just cruising to make mischief, the Ranger pulled away.

Having been introduced into this world of estates and fundraising garden parties, I preferred the time I spent driving the streets in the poorer neighborhoods. Yes, I was a product of a poor neighborhood, but mostly, I liked driving through these neighborhoods, because that's where the photographs were. The opportunity to make photographs was always the most important part of my workday.

In the suburbs, I rarely saw anyone outside their home unless they were mowing the lawn or washing a car. The inner city was full of photo ops. One day, as I was finishing up an assignment on Vine Street, a police car went speeding by. Minutes later, officers with drawn weapons were approaching a vehicle that had pulled to a stop. It made for a dramatic photo. On another occasion, I was walking on Walnut Street in the downtown business district, when I heard a woman scream. A guy ran past me with her purse. He rounded a corner, and as I caught up, several citizens had grabbed him. While he was being held, he asked me not to take his picture. Soon a couple of plainclothes officers arrived, and they asked me not to take their picture. At that point, I had all I needed, so I agreed. If I remember correctly, the spot news picture ran in the Saturday paper.

Back in the day, Washington Park was home base for many of downtown Cincinnati's characters. The benches were often occupied by homeless men and women, or someone just sleeping off whatever they had had too much of. I took many photographs in the park, a large green space with a gazebo style bandstand and at least six acres, including a public pool and elementary school. As I write this, the park, along with a great deal of the Over-the-Rhine neighborhood, has been gentrified. The many shops and restaurants are much favored by those who can afford to patronize the establishments. It seems more like a shopping mall than the neighborhood I knew back then with its street life and characters. Progress?

In 1974, and for a while later, *The Post* had its own fleet of staff cars and mechanics to maintain

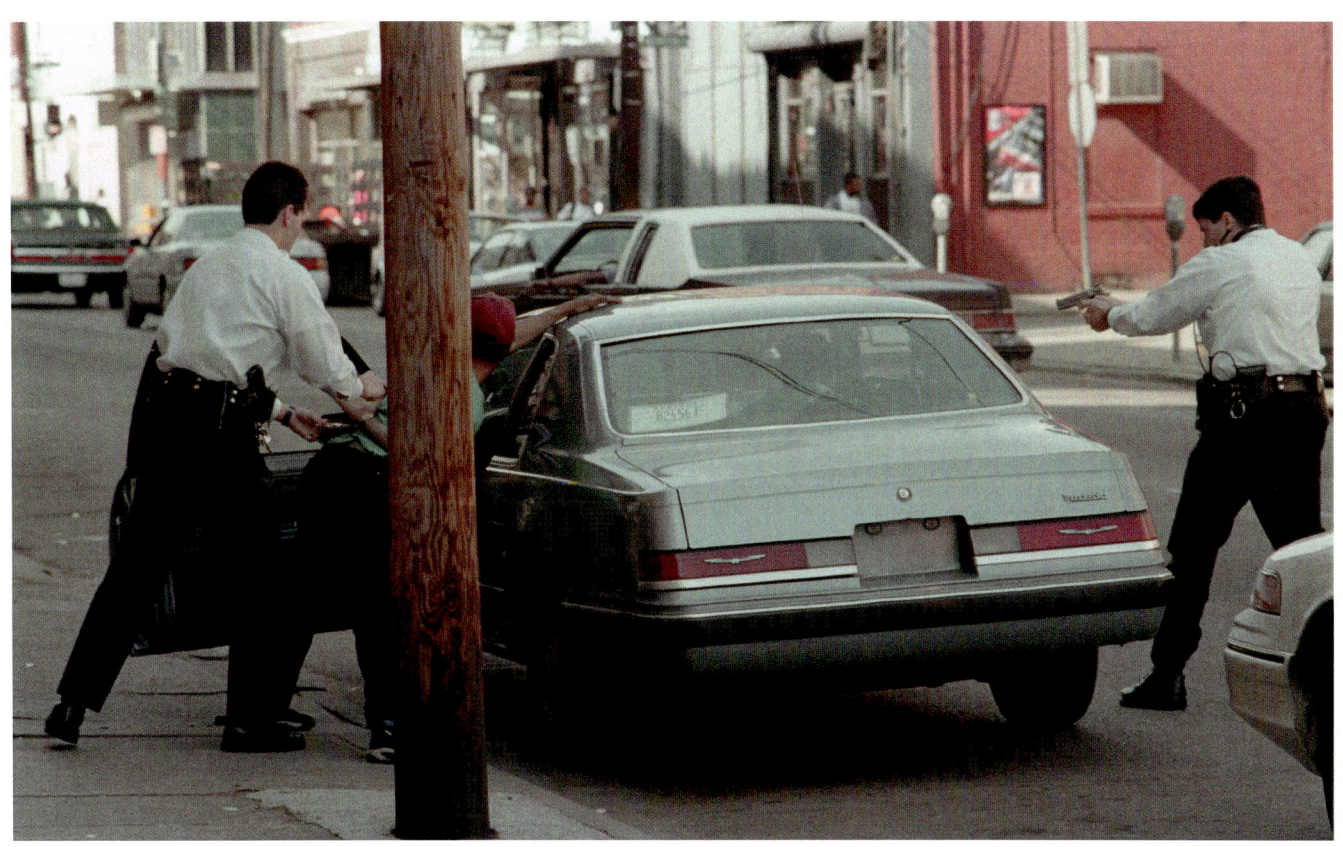

Cop stop on Vine Street in Over-The-Rhine.

them. At first, it was a point of pride to check out a key for one of the medium-blue cars that had *The Cincinnati Post* emblazoned on its exterior. However, each car had its own idiosyncratic issue. Car #111 was particularly hard to drive and had no air conditioning. One hot summer day, I was told to go to the city jail known as the "workhouse" for a tour, because there were discussions about closing it. An editor said he wanted to ride out with me, and I was told to make sure I checked out a car with AC. Of course, I did the opposite, and when the editor asked to have the car cooled down, I let him know that luxury was not available. I can't say that made a difference, but he did get a taste of what we had to put up with.

Another luxury absent from staff cars were broadcast radios. There were only two-way radios for *Cincinnati Post* communications, which meant we shared the radio frequency with the business side of the paper. When driving, I got to hear exchanges between the base and carriers about delivery issues, not very entertaining. Eventually, I brought a portable, battery powered boom box that I put in the back seat and played cassette tapes of jazz and funk such as George Clinton from my collection.

Eventually, we transitioned to our own vehicles, which meant more accounting for mileage plus a weekly fee for the use of our vehicle. For some inexplicable reason, I decided I wanted an Audi complete with a sunroof. It was totally impractical for newspaper photography work. Almost from the start, I would notice in the rearview mirror a round piece of aluminum bouncing on the street behind me, and sure enough, it was one of the wheel covers. Eventually, I settled on cars that could take tough wear and tear—first a Chevy Blazer, then an Isuzu Trooper, and best of all a Subaru AWD Legacy that I drove into retirement.

Aside from my mode of transportation, two big changes during my 33-year career were communication technology and color photography.

When I started at *The Post*, we relied on two-way radios, which we wore on our belts (and that made us look like cops). We were required to end each conversation with the radio's numbers KJJ801, which we shortened to KJ. This communication had its downside though. Editors could find us anytime, anywhere. One photographer repeatedly asked the editor if he could call back. Request denied, the photographer made sure the editor heard the toilet flush. For the really annoying editors, we employed a little trick of crumpling cellophane paper inches from the headset that sounded like static. "I can't hear you, I'll have to call you back," we'd say to buy some more time.

Photographers love gadgets, so as soon as the first version of cell phones were available, several of us had them installed in our cars. We worked out an arrangement with *The Post* to pay 75% of the cost, until they realized how valuable they were and picked up the whole tab.

In the days before GPS, I relied on my handy *Graphic Street Guide of Greater Cincinnati*, but I knew the city pretty well. In fact, I would have made a hell of a taxicab driver—I even knew what routes to take to avoid potholes. That said, when it came to the West Side of town, I often got lost. One service station owner got used to me stopping in for directions.

I was not thrilled when we were told to shoot in color. I am not a techno-minded photographer. I shoot like driving a car, instinctive not cerebral. Chrome slides, with their demands for accurate exposure and lighting, meant we had to pay attention to artificial light, and use filters to remove tint. We were so busy worrying about this shit, that we sometimes forgot to pay attention to what we were shooting. Thank God, we moved from chrome slides to color negative film, which was very forgiving, plus we could make black-and-white prints. My favorite film was Fuji 800 because it could be pushed to 1600 and performed well in low light.

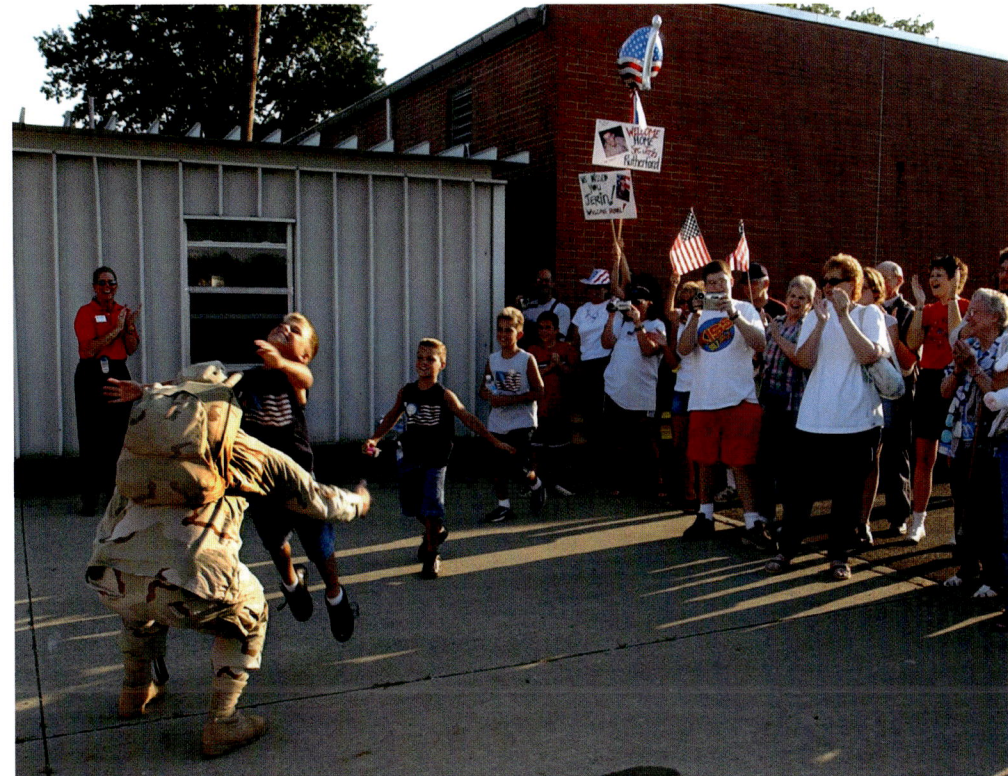

In Fort Thomas, Kentucky, a boy jumped into his father's arms after his dad got off the bus that brought him home from the Middle East.

Because color was expensive, only the front-page and section covers were in color. Since you never knew where your photo would be displayed, you had to shoot in both color and black and white. And you had to pay attention to the colors. Red was always popular, in fact *National Geographic* almost always had red in a photograph. We joked that they probably carried around a red umbrella just in case.

Many of my colleagues left for bigger and allegedly better papers. I had my chance. In 1985, *The Los Angeles Times* was interested and flew me out twice, the second time with Brenda, to tour the area. One of the photographers told me about a nice place to live that was "only" 90 minutes away from the newsroom. "You got to be kidding, I live ten minutes away from *The Post*," I replied.

When an L.A. editor finally called to offer me a job, he was shocked into silence when I turned it down.

I decided early in my career that I wanted to make photographs in the style of Henri Cartier-Bresson who wrote, "There are those who take photographs arranged beforehand and those who go out to discover the image and seize it." Of course, he traveled to exotic locales, and I lived in Cincinnati. One reporter, when I shared my desire to travel, told me I could not do it at *The Post*. I thought why the hell not, don't we have an airport?

FOREIGN TRAVEL: FINDING THE LOCAL CONNECTION

I never regretted that decision to turn down the L.A. editor. I could do anything I wanted to in Cincinnati and would figure out the local connection to get the paper to send me to Sudan, El Salvador, Vietnam, and more. The only spot on my wish list that I never got to was Rio de Janeiro. I thought there might be a Procter & Gamble connection to get me to Brazil, but to my regret, I didn't pursue that idea.

My first foreign trip was to El Salvador in Central America in 1984. I found out about it while waiting for an elevator in our new office building at 125 East Court, a far different environment than the art deco masterpiece at 800 Broadway. Karl Kuntz, our photo boss du jour, said they wanted me to go to El Salvador to cover the election between José Napoleón Duarte and Roberto D'Aubuisson. Bam!

Now what? I called Brenda, and of course she said, "What can I do?" My colleagues at the paper in a show of support had a T-shirt printed with the words "Press DON'T SHOOT" or words to that effect. I never wore it. Fellow photographer Bob Dickerson came up with a bulletproof vest. I took it.

The morning came for me to leave for the airport. I was unprepared for the range of emotion. I felt happy to be realizing a dream, but sadness at leaving my wife and young son, Miles (the night before I had recorded Brenda as she bathed Miles, and during the trip often listened to the audio recording).

We had added Miles Parks Grier to our family in 1978. He was four months old when we adopted him, and my influence was responsible for naming him for Miles Davis and Gordon Parks. Five years later, Brenda gave birth to Samantha Leslie Grier. I photographed the birth until the O.B. nurse insisted I put down my camera, and bond with the newest member of our family.

Photographer Gordon Baer met me at the airport and handed me a couple of dollars, saying "I want

Miles Parks Grier was four months old when he joined our family in 1978.

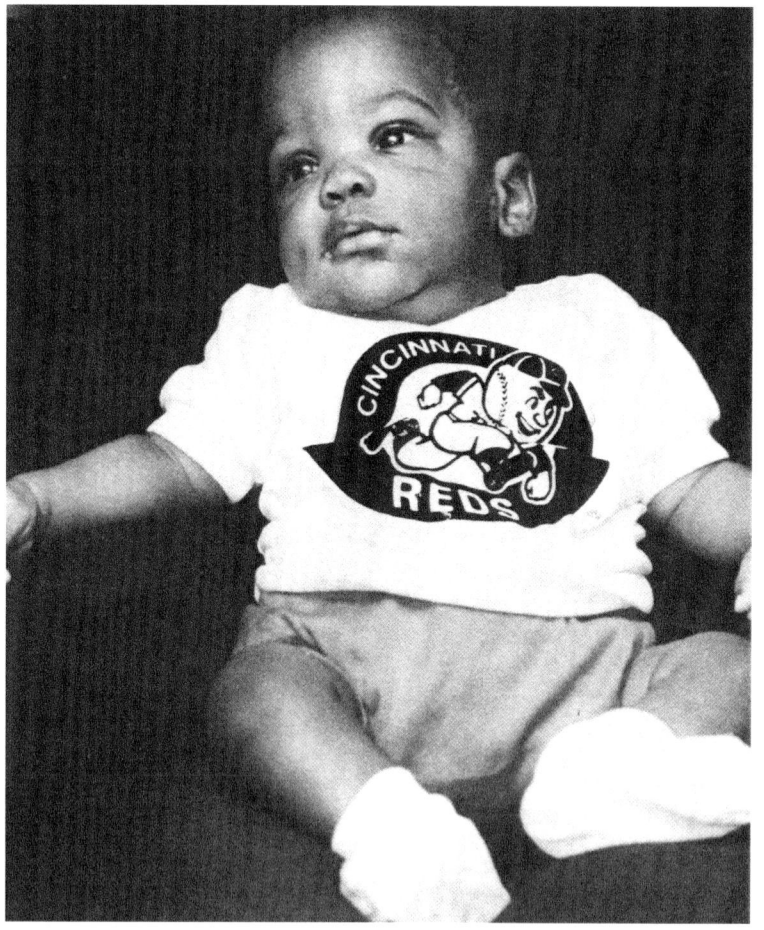

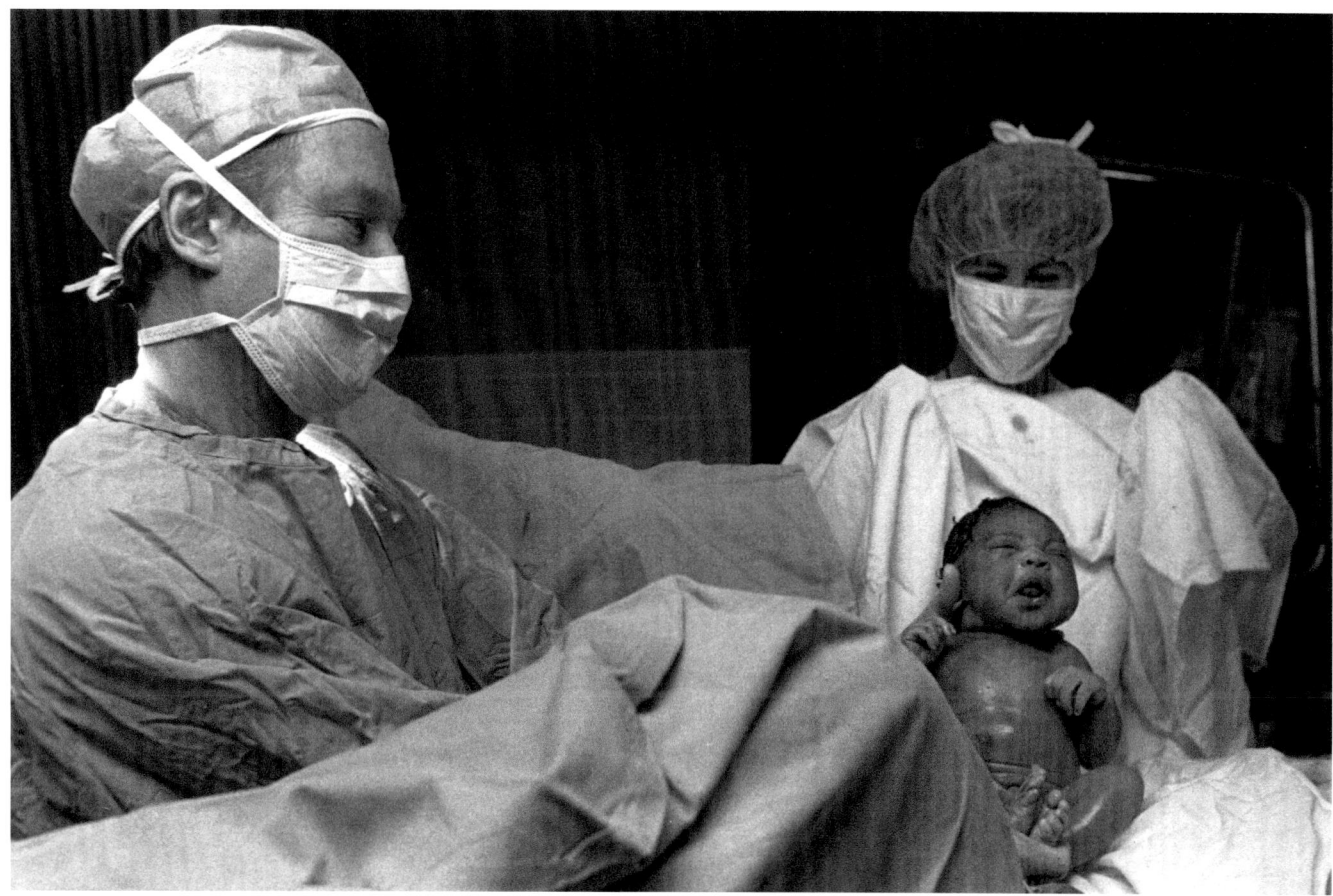

Samantha Leslie Grier was born on Mother's Day, May 8, 1983.

you to bring them back to me." I got the significance of his gesture.

On the flight down, I had to change planes in San Pedro Sula, Honduras. A few of us were talking about our intended destinations. When I said San Salvador, an older woman made the sign of the cross. Well OK!

As I mentioned, I had a bulletproof vest on loan. When we landed in San Salvador, the Customs officer opened my suitcase, stuck one hand in, felt around, stopped abruptly, gave me a hard look, and said something in Spanish. We were soon joined by other personnel in uniforms all speaking rapid Spanish and occasionally giving me hard looks. They confiscated the vest, then another guy—probably a bootleg cabbie—came up, spoke to the officers, then spoke to me in English asking where I was going. I told him the name of my hotel, we got my suitcase, and I followed him to his car. I got in, he started the engine, and to my surprise a song by Rick James came blasting from the radio. Getting to my hotel, I hooked up with Scripps Howard reporter Alan Thompson.

I don't recall the name of our hotel, but suffice it to say, in better times, it would have catered to tourists. When we arrived, it was crawling with media types. Alan and I went to some type of reception that first evening and got a ride back to the hotel with a guy dressed in civilian clothes with a handgun sitting on the console. One mishap occurred when we went to a restaurant in La Libertad, a village on the Pacific Ocean, and I made the rookie mistake of drinking local water. Enough said, but lesson learned.

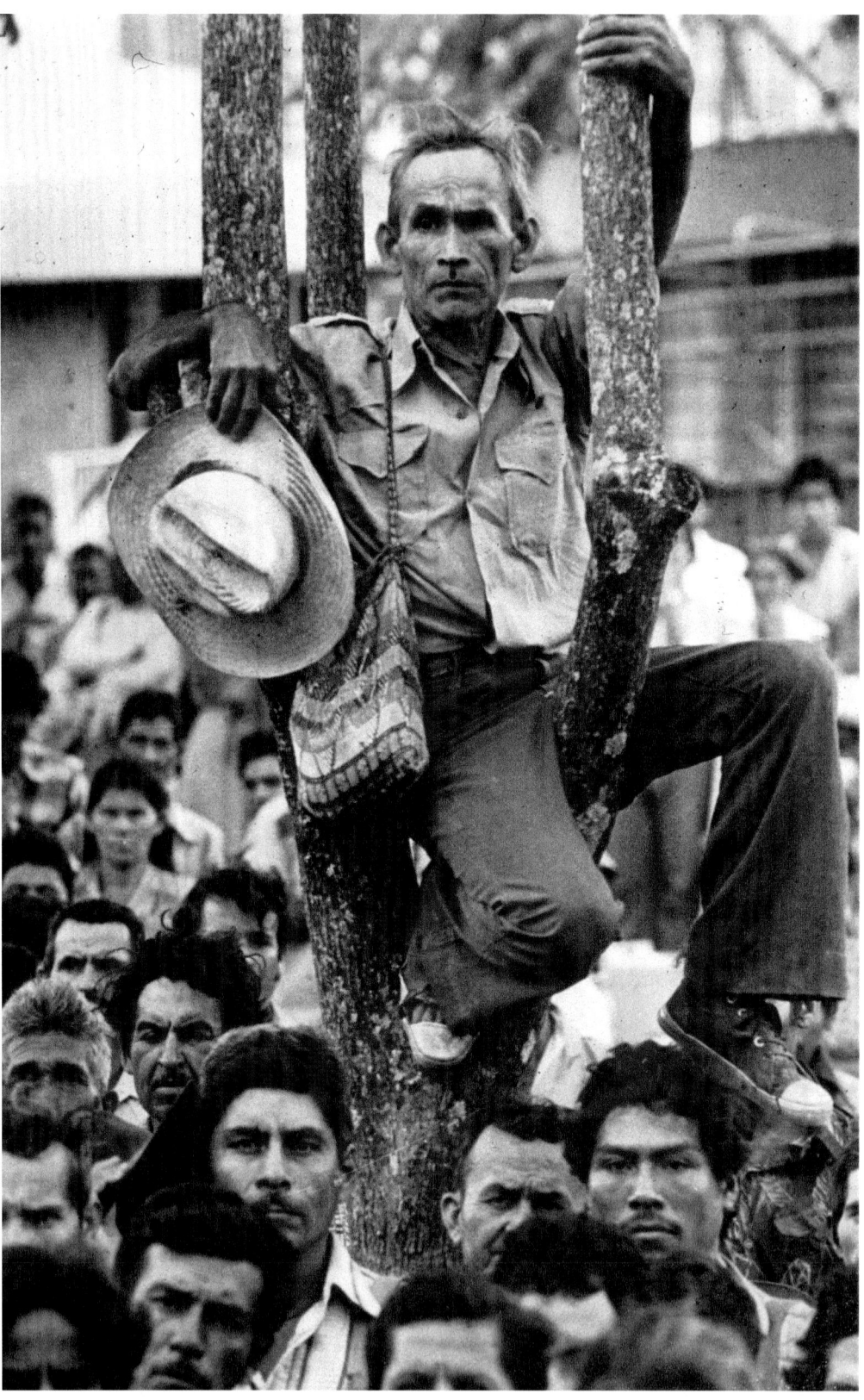

A political rally in El Salvador when José Napoleón Duarte spoke, mentioning that his visit was so important that the international press (i.e., me) was there.

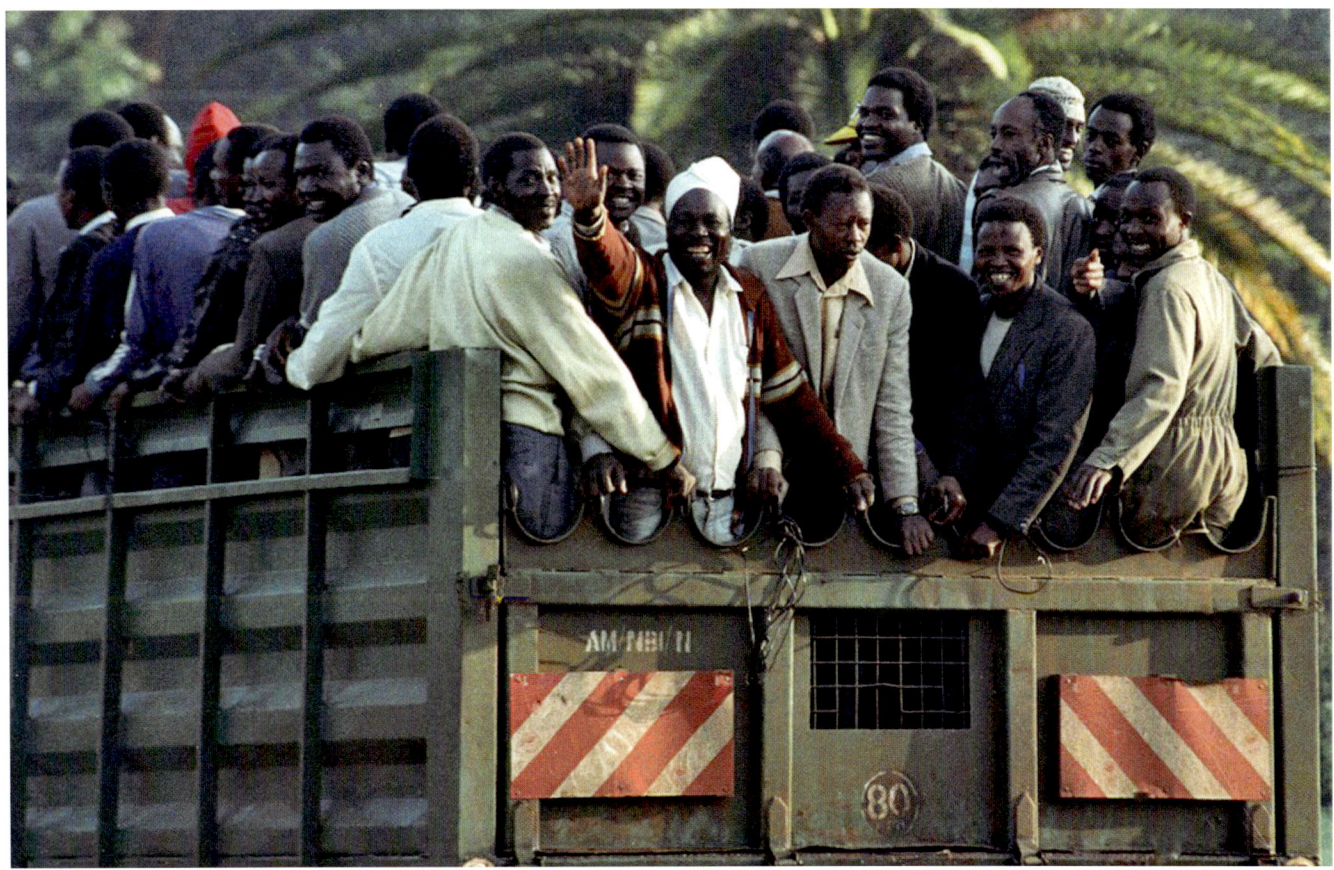

One morning in Nairobi, I saw a truckload of men off to an unknown destination.

I went to Sudan in 1985 with reporter Lisa Cardillo Rose, because Cincy Reaches Out was sending supplies to the country. Now I was leaving Brenda at home with two children—our two-year-old daughter Samantha and Miles, now seven.

I went to Cuba in 1998 with Caring Partners, a group of Middletown medical professionals who were also religious. We spent our days in hospitals and our nights in churches. It was a good trip; except they didn't drink alcohol.

This time, I knew to be careful about the water. Along with little cans of beans and wieners, and granola bars, I brought packets of Kool-Aid that I added to the water in the hope it would drown out any aftertaste and germs. I guess it worked, because I never got sick on an overseas trip. My other good-luck charm was collecting foreign currency and stuffing the money into my camera bag (I imagine if I dug deep into those bags even today, I'd find some old paper money).

Scripps Howard sent me to the *San Juan Star* in Puerto Rico to mentor photographers at the Scripps paper about shooting fashion. Brenda came along for a mini vacation. I would show up every morning at 9:00 a.m., and around 11:00 a.m., the photographers would come in. We'd have a brief meeting, and then they would leave for lunch. So much for showing them my stuff, but Brenda had a grand old time.

On my first trip to Africa, I stayed in an open-air terrace in Port Sudan. One day it started raining, a rarity, and this boy began playing.

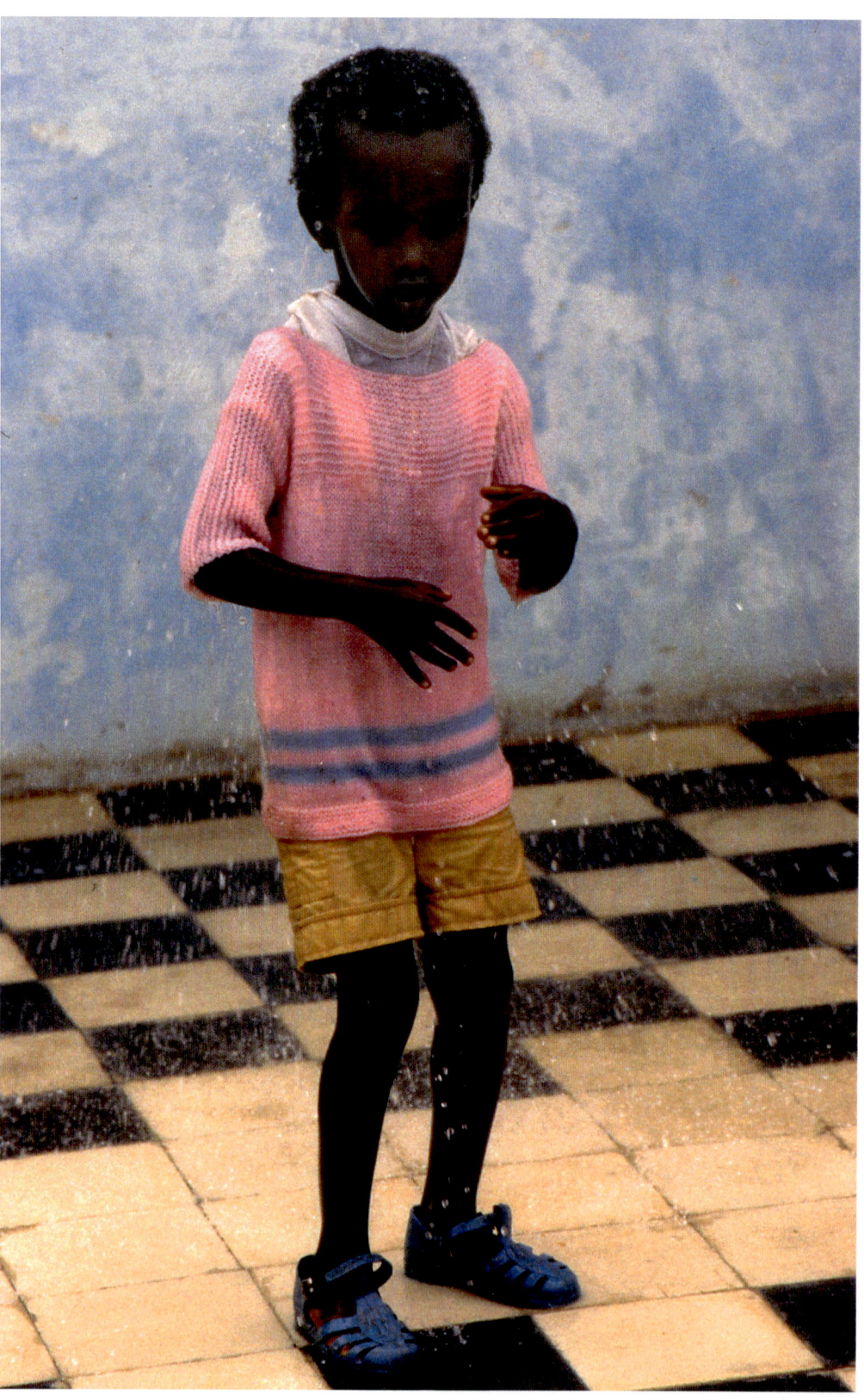

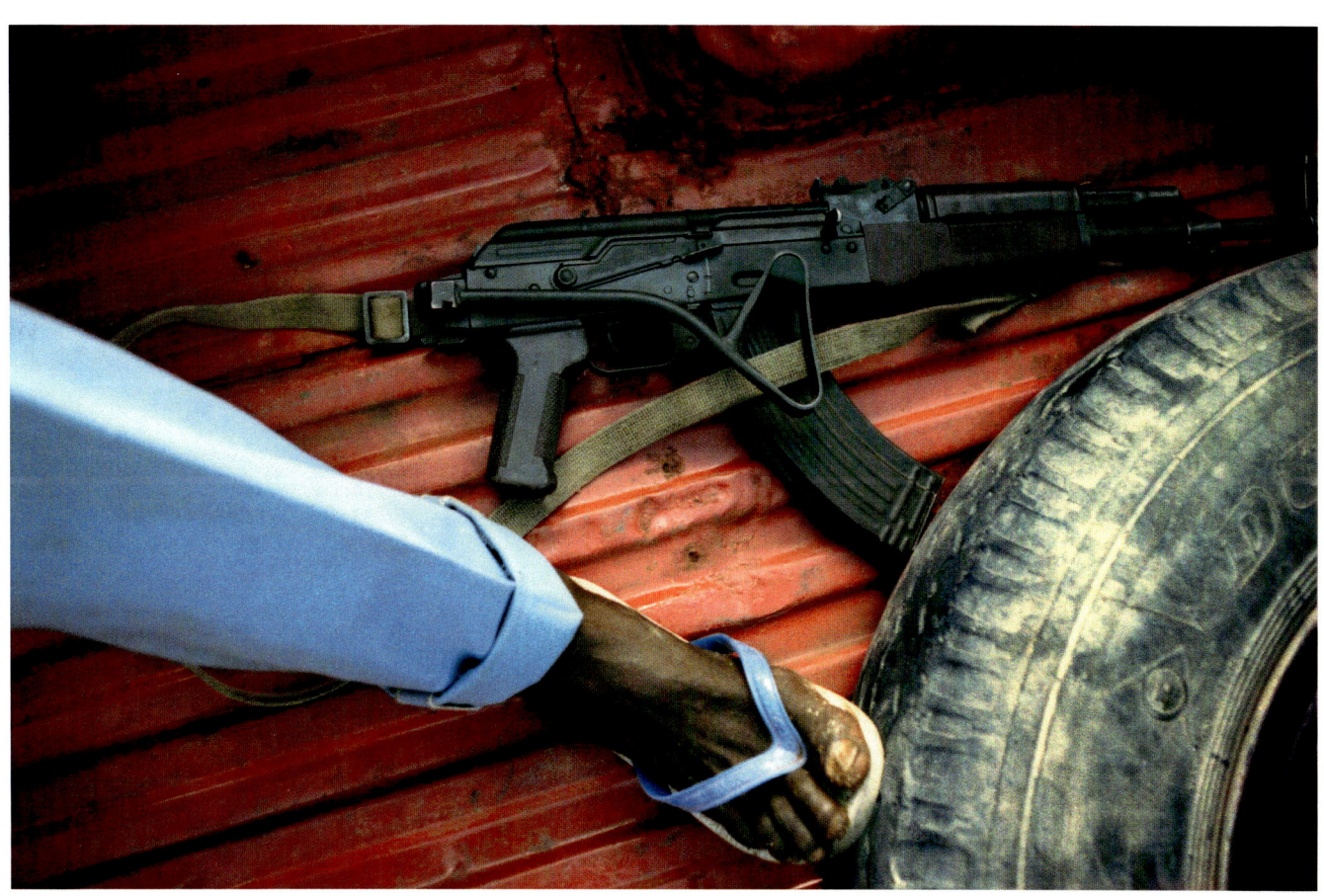

On my second trip to Africa, I made this photograph of our bodyguard while riding in the back of a pickup truck after landing near Baidoa, Somalia.

During a visit to a clinic in Somalia I walked through a doorway and happened upon this woman caring for a starving child.

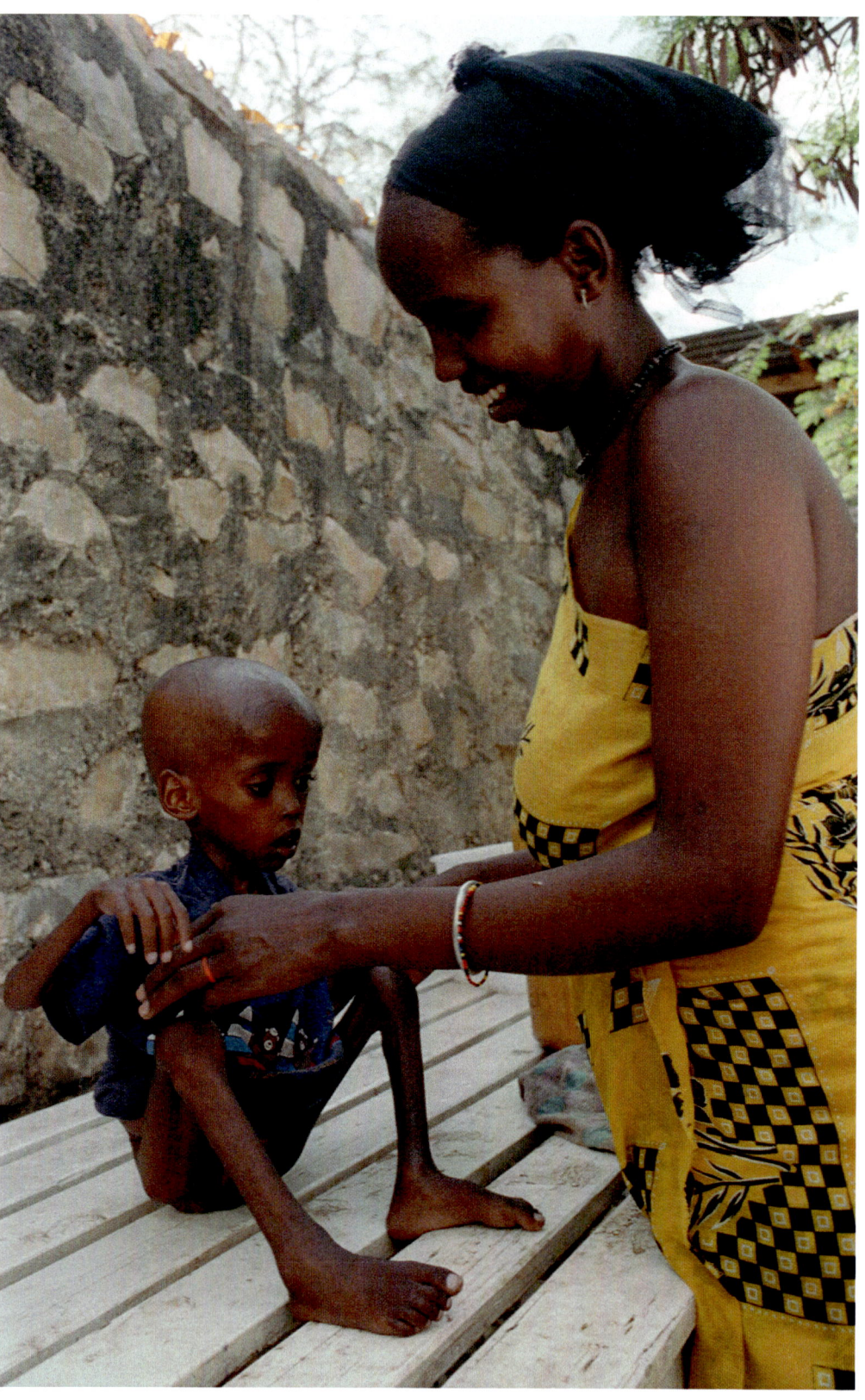

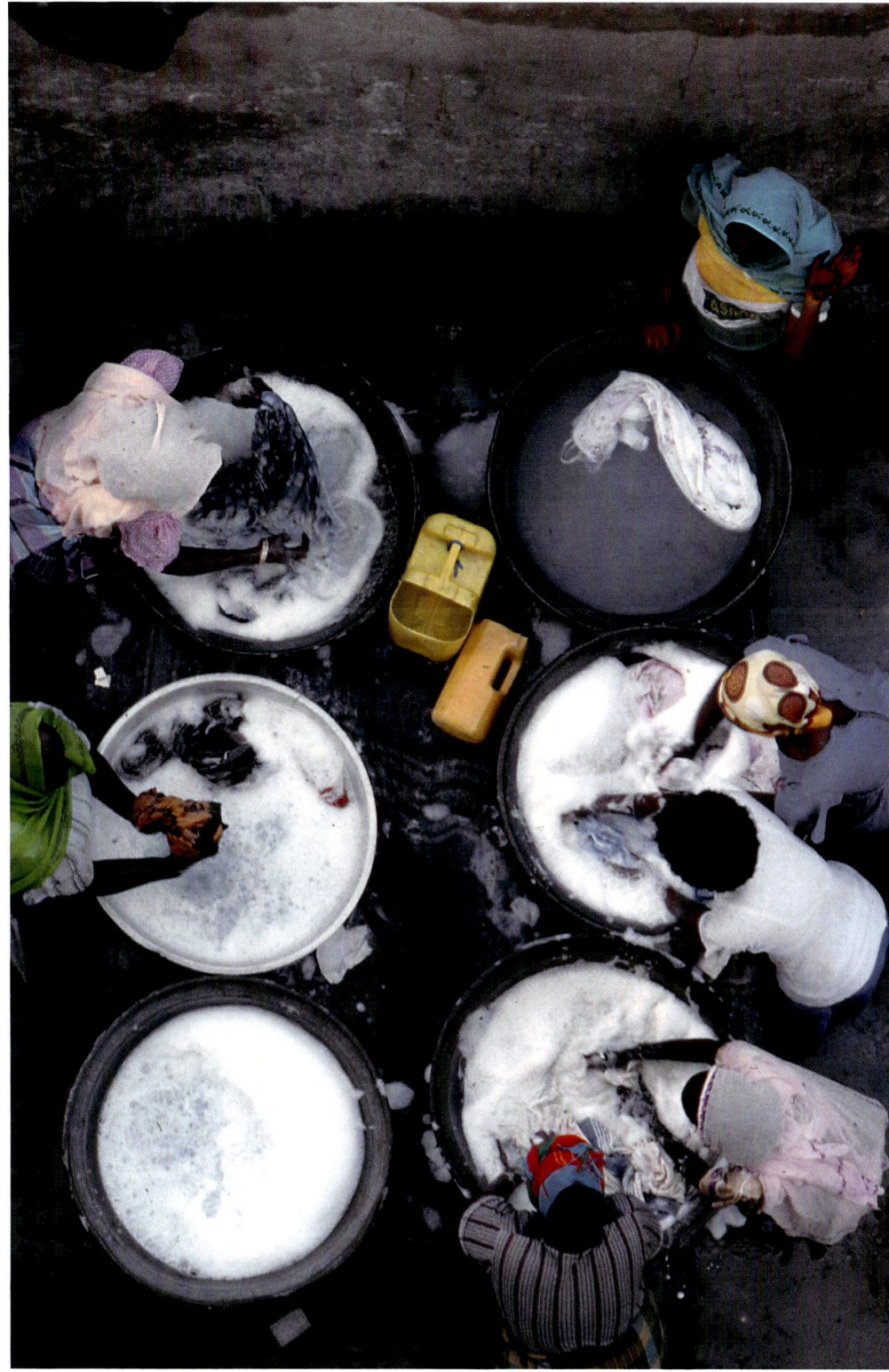

One morning in Port Sudan, I heard laughing and water splashing. Looking for the source, I walked to the edge of a terrace that gave me this view of Eritrean women doing the wash.

FASHION WITH THE INDOMITABLE MARY LINN WHITE

I have always enjoyed photographing attractive women. When I saw Nancy Pratt walk through *The Post* lobby, I stopped her and asked, "Can I take your photo?" She worked on the business side of *The Post* and had a "dare you breathe the same air" attitude. She said yes and came to *The Post*'s shabby studio for a fashion piece on jeans. She was often a model over the years.

But my main partner in fashion was Mary Linn White. She was a reporter for the Accent section, the successor of the Women's section. Accent featured anything of general interest to readers such as movie and theater reviews, human interest stories, articles related to food, and the society fundraising events which Mary Linn usually covered.

My first fashion assignment with Mary Linn involved a woman named Bobbie Corbean, who had just returned from a stay in Scandinavia. I drove

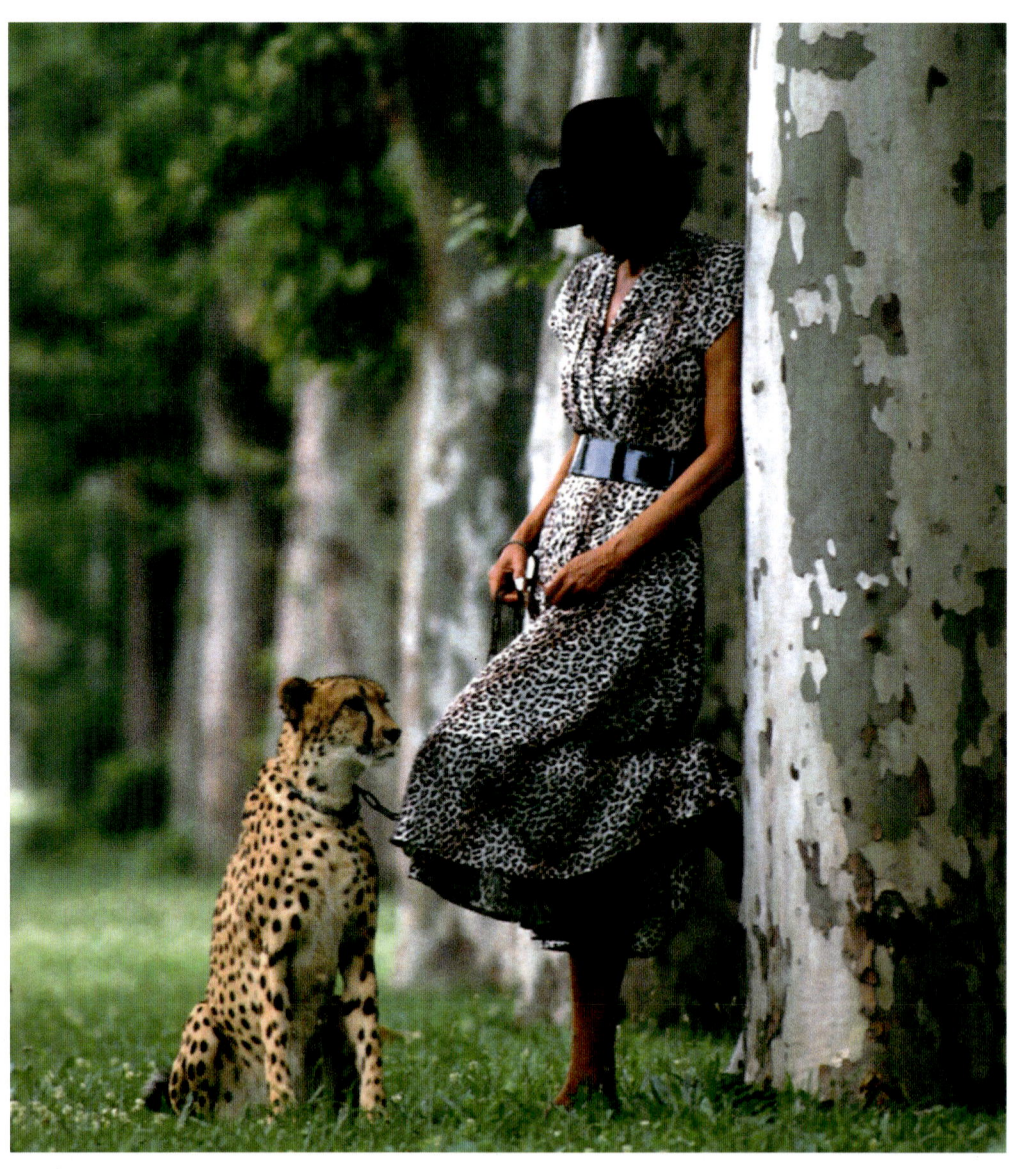

We did an animal-print shot at Triangle Park with a live cheetah, compliments of the Cincinnati Zoo (for safety, the zoo insisted the handler be the model).

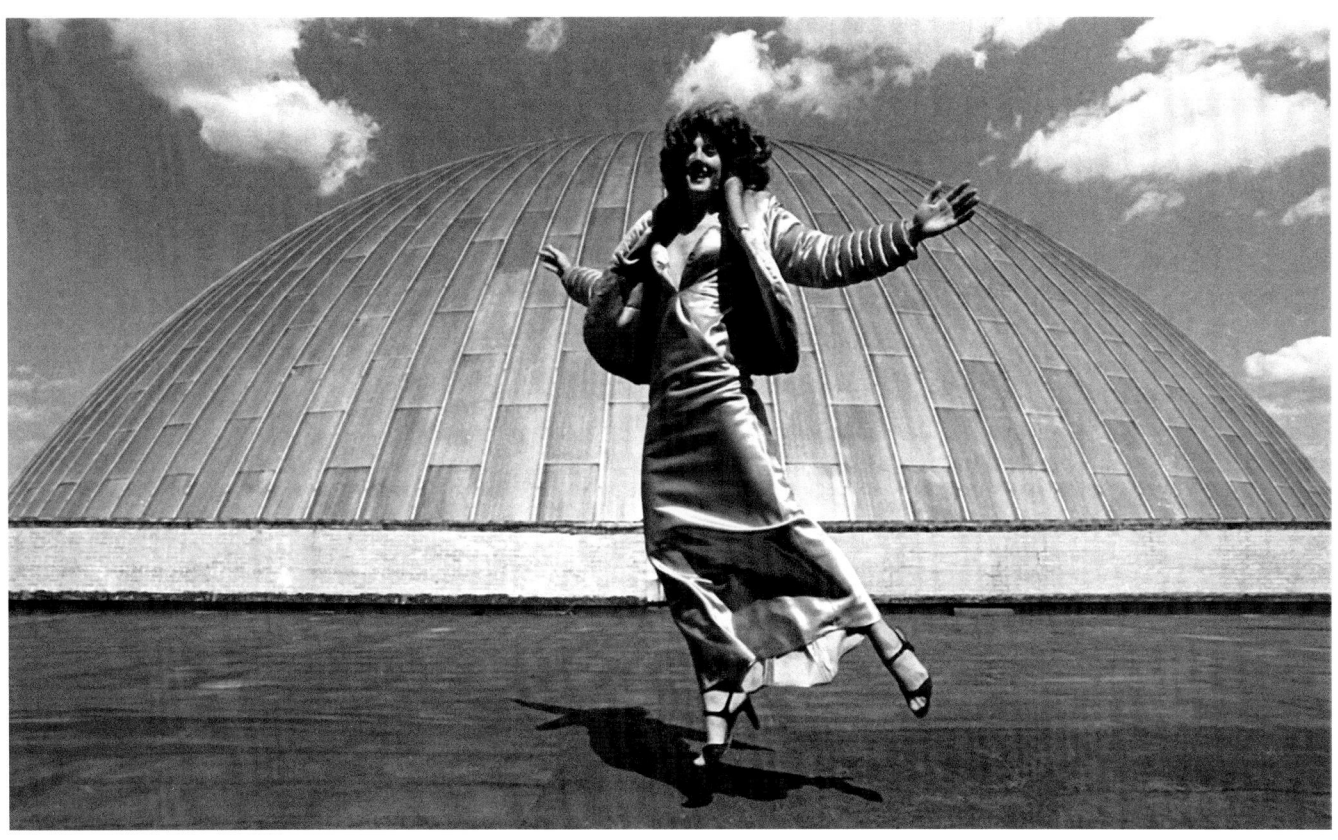

I knew the back of Union Terminal with its semi-dome shape would be a great spot for a photo, and the model jumped the way I had imagined (years later the photo was used for my fashion exhibit called "Clothes Encounter").

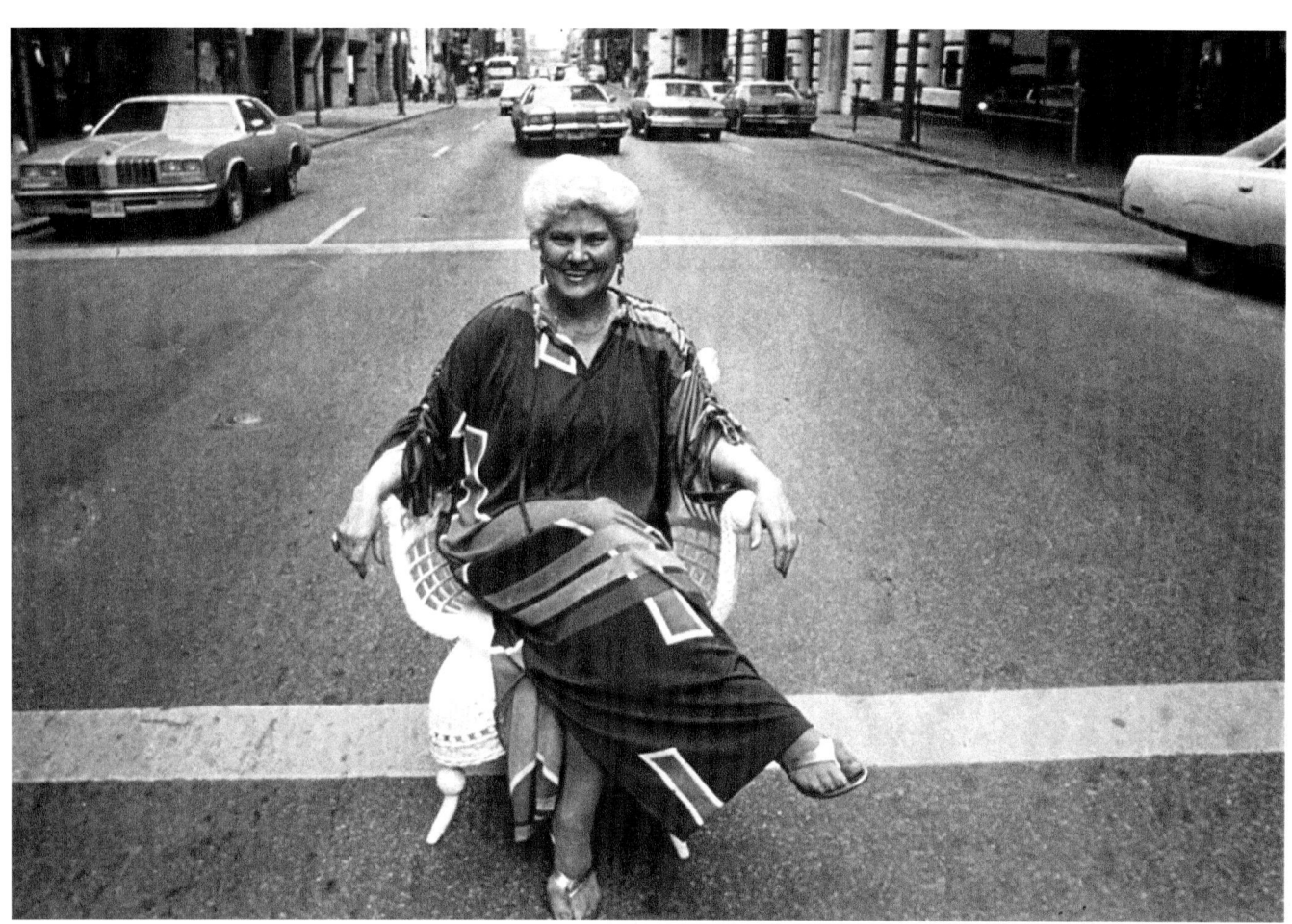

We timed the duration of the traffic signal. When vehicles came to a halt, I quickly carried the chair to the middle of the street, the model sat, and I shot.

to Bobbie's house in Kennedy Heights and decided to shoot her in the backyard, having her take wide steps to show the detail in her print wool skirt, per Mary Linn's photo request. Mary Linn liked the photo, and I told her of my love of fashion. A working relationship was born.

I'd stop by Mary Linn's desk, ask her what she was working on, and we'd bounce around ideas for the assignment. As I drove around town for assignments, I was always making a mental list of possible locations, from scenic parks to obscure loading docks. Mary Linn worked with Pogue's, McAlpin's, and other department stores to borrow clothes, shoes, jewelry, and sometimes even a model.

We did a feature on prom dresses at the old reservoir at Eden Park, and the wind blew at just the right movement to billow out the dress. Serendipity is a wonderful thing. Another prom feature was at Grammer's bar and restaurant in OTR. Two white

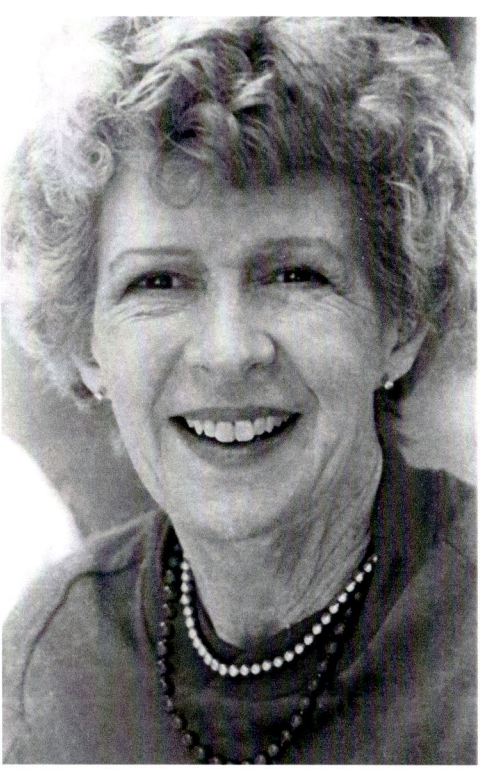

One thing I always appreciated about Mary Linn, and this we never talked about, was the importance of using white and Black models. It was just mutually understood.

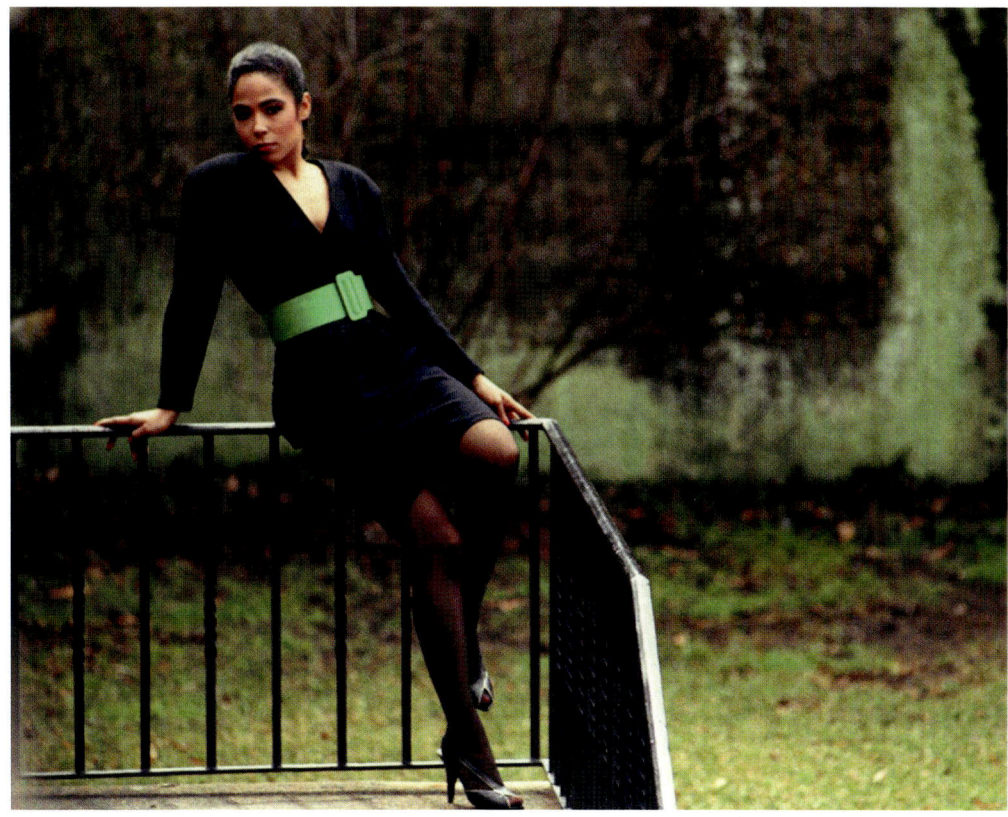

This is from a portfolio of fashion photos commissioned by the model Angela Boone. I shot this at Fleischmann Gardens in South Avondale, a great location for shooting fashion.

I hosed down a walkway at Fleischmann Gardens for this photo on plaids.

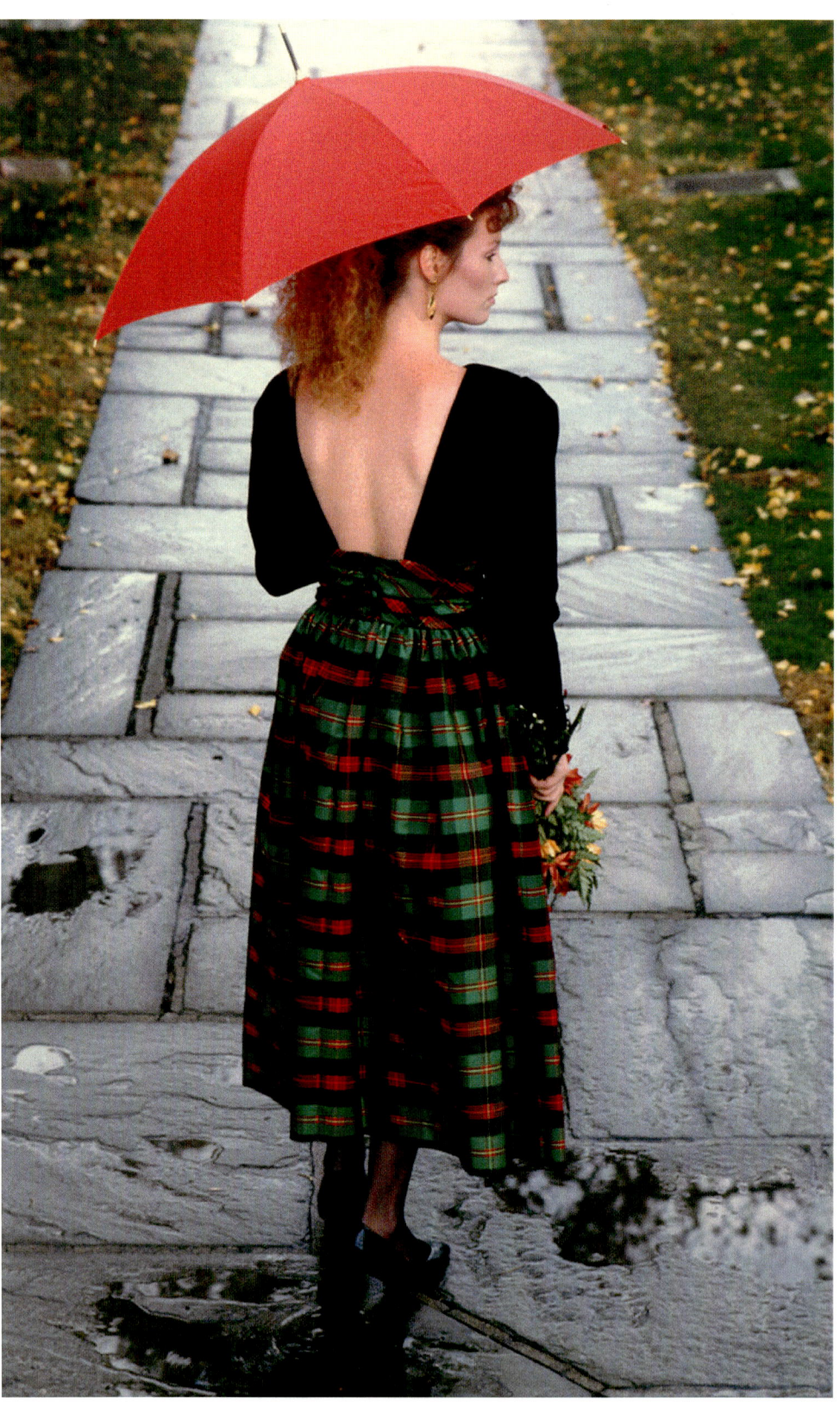

high-school students said their parents had told them OTR was dangerous. I was hoping they'd hear a gunshot or see a fight, but alas no such luck. But Grammer's did not disappoint. Now closed, it was known for its beautiful windows that faced north giving a beautiful soft illumination, a particular favorite for portrait and fashion photographers.

Mary Linn found a businessman who had a car phone—a rarity in those days—for a feature on furs. We met at Garfield Park, and he only had a few minutes to spare, so the model stepped up to the car door, and I clicked.

One of the most notable fashion photos that Mary Linn and I did involved a caftan. We were at McAlpin's, our brainstorming coming up blank, and as usual, we were in a time crunch. Then I looked through the window at the passing traffic below, and said to Mary Linn, "Why don't we put the model in a chair in the middle of Fourth Street?" Mary Linn laughed her approval, and we headed downstairs with the model and a chair.

Mary Linn was so much fun to work with, and we accomplished every fashion-photo dream we had except one. We wanted to have a model walk on water, and often when driving together to an assignment, we'd banter about it. Alas, it never came to be.

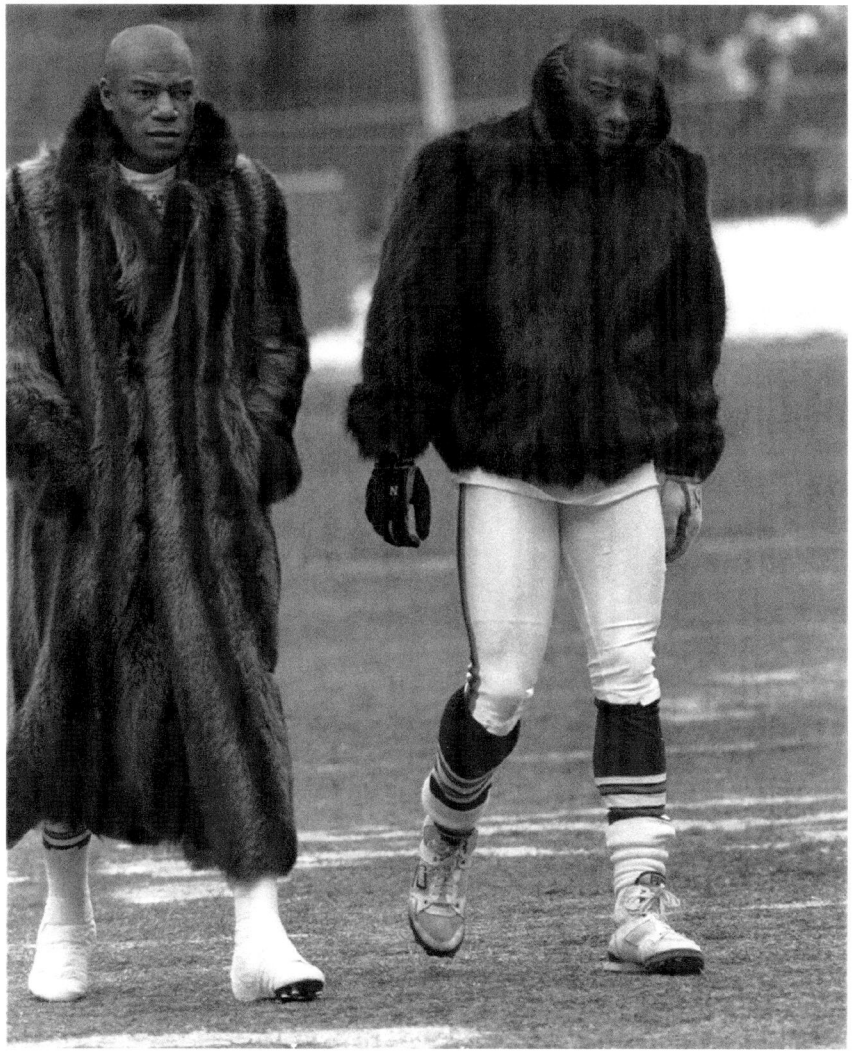

I wasn't looking for a fashion photo on a cold fall day in Cleveland, where I had been sent to photograph a Browns vs. Bengals football game. Hours before the game, two Browns players arrived wearing fur coats. Click. I can't recall if the photograph ran in sports or features.

SPORTS: NO LONGER A REDS FAN

Initially, I did not get many sports assignments, because they called for nighttime and weekend work. When first hired, I was assigned to straight days and no weekends. However, the time came when Jack Klumpe decided I was worthy of a sports assignment.

I was a huge Cincinnati Reds fan when I arrived at *The Post*. As a child, my dad and I would walk to Crosley Field for a game, and I was in awe of all the green grass, because there wasn't much green where we lived. But I mainly remember those times, because it was the only thing my dad and I did together.

When I was handed a Reds media credential, I accepted it both nervously and joyfully. My first time in the media dining facility at Riverfront Stadium was a revelation. There was free food and beverages available for the asking. My nerves would not let me relax enough to enjoy a meal, so I headed down to the field—close to the players I had only seen on TV or pictured in newspapers and magazines. I soon got over that fascination.

Since *The Cincinnati Enquirer* sent a photographer to cover the games, there was a casual competition to get the best shot. More than anything, you did not want to get beat by *The Enquirer* photographer. But sometimes this happened, because I had other assignments and arrived late. Say a big play happened in the first inning, and I was still en route, well, I missed it. You were assured, the following day, there would be a typewritten memo from Klumpe asking, "What happened?"

It didn't take long, however, for me to become a non-Reds fan. To put it mildly, I have never encountered a bigger bunch of "fill in the blank" than some of the Reds players. They were rude, cheap, sexist, just plain nasty.

Even if I had remained a fan, it was unprofessional to root while working. Ditto for asking for autographs, which I did under duress once for one not-to-be named managing editor who insisted a staff photographer (me) get Johnny Bench's autograph for one of his friends. When I got to the Reds clubhouse, Bench pretty much ignored me, eventually turning my way and rudely asking

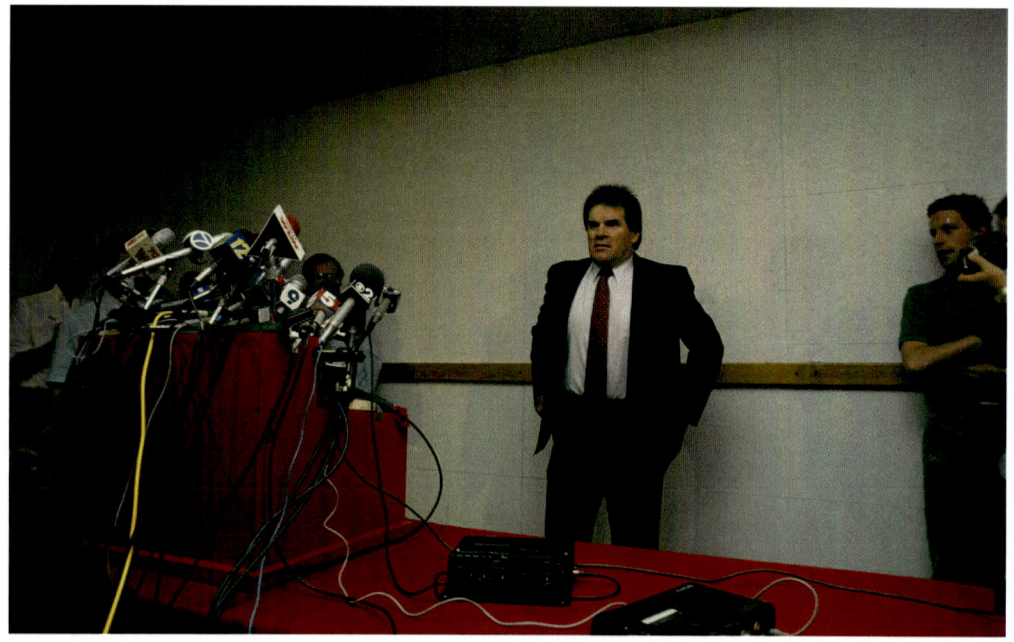

On August 23, 1989, Pete Rose accepted a lifetime ban in a settlement with the Major League Baseball Commission for gambling. Afterwards, the former Cincinnati Reds manager held a press conference looking quite defiant.

what I wanted. I got out the provided photo for him to sign. Pure humiliation.

For a completely different reason, I never asked to go to spring training, which was considered a plum assignment. My reason? In all those years, I only saw one photo from spring training that I thought was worth a damn. *The Kentucky Post* photographer Jim Osborn took a photo of the Reds outfielders with a few Amish men looking on. I wish I had shot it, which is the highest compliment one photographer can give another.

Sometimes, when I received a sports assignment, I was told it was a big game. As a new staff photographer, I took that to heart. After a while, I came to realize that all games were big. It didn't matter if it was for a championship or a homecoming. We also photographed a fair number of practices, which we dubbed as getting ready.

Not being emotionally invested helped me focus. So did a gift from Sandra Boulanger, a ballet dancer with the Cincinnati Ballet. When I met her, she was on leave from the company because she

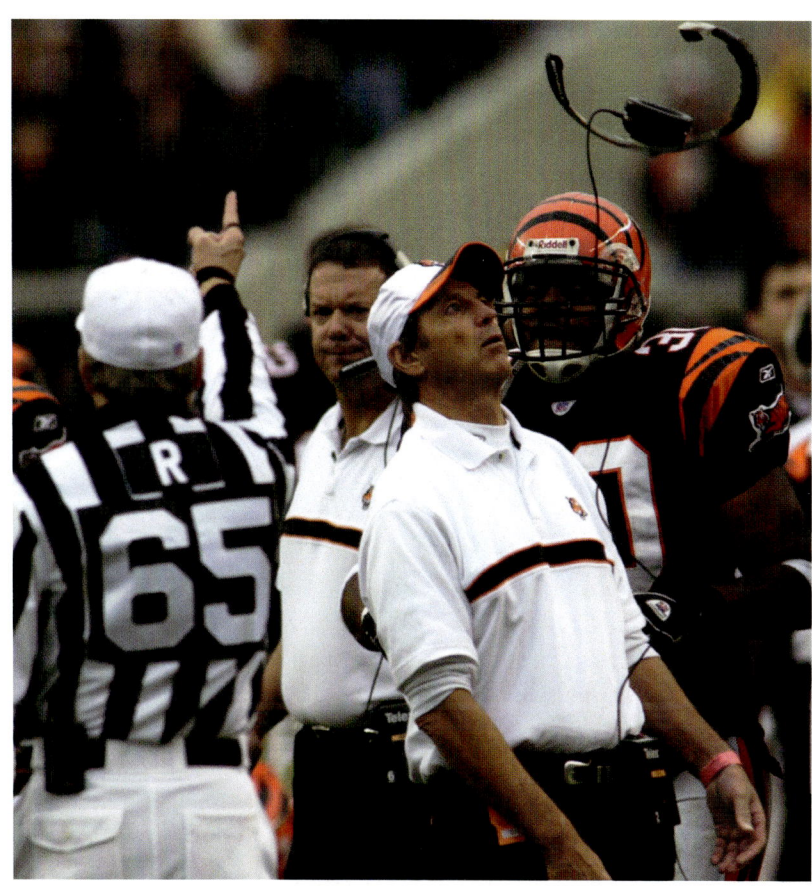

A frustrated Cincinnati Bengals Coach Dick LeBeau.

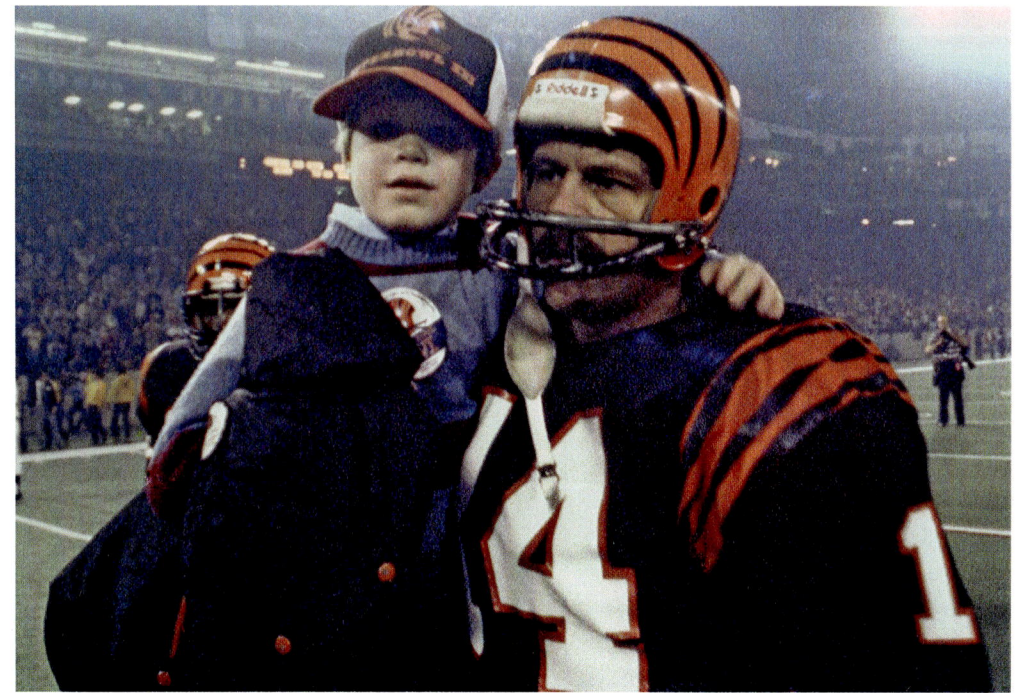

After losing Super Bowl XVI to the San Francisco 49ers 20-16, Bengals quarterback Ken Anderson walked to the stands, picked up his son, and carried him off the field.

Cincinnati Reds owner Marge Schott visits with players pregame while her St. Bernard Schottzie gets a drink.

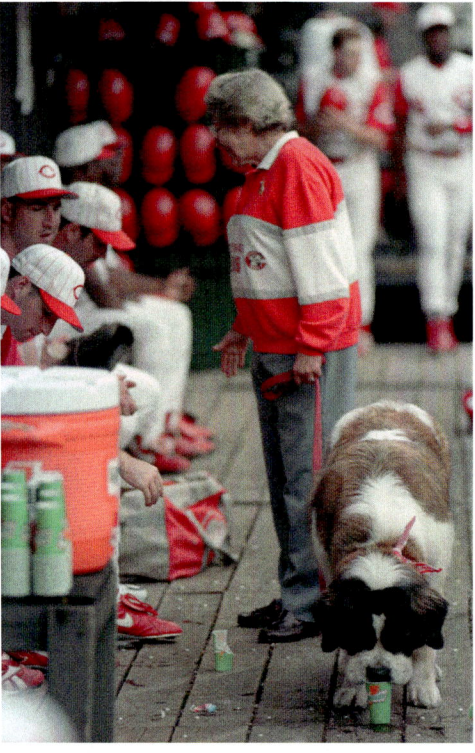

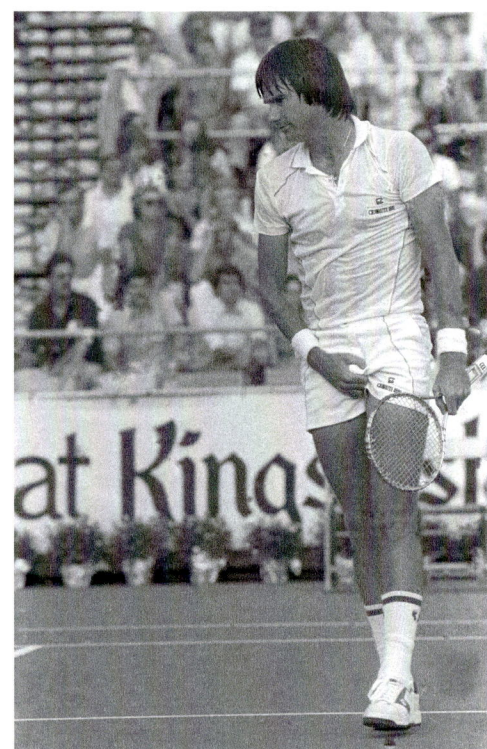

Jimmy Connors makes an adjustment during an Association of Tennis Professionals match at Kings Island in Mason.

Cincinnati Reds first baseman Tony Perez celebrates winning the 1976 World Series against the Yankees at Fountain Square in downtown Cincinnati.

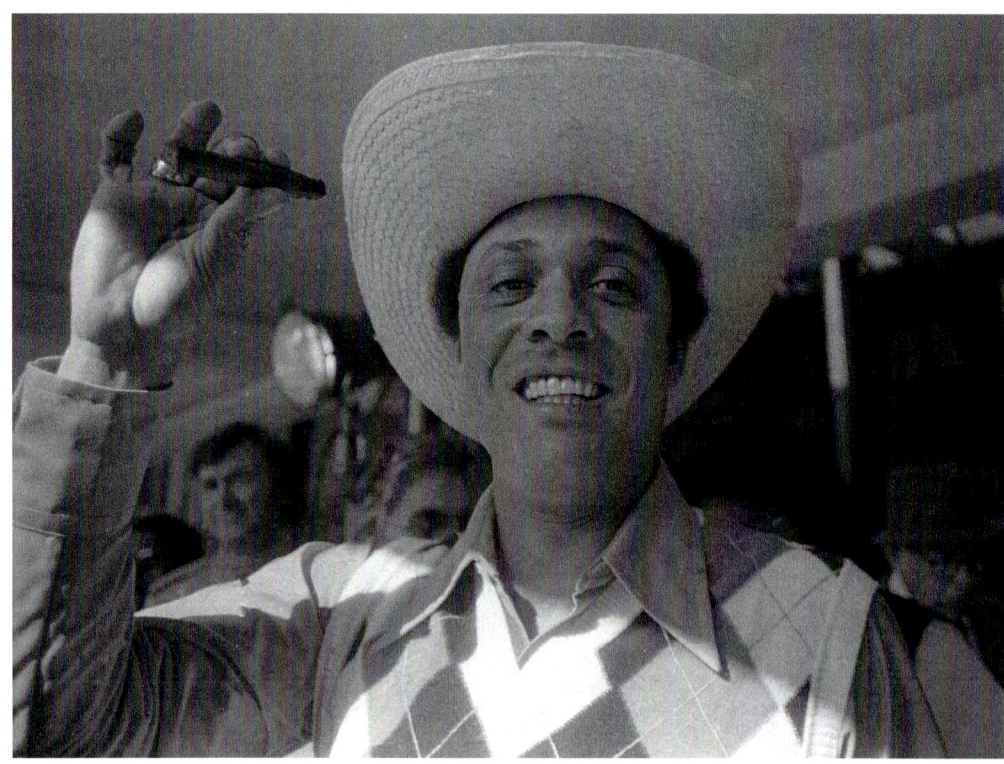

was recuperating from an injury. She expressed an interest in learning photography and began hanging out with me in the darkroom and on occasional assignments. It was my custom to have music playing in my car as I drove to assignments, especially Brazilian music by Flora Purim and Airto, George Duke, Antônio Carlos Jobim, and others.

It was my turn to work the 3:00 p.m. to midnight shift one summer night, which meant covering a Reds game, and Sandra brought me a mix cassette of Brazilian music. I decided to take the tape and a portable player to that night's game. Once I got settled into my usual spot down the first-base line, I put on the headphones, inserted the tape, and everything changed. From then on, I listened to music at baseball games and all sporting events. One of many favorite memories was an afternoon game between the Reds and the Cubs. A fight broke out while I was listening to "Tenderly" by Sarah Vaughan, and the irony made me smile.

By now, our children were young adults. As our daughter Samantha was winding up her time at Saint Ursula Academy and looking at universities, I asked Brenda what Sam had decided

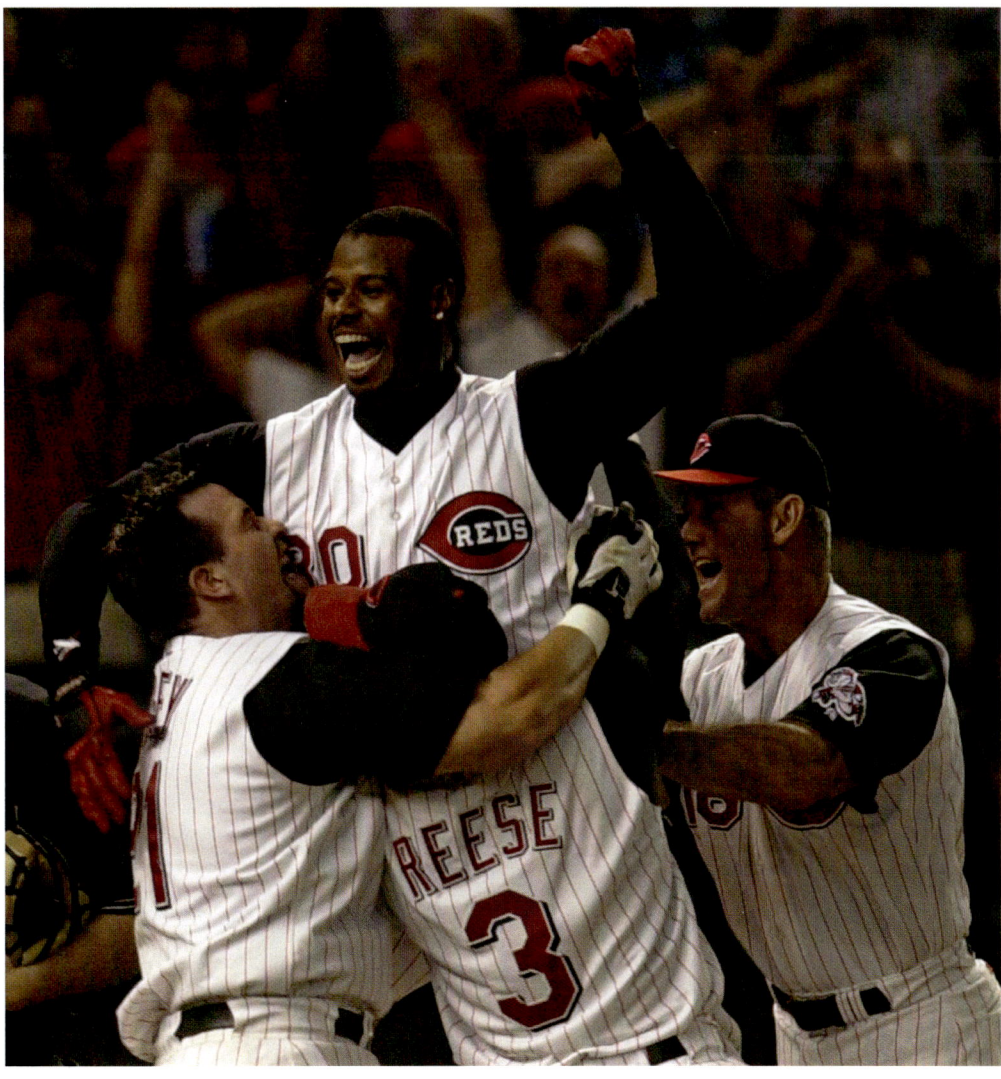

Ken Griffey Jr. celebrates hitting an inside-the-park home run at Riverfront Stadium, the Reds former home, on August 20, 2001, against the St. Louis Cardinals in the bottom of the 11th inning to win the game.

she wanted to study in college. I was surprised she said photojournalism. Sam applied to the School of Visual Communication at Ohio University in Athens, only a three-hour drive east of Cincinnati, so the three of us made the trip to visit the campus. I knew several professors at O.U., including former *Post* graphics director Larry Nighswander, and it was great to see them. Eventually, Sam got her acceptance, and the day came when Brenda and I were empty nesters. Our son Miles was doing graduate studies, and Sam was starting four years at "Harvard on the Hocking." Brenda continued her social-work career, while I tried to enjoy work and be productive as my time at *The Post* counted down.

-30-: THE END

By the time I retired, I had had 13 bosses lead or attempt to lead the photo department. The newsroom had dwindled from a staff of 130 to less than 30. Another sad reality is that no African American photographer followed me until my daughter Samantha briefly joined the staff in 2006, some 32 years after I was hired and a year before *The Post* ceased publishing.

Long in advance, we knew the date of our last edition, December 31, 2007. *The Post* and *The Enquirer* had entered into a joint operating agreement (JOA) in 1977 as part of the Newspaper Preservation Act. The Act was put into place to help floundering papers, most often afternoon publications like *The Post*, survive. The agreement was for 30 years, so we all knew when the JOA was slated to expire, but there was always a sliver of hope it would be renewed. That hope was dashed in early 2004, when *The Enquirer*'s owner, Gannett, announced it would not renew the agreement. The newsroom exodus began.

But let's back up a minute to 1977. One day, soon after the JOA was signed, the arrangement became real when I returned to 800 Broadway and witnessed the presses being moved. One had to be removed through a window. That was one of the saddest days in my entire career. One of the editors invited us for a tour of Western Avenue, where *The Enquirer* was printed and now *The Post*. I said no thanks, sharing presses was like sharing a wife.

In 1984, *The Post* newsroom moved down the street into a new building at 125 East Court Street. While it was just a few blocks in distance, it was a world away from the odor of ink, the rumble of presses, and the general newsroom disarray. At 800 Broadway, there were large letters painted gold that announced *The Cincinnati Post* above the entry doors to the lobby. When we moved to 125 Court, new letters were posted on the fifth-floor wall opposite the elevators. I often joked that when *The Post* closed, I would take that sign with me.

The Post occupied the fourth and fifth floors, above offices, a bank, and restaurant. We gained a spanking-new photo department with large individual lockers and a shared darkroom that had a large sink for the print trays, but each photographer had their own enlarger. Most importantly, we were provided with free parking in the attached garage a few steps from the photo department's back door.

As the JOA neared its termination, *The Kentucky Post* and *The Cincinnati Post* merged. The KY people moved across the river to the Cincinnati newsroom. Photographers Jim Osborn, Joe Munson, Terry Duennes, and Dale Dunaway joined our photo staff, which by then only included me, Bruce Crippen, and Bob Dickerson.

There were still great assignments to be had, if I could find the local connection, but it was frustrating to know that so few people read our paper, a circulation of 40,000 and declining

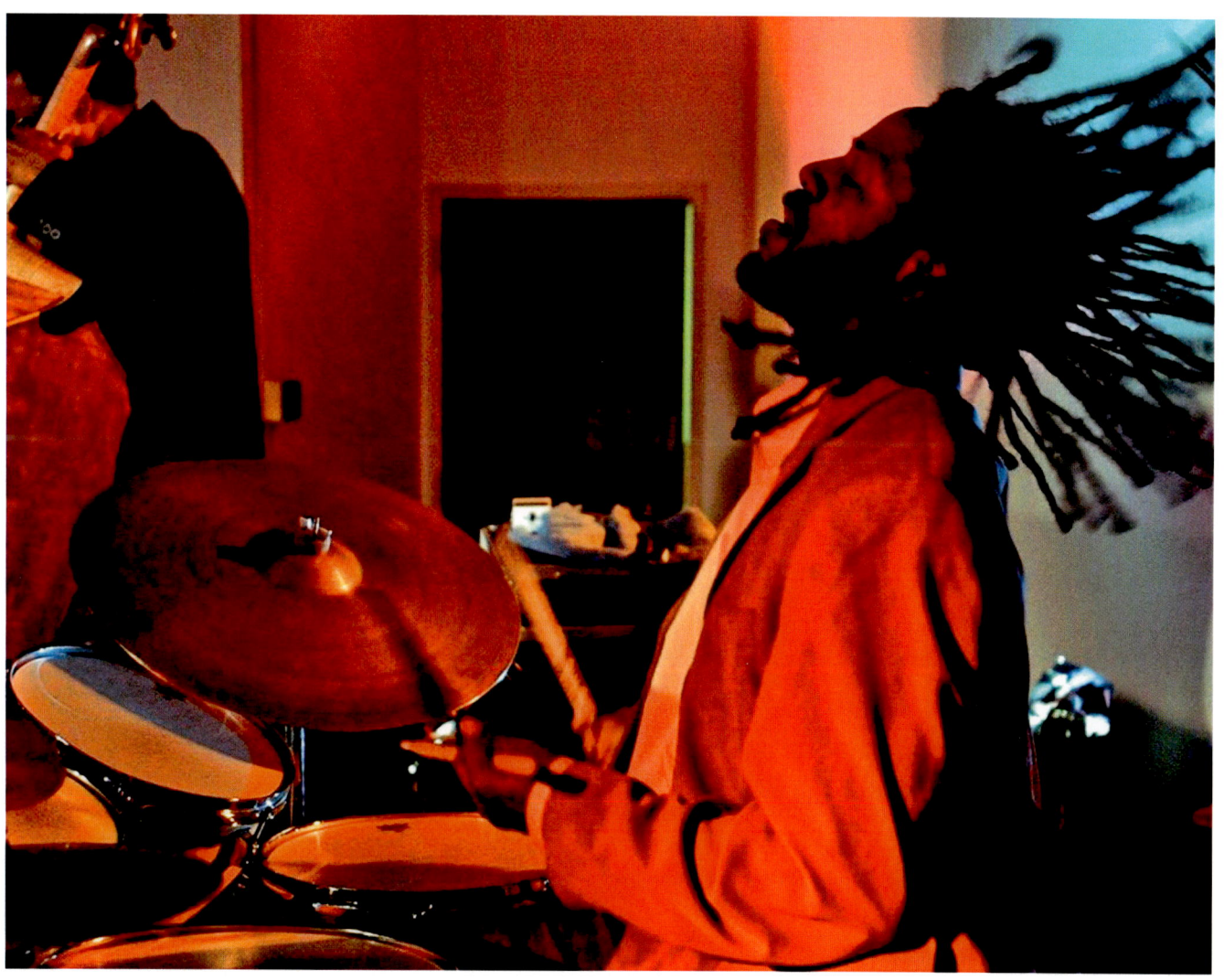

This photo of drummer Mark Lomax was difficult because of the low light and trying to get his dreadlocks flying.

Black and white will always be my favorite medium particularly when an unexpected opportunity presents itself like this photo. I was in my ride, sitting in a parking lot on Central Avenue in the West End, when these three came walking up. I asked what they call themselves and one answered, "Ninja," so I titled this photo "Urban Ninja."

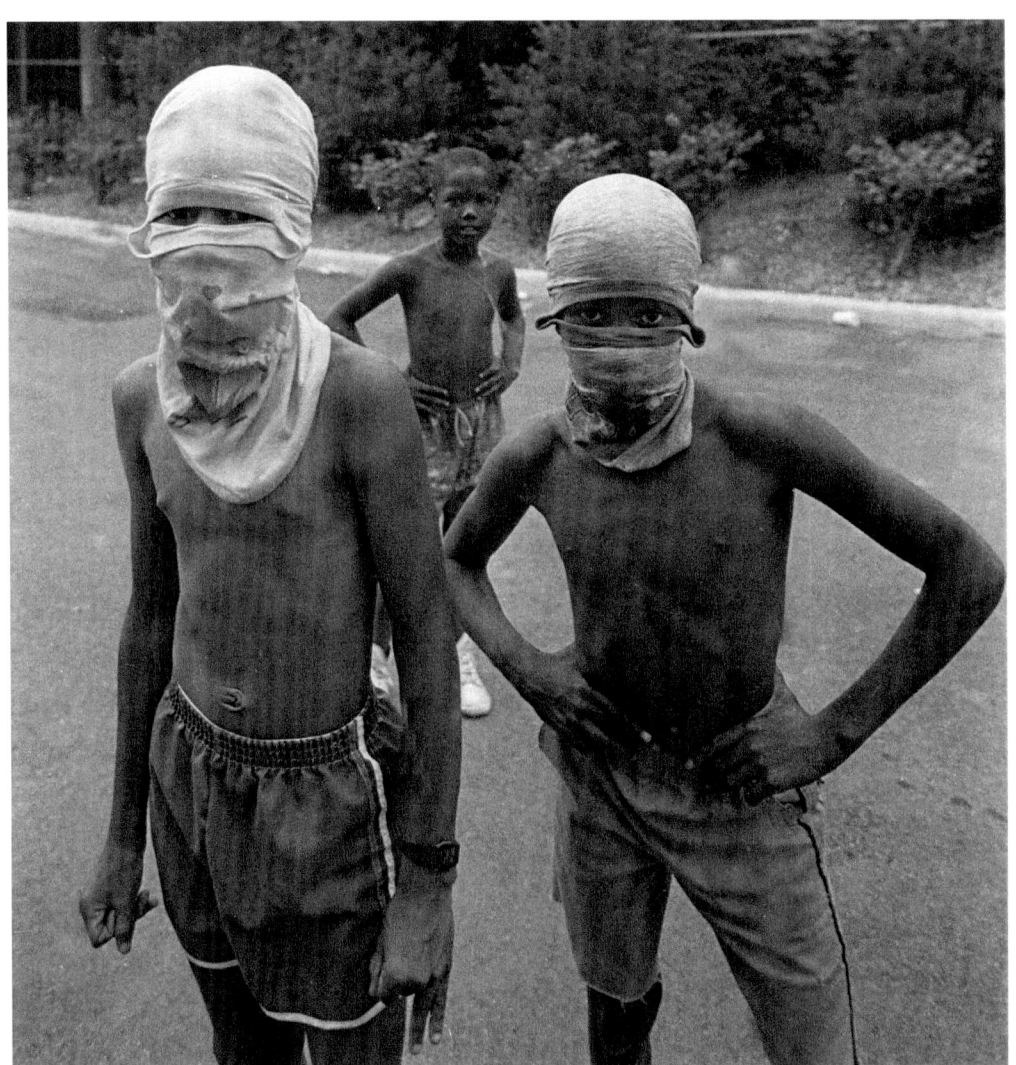

almost daily. Still, I remained motivated to do my best with the goal of at least one really good photo a week, which was harder than I thought it would be.

Prior to working at The Post, I visited favorite locales that would sometimes have interesting subject matter. I would walk the streets in the Over-the-Rhine and West End neighborhoods, where lower-income people were more inclined to spend time outside on the streets. As the number of assignments decreased, I once again looked to these sites in the hope of finding photographs.

I was also dedicated to my own projects. My most frequent were storefront churches and jazz clubs, because they were accessible during my free time. A series of my storefront-church photos were exhibited at the Contemporary Arts Center in "Strategies, Artists in the '80s."

Those personal projects eased my mind, as The Post moved into that final year, then last months, and that last saddest of all days, the final edition. There were employment-termination papers to sign, hands to shake, a quick goodbye embrace. Much as I disliked it, I joined some of the other staff to watch that final press run at Western Avenue.

When I opened the final copy of The Post, I was surprised to see a photo that I shot while on feature patrol. I had made a photo of a guy working on a building in Covington that a copyeditor cleverly titled "Finishing Touch." The paper also generously included a page of each photographer's work in that final edition, -30-, the newspaper symbol denoting the end.

Photographers were allowed to select some camera equipment to take as they departed. We were also asked to give our negatives to the Cincinnati Historical Society. With concern for my life's work, I handed over just two boxes.

Even some 15 years later, that last day is a blur of faces and formalities, and I still regret that The Post is no longer here. The popular cliché is, it's the people that you miss. To a certain extent, that was true, but when that first week of 2008 came, and I had nowhere to go and all day to get there, I missed just being out in the streets. One thing I didn't miss was expressway driving. I made a promise to myself to stay off the interstates, a promise I have pretty much kept.

Since I was friends with the security guard who manned the reception desk in the lobby of 125 East Court, I returned there on a couple of occasions, and he permitted me to go back up to the fourth and fifth floors. It was incredible how quickly all traces of The Post had been removed. That provoked a feeling of remorse that all I had were the memories, but I also felt good that I had held onto most of my negatives.

During my time at The Post, I covered other organizations closing and the loss of employment that came with it. Now it was my turn. I was in a good position to make the transition to whatever awaited me. I was 66 years old, I had a pension, Social Security, health insurance, and Brenda was working as a social worker. Our home was paid for as were our two vehicles.

Now it was time to move onto the next phase of my life.

One of my last assignments was to photograph Santa Claus arriving via helicopter at the University Hospital helipad in Cincinnati. Turns out it was not a real landing but a publicity stunt, which I refused to shoot. When I called Tim Stein, my graphics director, he backed me up, and I left the helipad without a photograph.

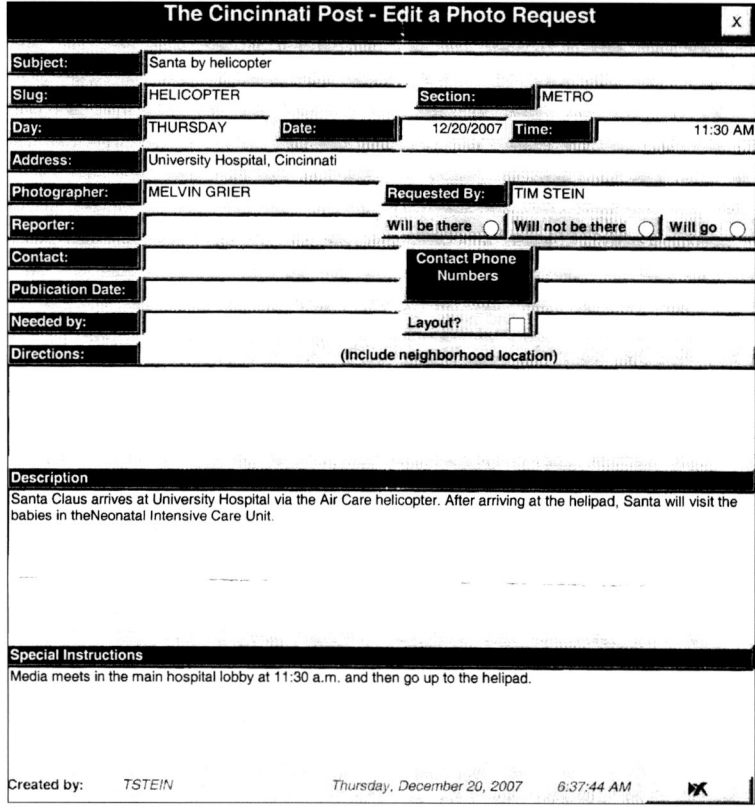

CHAPTER 4: ART LIFE

With my days at *The Post* over, I could now return to the world of art that I had dabbled in, sometimes intensely, over the years. As my career had progressed at *The Post*, I came to realize that I wanted the public to see my photographs as I intended them to be presented. Newspaper reproduction sometimes left a lot to be desired, and space in the paper might mean a crop I disliked.

I was also trying to establish myself in the Art world—with a capital A. I wasn't sure I belonged; however, I was quite happy as a newspaper photographer working the streets and roads of the tri-state area where Ohio, Indiana, and Kentucky meet. I was comfortable with street photography, and a rare trip abroad was sufficient adventure. In 1976, I was happy to join my fellow *Post* photographers, Terry Armor, Alex Burrows, Mimi Fuller, and Ken Stewart in a show entitled "Photography and Light Hauling," an exhibit at the Contemporary Arts Center.

While I had never thought of myself as an artist, I had a growing desire to be one. Henri Cartier-Bresson, whom I greatly admired, was arguably one of the greatest street photographers. Among others, he elevated photography to an art form.

Years before my retirement, I was invited to have my work displayed in the "Cincinnati Invitational Exhibition: Photographs and Watercolors" at the

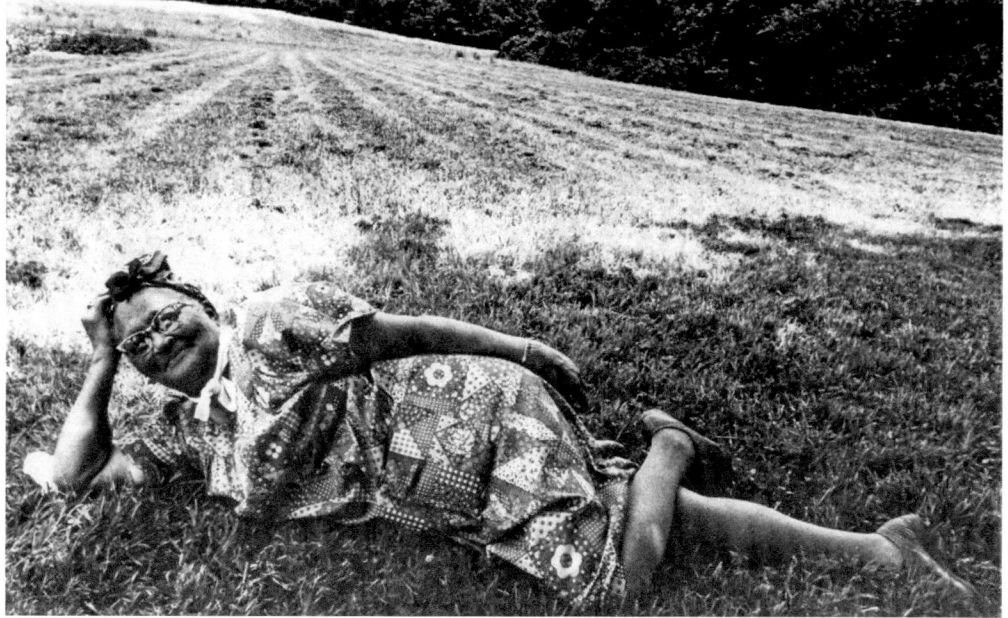

Gardener resting after work, one of three of my works selected for the Cincinnati Invitational Exhibition, "Photographs and Watercolors."

Cincinnati Art Museum. There were several other artists included such as Tony Walsh, Thom Shaw, Cal Kowal, Barry Andersen, and Tom Schiff, whom I would cross paths with my entire career.

During three-and-half decades, I always made sure I was aware of photo opportunities that might make my daily assignments stand out. It could be as simple as standing away from the other photographers at a press conference so that my photo had a different look. Sometimes that might backfire, but most times, it worked. For instance, during a halftime ceremony honoring retiring Bengals wide receiver Isaac Curtis, I stood away from the pack of photographers and using a long lens got a tighter—and I think different—photograph.

The daily work went on as I lobbied for something a little more exciting. I eventually established a goal of making at least one photograph I liked every week.

Let me be clear, on a day-to-day basis there were often assignments that satisfied the needs of *The Post* but were not real keepers. It could be something as simple as a ground breaking or a shtick presentation, which we dubbed a grip-and-grin. I tried to elevate these assignments, but most times, it was impossible. Most rewarding were those unexpected opportunities when a great photo was there just for the taking. Whenever possible, I tried to be the first photographer to arrive and stayed as late as I possibly could, because that was when people reverted to their true selves.

Often, when I first got to an assignment, the subject would ask, "What do you want me to do?" I would reply, "Whatever you were doing before I got here, please just continue to do that." It would take a few minutes of my waiting without shooting even one frame, and the subject would then get busy with a particular task. This worked for larger groups too. Of course, there were those times where it was appropriate for me to pose people for a portrait. But I mostly enjoyed letting the right photo come to me.

Sometimes, while driving to an assignment, I might see something. I recall a Sunday when I was on my way to a basketball game in the western part of Cincinnati, and I saw a man riding a bike with a monkey sitting on the handlebars! Ridiculous, I admit, but more upsetting was that I didn't immediately stop. When I turned around, he was gone. That missed opportunity is to this day hard to explain, and even harder to accept.

As I look back on the many exhibitions I have done post-*Post*, there are a few spaces and opportunities that have been extremely meaningful to me—Kennedy Heights Arts Center, Taft Museum of Art, and Arts Consortium of Cincinnati, to name a few. I also enjoyed creating unique exhibitions. To date, I've included spoken word, written word, music, or movement with my exhibitions. Let's start at the beginning.

During my two trips to Africa in 1985 and 1994, I had amassed a large body of work that had never been published, except for those photos that ran in *The Post*. I decided that I wanted to take on an exhibit of the unseen images. Also, I wanted to go a couple steps further than just hanging photos on walls. Exhibits were run-of-the-mill. Everybody did an exhibit. I wanted to do something more, and something different, particularly for the opening reception. I wanted people to be immersed in African thought and culture as they viewed the photos, to experience some of what I had seen on my trip.

I had worked with a friend, freelance video producer Meg Hanrahan, on a couple of other projects, so she agreed to help with African proverbs that would serve as captions to be displayed with the work. Dean Tabler was a theater producer who presented plays at the Arts Consortium, so I

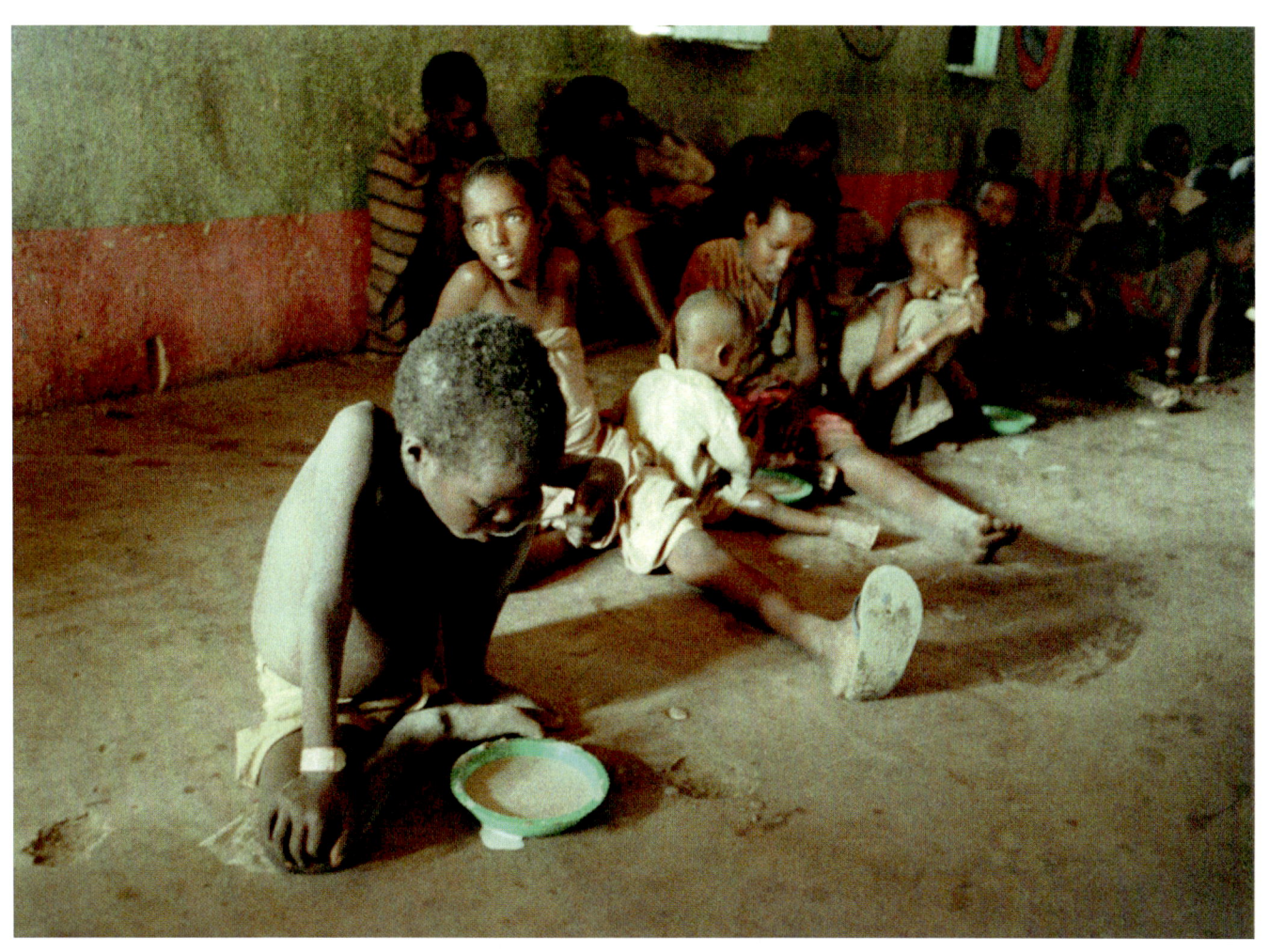

A feeding station in Sudan.

approached him with another idea—two or three spoken-word artists who would mingle with the opening-night crowd, and just suddenly erupt with a poem or prose. This turned into my first solo exhibit, "Souls in Bondage: Essays of East Africa," at the Arts Consortium in the West End. "Souls in Bondage" helped me to think of myself as an artist and started me on a path of believing that some of my photographs were worthy of being displayed in galleries.

This two-month exhibit in 1994 was significant for a couple reasons. Brenda grew up across the street from the space in Laurel Homes public housing. As aspiring young painters and photographers, we did not have access to an art center when I was growing up. We made do with any area open to us. Eventually, as a result of local activism, a building was acquired and converted into a center for exhibitions, a dance studio, a theater, a darkroom, and a conference room.

Located at 1515 Linn Street, the Arts Consortium (originally named the Resident Arts and Humanities Consortium) opened in 1973 in an old Kroger building and sat in the heart of what was left of the West End of my youth. That was important to me. Today, we would say the Arts Consortium was located in an underserved Black community. The fact that it provided all the essentials for aspiring and working artists under one roof made it special. It not only offered exhibit and working spaces, but it also offered free instruction in weaving, sewing, graphics, dance, drama, photography, and other artistic disciplines. Over time, white artists and art lovers came to the center, too. Unfortunately, the Arts Consortium lost its lease and closed in 2004.

Long before I started at *The Post*, I had developed a working habit of doing photo projects that would feed my need to pursue some form of photojournalism. So, on days where I was free, I would catch the bus downtown with my camera, and wander the streets. One day, as I walked through the projects not far from where Brenda grew up, I found two elders playing checkers. This memorable

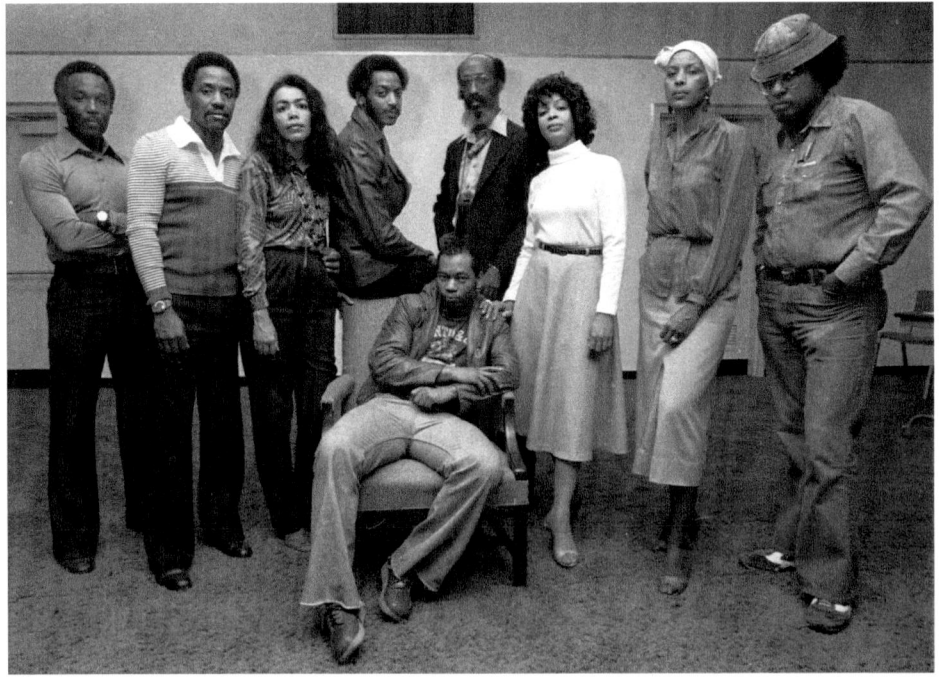

I was honored to be a member of Mixed Media, a group of distinguished artists: (left to right) LeRoy Porter, Gilbert Young, Joyce Young, Cornelius Lindsey, Bing Davis, Irene Bryant, Pat Rambo, me, and Thom Shaw (seated).

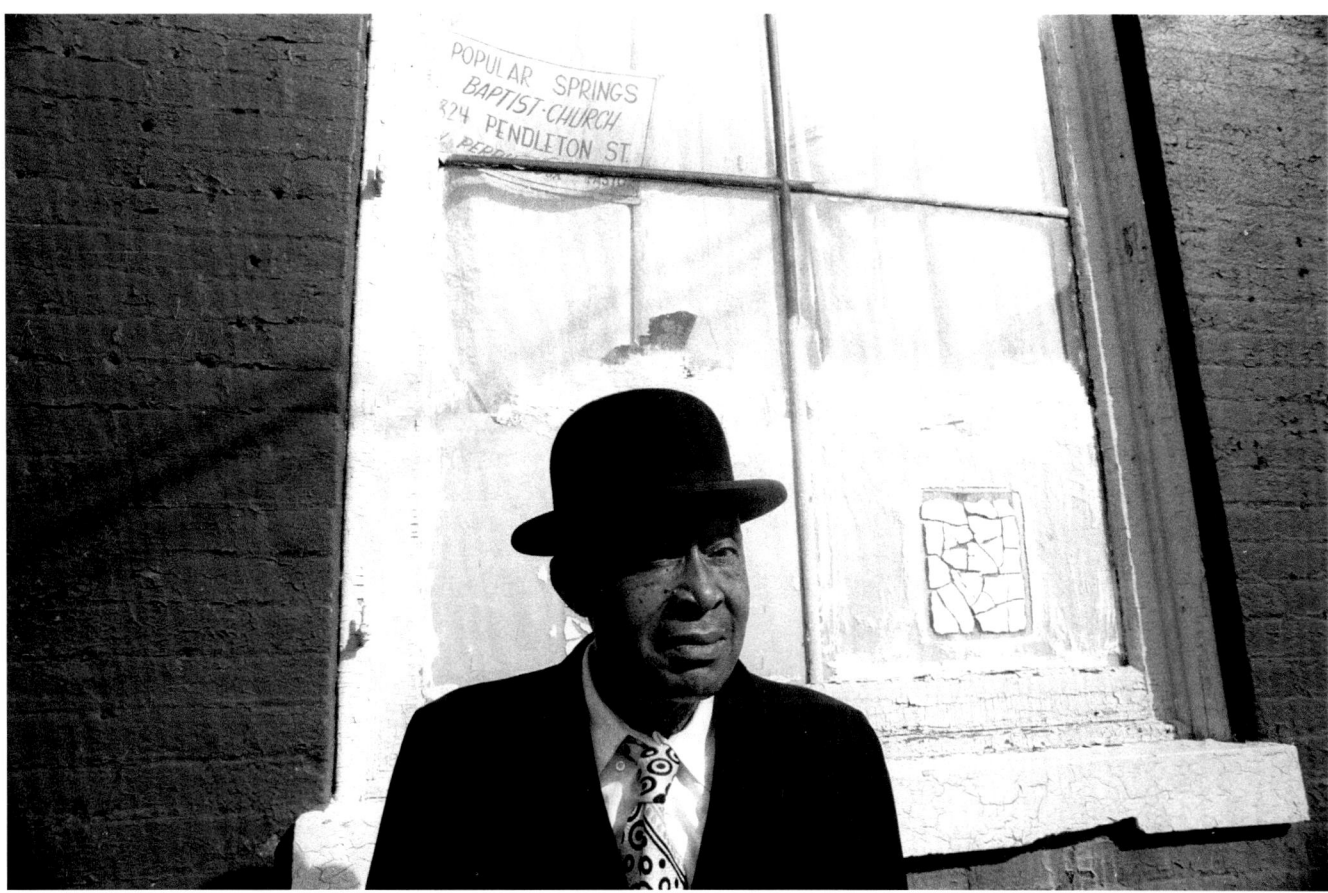

Reverend Perry Locke, pastor of Popular Springs Baptist Church in the Pendleton District, was a perfect portrait subject with his derby and somewhat-aloof countenance.

photograph now greets visitors when they walk through our front door.

I grew up across the street from the Bibleway Church of God in Christ, one of many small, here-today-gone-tomorrow places of Godly worship in the West End. It was only natural that I would pursue a deeper dive into distinct but very different styles of worship, and I put together a series of photographs for a 1979 exhibit. I often include these storefront-church photos in other shows.

What I most craved was the shared experiences of others who might be struggling as I was to find a path to fulfillment as an artist. To this end, I joined a few different artist groups formed in that period, most with African names. The first meeting would bring us together with a common purpose, but soon the question of how to achieve that goal was debated to the point of disintegration. I like collaboration (and still do), but I learned that sometimes group dynamics do not work, and at times, it is best to formulate my own goals, and work to achieve them.

One day, I was working in our front yard, and Brenda came out to say I had a call from Joel McCray, co-founder of the Robert S. Duncanson Society at the Taft Museum of Art. When I picked up, I was greeted with good news. "Hello, Melvin. You are the 2004 Duncanson Artist-in-Residence." I was very happy to become the museum's 18th artist-in-residence.

Robert Duncanson was a famous African American artist who created the murals that adorn the original entrance to the Longworth residence,

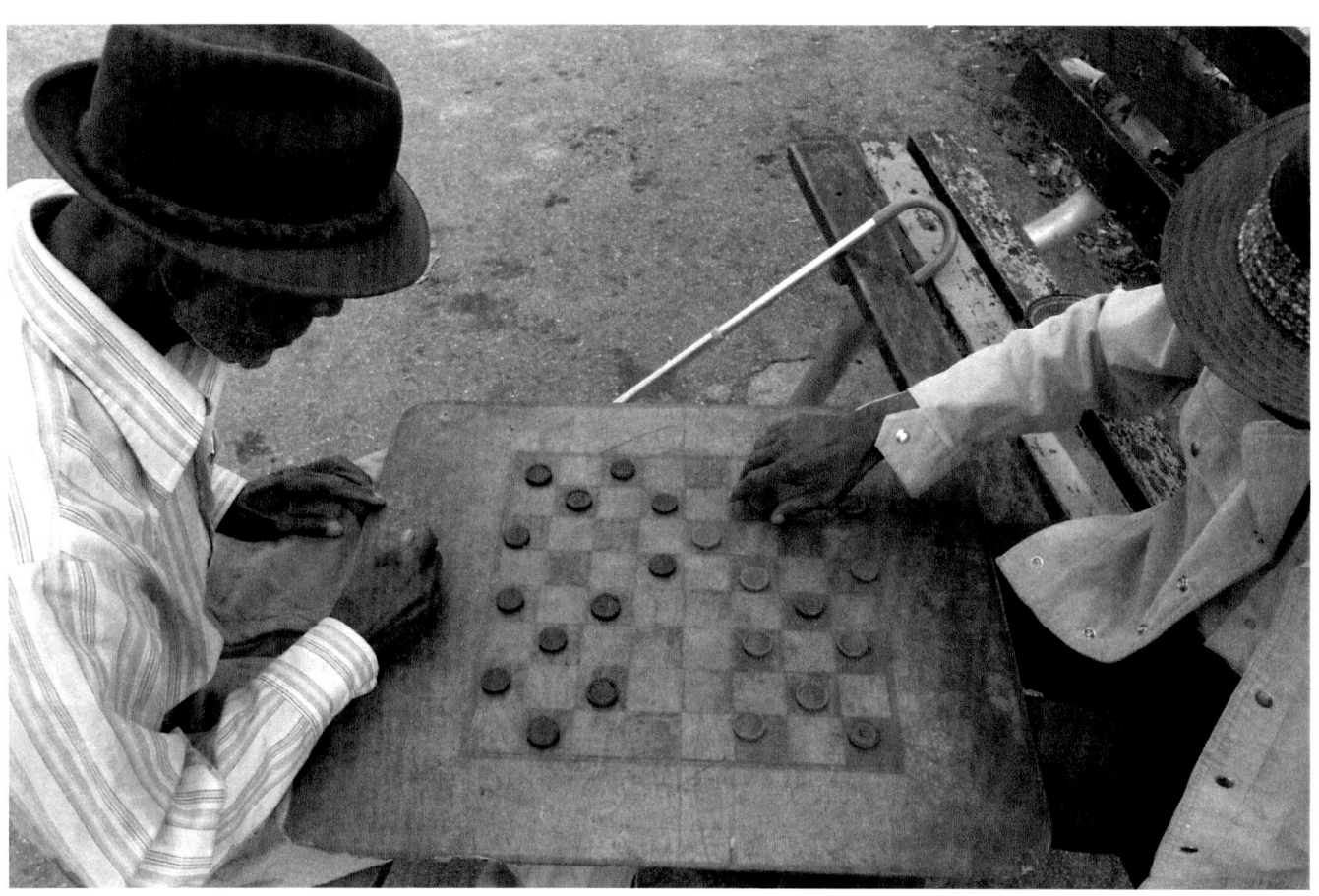

I took this photograph a few years before I started my career at The Post, and it remains one of my most cherished.

now part of the Taft Museum of Art adjacent to Lytle Park. The program was established to honor the achievements of contemporary Black American artists. It was an honor for me to be among the previous artists, such as Nikki Giovanni, Kathy Wade, and Annie Ruth.

We had our first meeting at the museum to discuss what was expected of me. There were several requirements. I would have to present information about myself and the Robert Duncanson murals. One suggestion was a PowerPoint, which I immediately vetoed. My solution was a video. At that time, I was mentoring a young student, Una Karim Cross. I mentioned my idea about the video to her, and she asked that I let her and a friend, Hye Yon Moon, do the edit of the video footage. I had first planned to shoot the video myself with my Canon XL 1(s) but decided it would make more sense for someone else to be behind the camera.

I commissioned a young man I had met in the early 1990s, when Molly Kavanaugh and I were "on loan" to a Cincinnati Public Schools journalism program. The program was overseen by mutual friend Jene Galvin. In 2004, there was a hip-hop cultural arts center that served as a gathering spot for young people. It stood next to Enzo's, the coffee house I frequented. One day on the sidewalk, I ran into Ageymang Sparks, who I had met at Hughes High School, and asked if he would be willing to operate the camera for my video. He agreed, and we met at *The Post* to shoot a typical day of mine at the paper, with no script. Then we hit the streets.

Another requirement of the residency was making several presentations to local students. I wanted to include music. Young people have a short attention span and respond favorably to hip-hop beats. Sure enough, after a couple minutes of Dave Brubeck jazz at the beginning of the video, their focus started to wander. But then the beats started, and the students focused right back.

In addition to the video, I produced an exhibit titled "15 retro/15 active" to be displayed at the Taft Museum of Art. This exhibit led to the first time one of my photographs became a permanent piece in an art collection. Of the 30 photographs that were part of the exhibition, one photograph entitled "Red Hat" was purchased by the Cincinnati Art Museum's Sowell Committee and added to the permanent collection of the Cincinnati Art Museum.

I would also be expected to give an artist talk. I had learned from an awful experience that I could not work from a script. After my first trip to Africa, Annunciation Catholic Church asked me to do a talk. My two children, Miles and Samantha, were enrolled in Annunciation School. I had to speak from the lectern in the sanctuary. Speech in hand, I walked to the lectern and began my talk. After a few minutes, I began to bore myself. Lesson learned. I'm better at speaking off the cuff, and, whenever possible, I work with images. After all, I am a photographer. At the Taft Museum, I riffed instead of using notes, and the audience responded with enthusiasm.

The evening of my talk at the Taft Museum, all the chairs in the room were occupied. I had decided that the theme of my talk would be "connections," allowing me to recognize members of the audience. Whenever I do artist talks, I always include someone I see in the audience. I had learned a great deal from my miserable performance at Annunciation.

The Duncanson Artist-in-Residence reunited me with Yvonne Thomas. I had done portraits for her at a studio I shared with local Cincinnati photographer Robert Flischel. Yvonne became my contact person for speaking engagements associated with the Duncanson obligations.

After Duncanson, Yvonne scheduled a speaking engagement for me at an Ohio teachers'

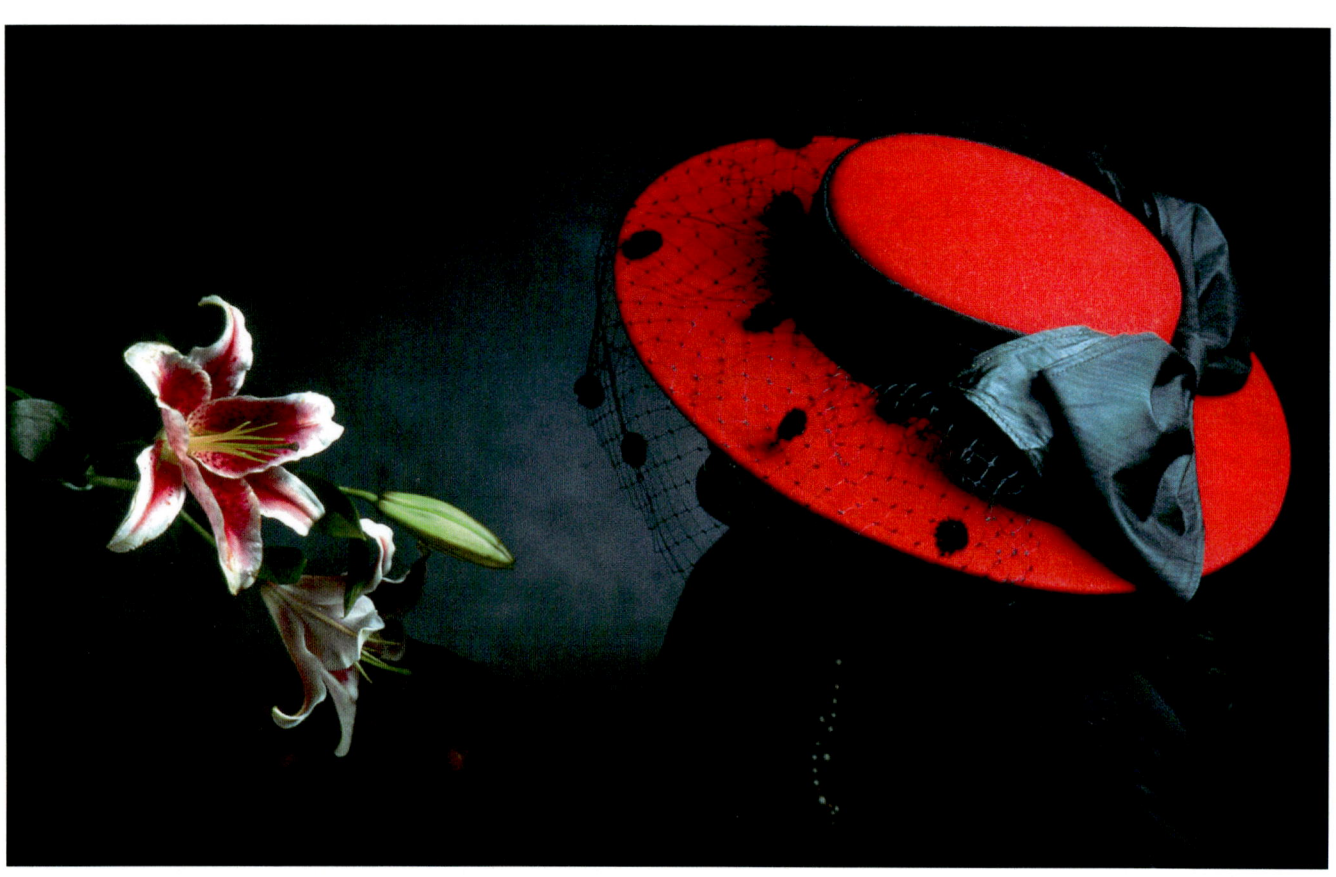

"Red Hat," one of four photographs I have in the Cincinnati Art Museum's permanent collection.

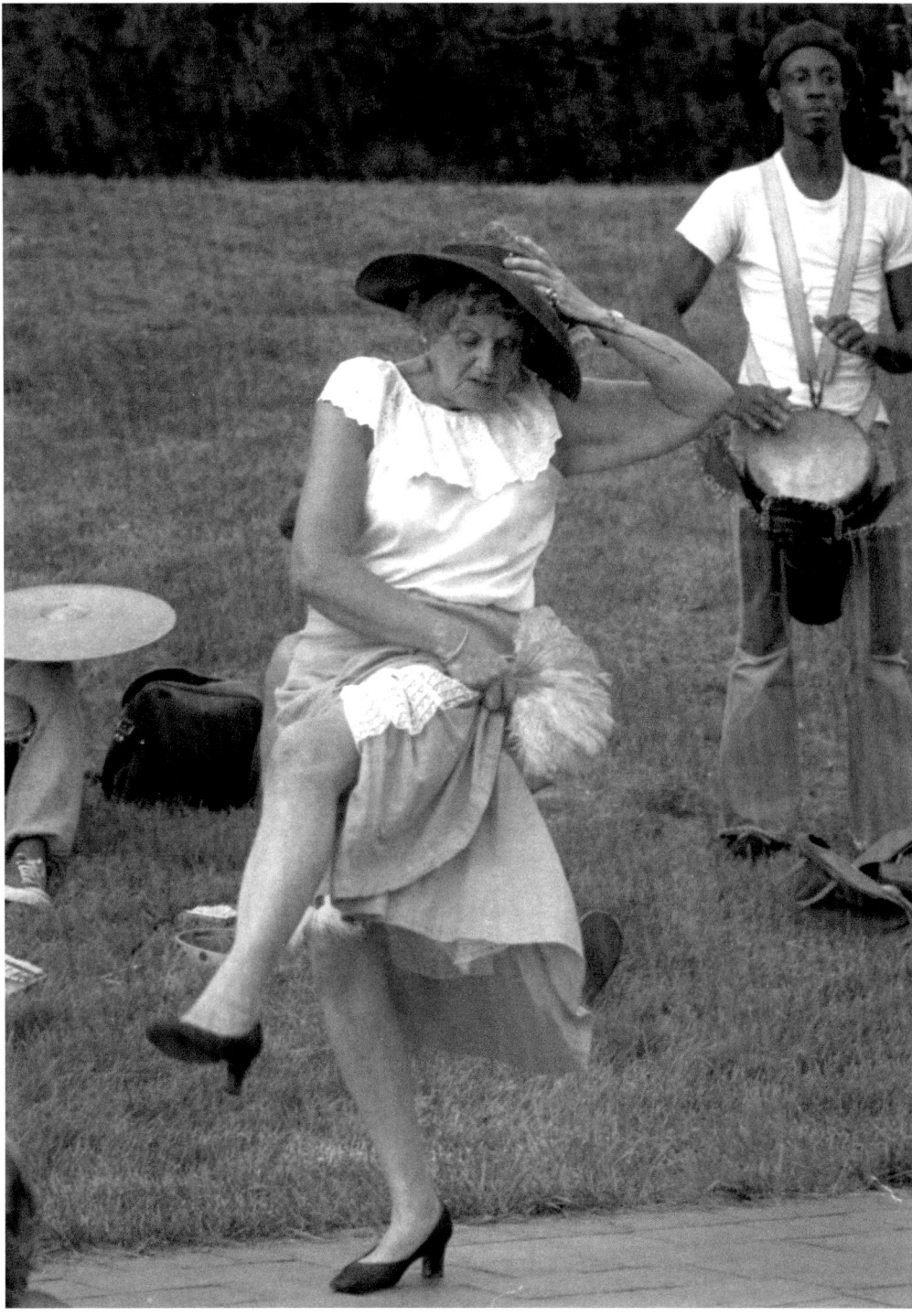

One image in the "Joyful Noise" exhibit was "Virginia Dancing." If there was music, she would almost magically appear and kick up her heels.

organization at the Hyatt in downtown Cincinnati. I was to speak about my career and show some of my photos on a screen. I hired a friend, jazz saxophonist Bruce Menefield, to improvise music during the visual presentation. Initially, there was a problem with a stubborn computer not working correctly, but we solved that, and all went well. As the applause faded, I asked the audience of three hundred adults to do something I had often heard and always wanted to do, "Put your hands in the air and wave them like you just don't care." They obliged—-some with puzzled looks—and I was satisfied that my crazy idea worked.

Another time, I had an exhibit in Covington, Kentucky, at the Cathedral Basilica Gallery. Entitled "Joyful Noise," it was a celebration of music dedicated to Jonathan Wilson (JW), a very good friend with whom I had attended many a concert and who unfortunately had passed away. I am grateful for these and so many other opportunities to display my work, sharing what brings me enjoyment and expands my artistry and perspective.

During my *Post* years, I had an assignment to go to the Kennedy Heights Arts Center to cover an exhibit of photos by the American Society of Media Photographers, a group of primarily commercial photographers. I was impressed with the exhibition space at the KHAC. At one time, it had been a funeral home, and the various rooms reflected it. I felt very comfortable there and thought how wonderful it would be to have my work on the walls. That dream came true in 2011 with my first solo show at the KHAC. "White People: A Retrospective" grew out of a conversation with my daughter. By then, Sam had left *The Post* and moved onto the *Hamilton Journal-News*. She mentioned that many times she was the only Black face present. I had noted this during my career and thought about doing an exhibit that featured only white people.

Many contemporary African American artists have featured work that depicts Black folks or people of color. My work was different. My roots were in a Black neighborhood, and we lived in South Avondale, a struggling predominantly Black community, but my photographs reflected a great

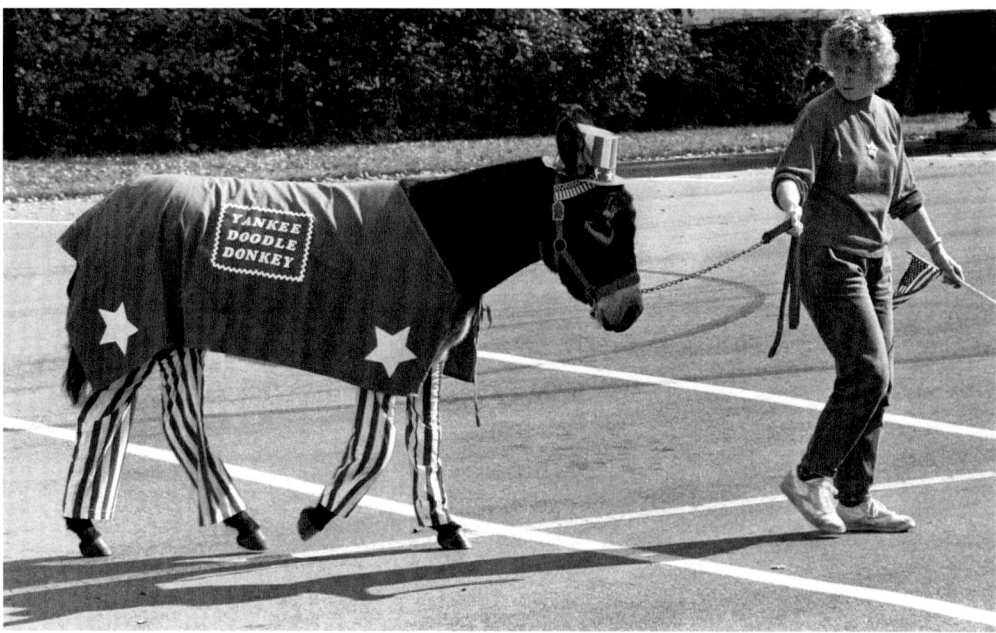

A photograph entitled "Yankee Doodle Donkey" used in "White People: A Retrospective."

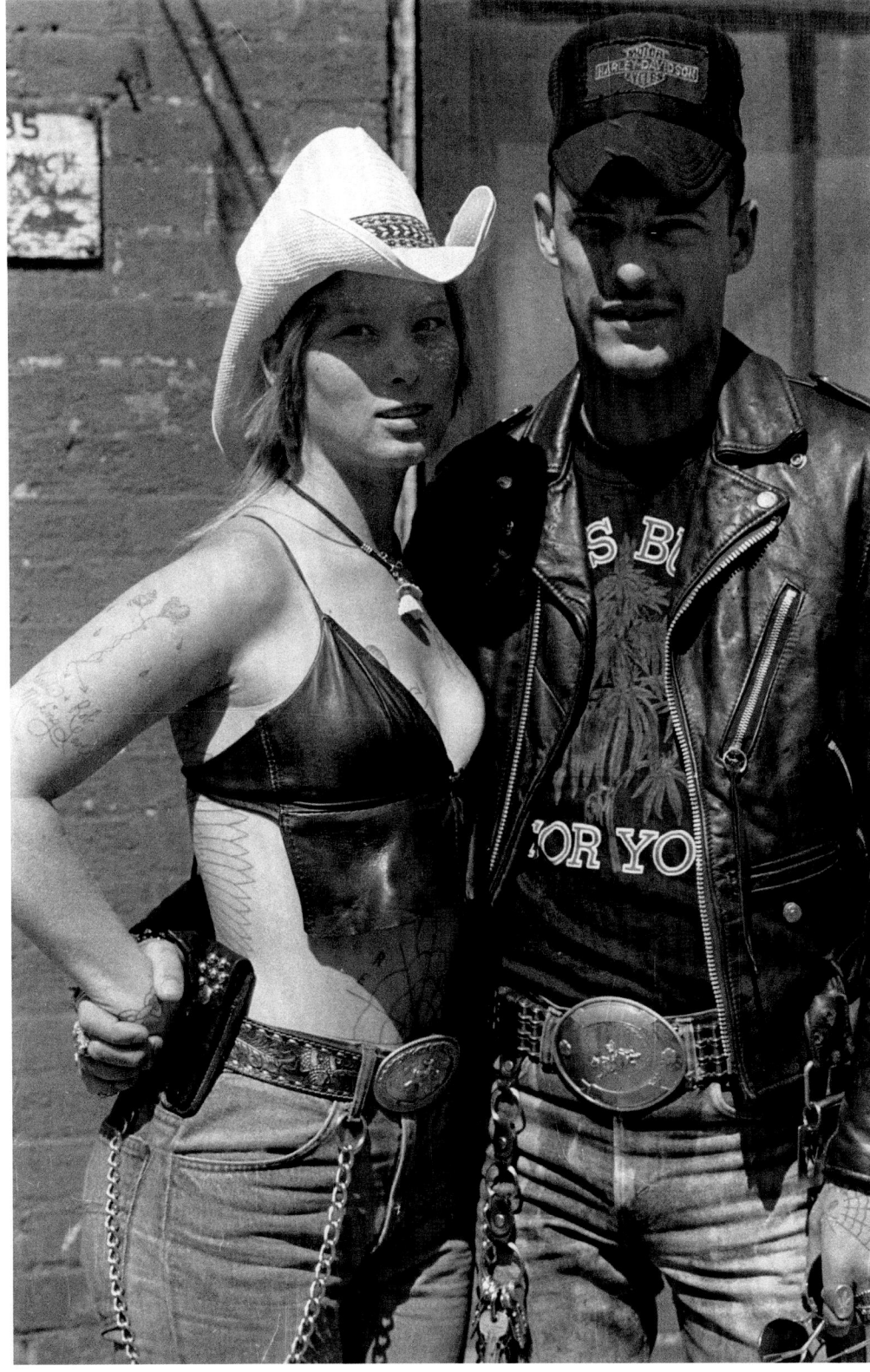

While I was waiting on a sidewalk in the Over-the-Rhine neighborhood, this couple came out of an apartment building. When I asked to take their picture, Rob said "F--- no!" Vonda said, "Oh, I want to."

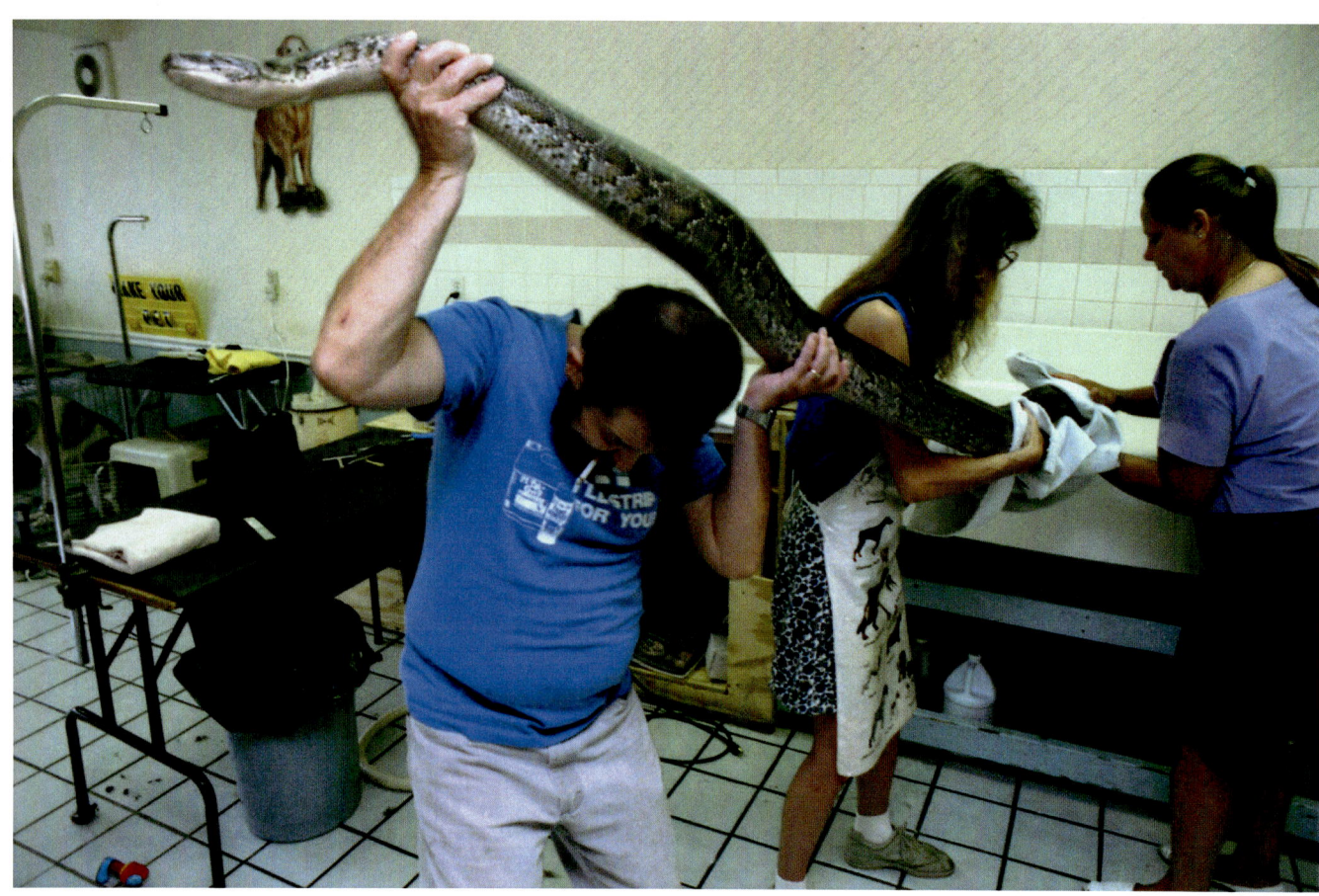

When I stopped at a pet-grooming shop in St. Bernard, a suburb of Cincinnati, I was looking to shoot something for a project about documenting Vine Street. I was surprised that they would be bathing this large snake.

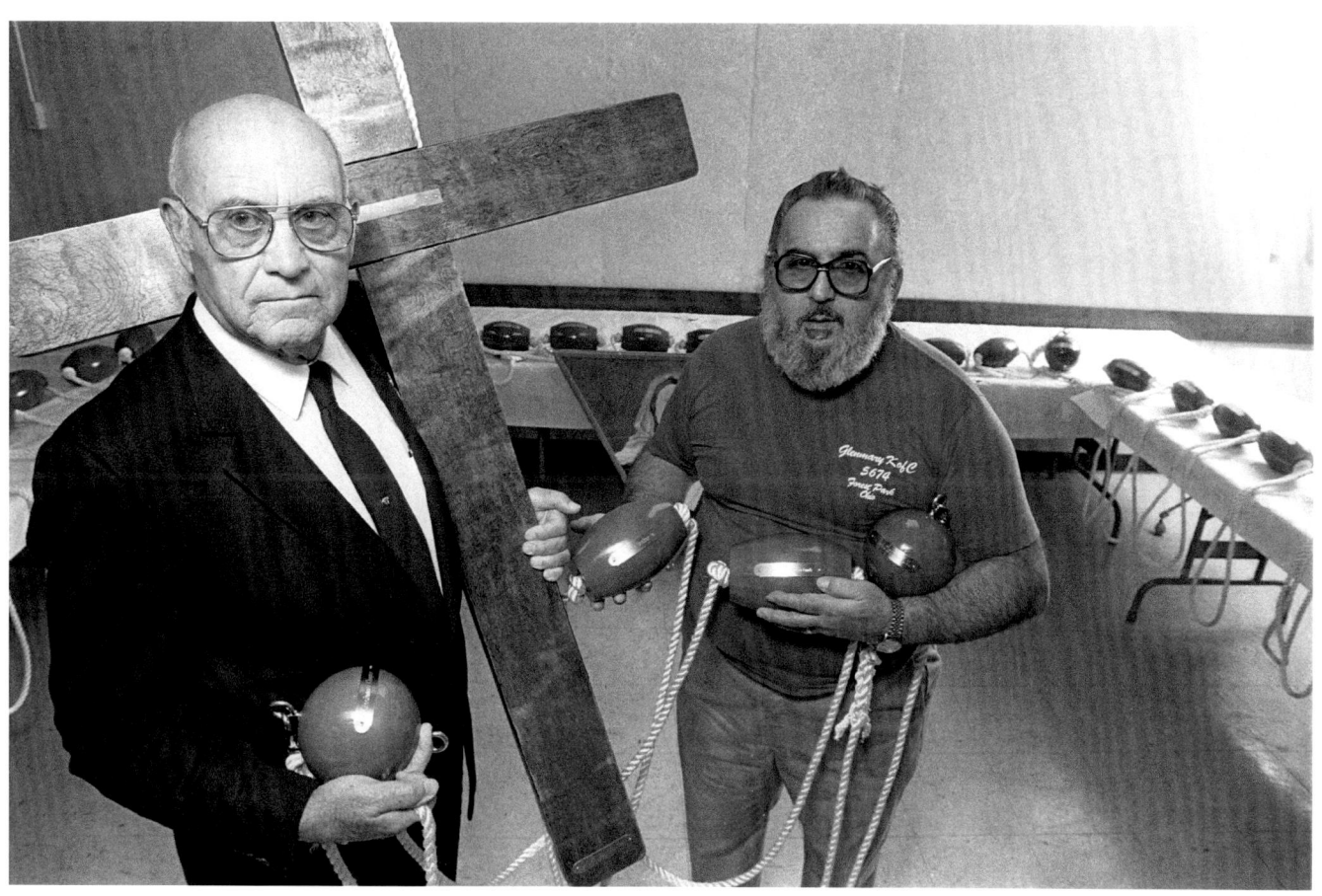

It was difficult to get this giant rosary and the two gentlemen in the photograph. I stood on a folding chair and hoped it didn't collapse.

ART LIFE | 81

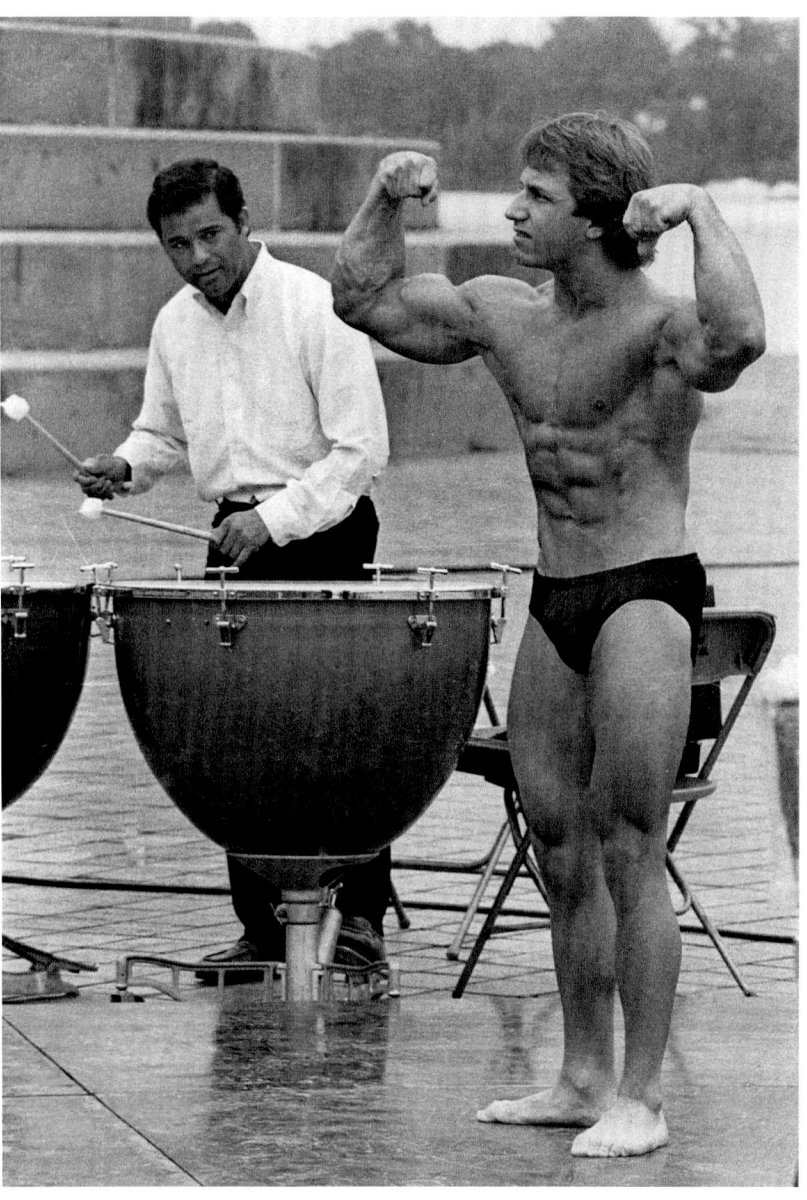

Shot near the Serpentine Wall on the downtown Cincinnati riverfront, a contingent from the Cincinnati Symphony Orchestra performed, and this bodybuilder flexed while the kettle drummer played along.

deal of the majority's happenings as reported in *The Post*.

During a meeting at the KHAC, I presented my idea. The initial question was "Will it be controversial?" My answer was, "It wouldn't be if I was doing Black people." So "White People: A Retrospective" was presented at the KHAC in 2011.

"White People: A Retrospective" was a great success, garnering media attention from as far away as the Netherlands. I got the sense that some white people approached the show with maybe a little reluctance, not knowing what direction my photographs would take them, but when they saw the many facets the photos depicted, they tuned in. My artist statement for the exhibit was "Observe. Compose. Capture. Move On." So, four years after my retirement, I had something to hang my photo hat on.

In 2012, I did a second show at the KHAC with two Michaels (Kearns and Wilson) called "Let's Face It." It was based on the premise that opinions about individuals are sometimes based on their appearance. We developed ten questions for each individual, and I made 10 large-scale prints. The portrait subjects answered the questions, which were displayed next to their portraits. Attendees could assess whether their initial impressions of the person were correct. My favorite photo was Bob. I had seen this gentleman at several art gatherings and was intrigued with his body art. I thought he would make a great subject for "Let's Face It." but I had formed an opinion that he would probably reject any approach by me. Finally, at one show, I somewhat hesitantly walked up to him, introduced myself, and asked if he would permit me to photograph him. To my pleasure, he readily agreed, and I was even more attuned to the notion of forming opinions based on outward appearance.

In 2016, I did another solo show at the KHAC. I have always had a love of jazz, so this time, I decided

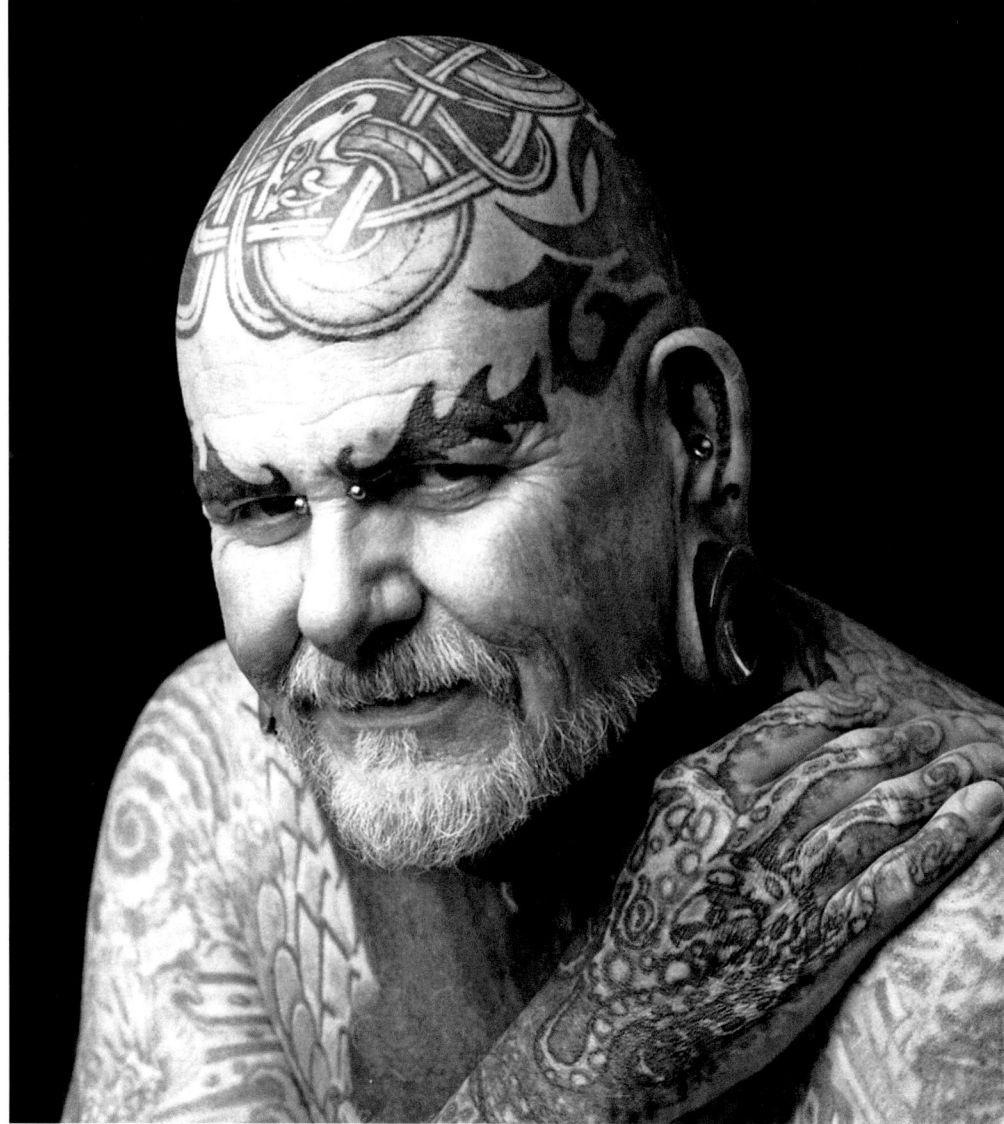

Portrait of Bob used in "Let's Face It" at the Kennedy Heights Arts Center in 2012.

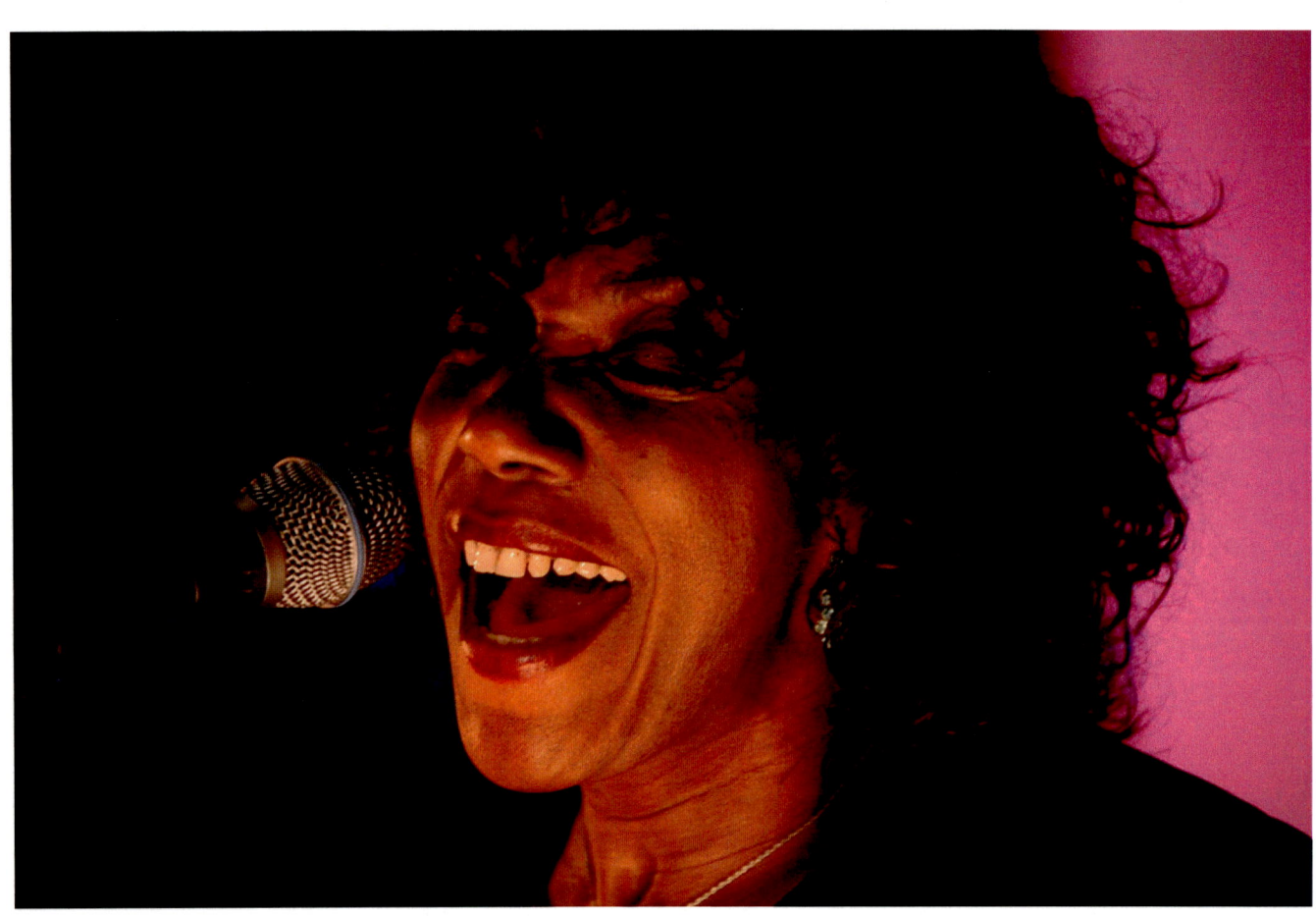

Carmen Lundy sings at a Friday evening music series produced by Walt Broadnax.

to feature some of my jazz photographs in an exhibit called "Homage to a Sound." My idea was to concentrate on local musicians and singers who were not often recognized for their talents. In addition to still photographs, I also shot video, because jazz is an audio art form. The video was used in a short film, also called "Homage to a Sound" (this is available on YouTube). I also did some interviews with a few of the musicians. It was more difficult than I had imagined getting them to talk on camera.

IN CLOSING

Those first few months after retiring were challenging. I sorely missed the daily interactions with colleagues and assignment subjects. Since I had quite a few books that had come to *The Post* library and had been gathering dust at our home, I decided to read a biography about Napoleon. It was boring, the pages filled with descriptions of gray cold weather, kind of like I was experiencing, so I retreated to the bedroom near a heat register and continued reading. Now this was a poor substitute for a day out and about covering the city with my Nikons.

I had developed an interest in gardening, but since it was winter, work outside was out of the question. I thought maybe I could volunteer at a plant nursery run by the city of Cincinnati, but no luck there. Jazz and storefront churches were weekend pursuits. What to do during the other five days? Eventually, I began spending my days pursuing a lifelong goal—getting my photography organized. (It remains a work in progress.) One of the joys of retirement is the right to say, "No, I'm retired" when asked to do something of no interest but say "Yes" to those activities of interest. I have often heard other retirees say how busy they are, and that has proven to be true for me as well.

In 2008, my first year of retirement, I very much wanted to volunteer in some capacity

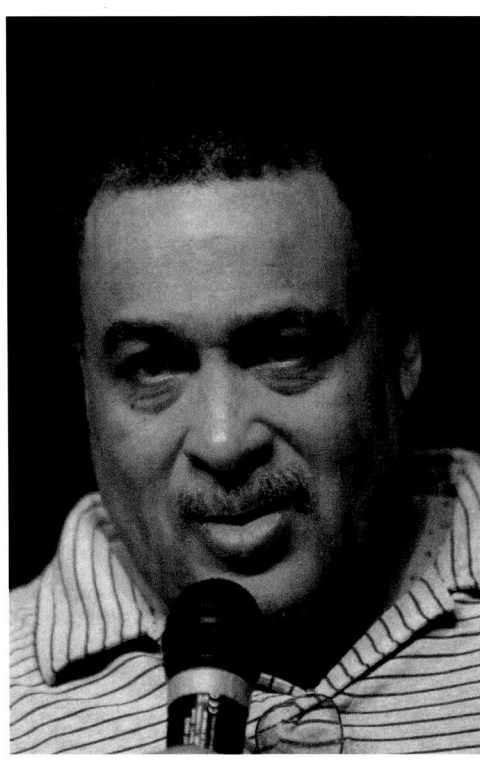

Walt Broadnax, known as Doc B, often started the concert by saying, "I know you didn't pay to hear me."

with Cincinnati Parks. I thought I could do some good for the public while learning about plants. I eventually became a member of the Cincinnati Parks Foundation. After a couple of meetings, I could tell I was out of my depth, because there were foundation members well-schooled and experienced in business and fundraising, qualities I sadly lacked. I hung in there to complete my term, but I was happy to move on.

In June 2014, I joined the FotoFocus board, which proved to be a better fit. FotoFocus was founded in 2010 and presents a biennial Cincinnati event featuring a wide range of photography at multiple venues. As someone who worked as a photojournalist, I had a particular interest in bringing reportage photos into the mix. This proved to be more difficult than I thought, since the FotoFocus board doesn't decide the main curatorial theme (that's up to Kevin Moore, artistic director and curator).

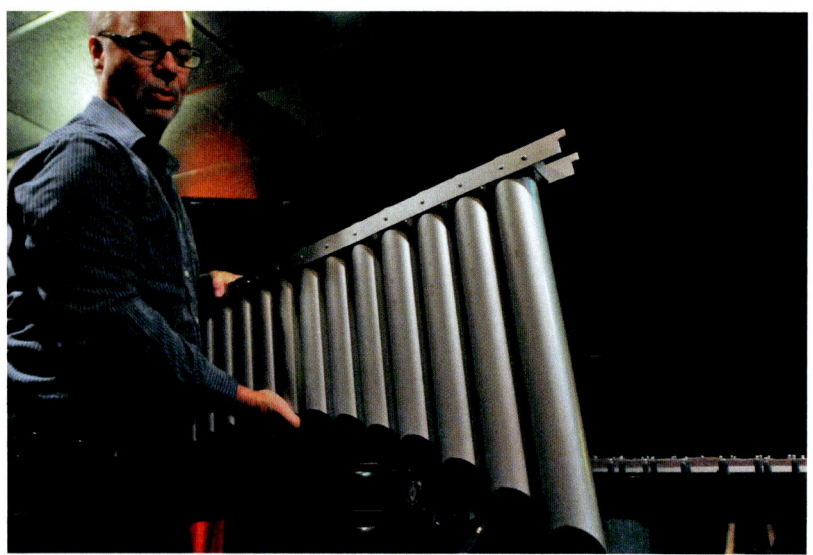

One of my objectives for "Homage to a Sound" was to include images that were atypical, such as Rusty Burge assembling his vibes.

I was concerned that local and regional photographers might lose their voice during the biennial, and I was not the only photographer with this concern. We sent the word out for a gathering at a downtown coffee house. A large group came. We had previously decided to have each photographer pick the name of an attending photographer out of a hat and that photographer would be their portrait subject. Thus, the "photographers by photographers" exhibit was born.

It was decided that local photographers would have to be proactive (after "photographers by photographers"), and five of us decided to form a committee called Local Eyes, which is still ongoing in Cincinnati. Now, once again, I was involved in photography.

However, if there has been one consistent disappointment, it has been the absence of African American photographers from news and art scenes, the exception being TV news videographers. It was encouraging to see that a recent exhibit at the KHAC in 2022 featured the work of two African Americans.

In 2018, I was pleased to be welcomed as a board trustee of the Cincinnati Memorial Hall Society. Memorial Hall is a 550-seat performance and event venue located in Over-the-Rhine. Built in 1908 as a memorial to war veterans, trustees are concerned with the preservation of the facility in matters of upkeep. Trustees also support the Longworth-Anderson series of concerts, which has introduced me to new music. I have also had some input to bring a little jazz into the programming.

For my 33 years of work for *The Post*, I wanted to leave something behind besides lamentations about the demise of print media. There had been a great deal of that in social-media posts from photojournalists and reporters. The reality was that the newspaper business I had loved was dead and no longer relevant. The first big change we saw was autofocus. When a freelancer showed us his film from an NFL game shot with an autofocus camera, most of the frames were tack sharp! By the end of my career, we were no longer making prints but just uploading images to a server. Some of the appeal of newspaper work was gone for me.

Even *The Cincinnati Enquirer* is but a shadow of its former self. The hoopla of the Pulitzer it won in 2018 was a great achievement, but its parent, Gannett, continues to reduce staff.

I participate in social media, i.e. Facebook, but I wanted a more-lasting legacy. Hence this memoir. I sometimes hear, "You ought to do a book," and have friends who have done beautiful coffee-table books, often sitting in boxes unsold. I wanted to do something different, just as I have my entire life.

I'm still pissed off about the demolition of the West End, and this memoir has given me a chance to highlight my roots in the West End and its destruction. It is a sad state of affairs when you have nothing remaining from your childhood. I have a neighbor who can drive through his old neighborhood and point out his childhood home and other landmarks. I can only point out what used to be.

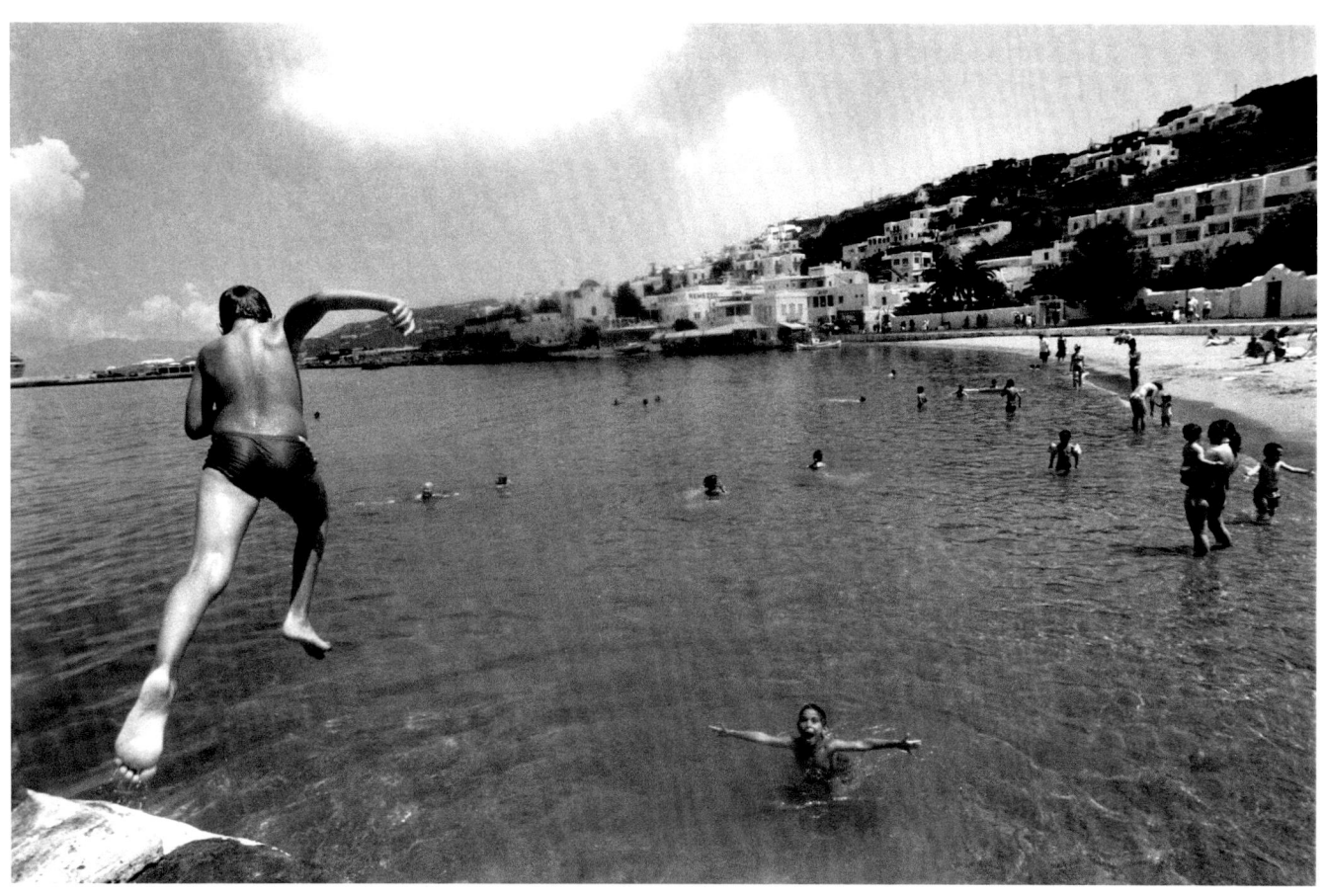

One of the joys of retirement is traveling. For our 40th anniversary, Brenda and I took a Mediterranean cruise, where I came across these swimmers in Mykonos, Greece.

This is the postcard announcing the "photographers by photographers" exhibit at Xavier University's main gallery.

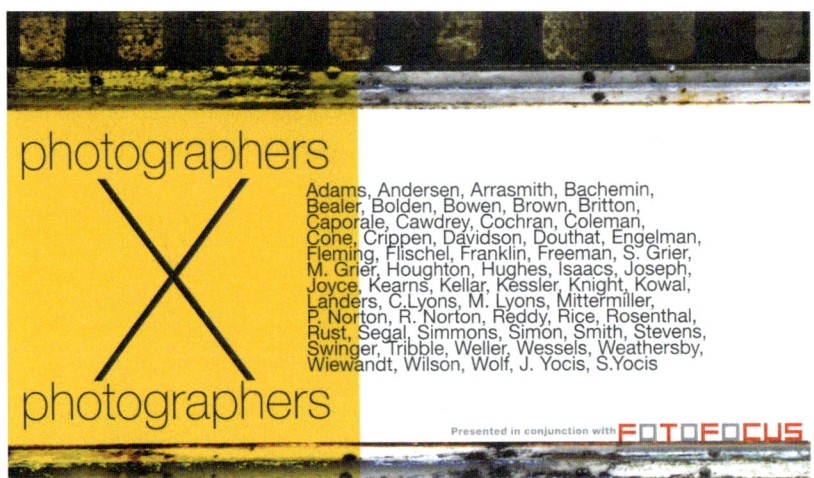

Frank Sinatra sang "September of My Years," and as I write this, that is where I find myself. From the realization of my dream, since I first stepped into 800 Broadway, I've had some very good years. I have every intention of continuing to make photographs and put together exhibits. By the time you read this, I'll probably be working on yet another project. I want to be like filmmaker Frederick Wiseman, who continues to create in his 90s.

After my first boss Jack Klumpe and I had both retired, I received a letter from him saying that ". . .it was a great day for *The Cincinnati Post* in 1974 when you came to work there. It was to your credit that you stayed till the bitter end, amassing thirty-three years on the job." I wrote back saying his hiring me made a huge difference in my life and my family's life.

My wife Brenda was more than supportive from the day she said it was OK to walk away from a perfectly well-paying job at Young and Klein lithographers to pursue a dream. First, she had to teach me to drive our new V.W. Super Beetle. In order to be available to our family, she started a house-cleaning business—Bucketts, Mopps and Raggs. Our son Miles came into our lives at age four months and at age 40 decided to leave and go his separate way. Our love for him is not diminished. Samantha, our daughter, has brought us joy from the day she was born. To my surprise, she chose to study photojournalism at Ohio University. She exhibited a special talent even before entering O.U. It's unfortunate that the failing newspaper business forced her to seek alternative employment. I was happy we got to work together on *The Post* photo staff for a year.

Bottom line: I gave *The Post* the best years of my life. *The Post* gave me the best years of my life.

POSTSCRIPT

MOLLY KAVANAUGH
Reporter for *The Cincinnati Post* 1982–1992

A week after arriving at *The Cincinnati Post*, I was assigned to interview the owner of Drew's Bookshop in Hyde Park. A man with an afro and a couple cameras hanging around his neck walked in after me. Figuring he must be *The Post* photographer, I introduced myself, then resumed talking with Drew Gores.

When I saw what I thought was the perfect spot to take a photograph of Drew, I motioned to the photographer with my index finger. He walked over, nodded, and ignored my suggestion.

Thus began my 44-year professional relationship and personal friendship with Mel Grier. (Disclaimer: He's known as Melvin Grier to the professional world, but he has always been Mel to me.)

First, let's set the record straight. Our manners are bad. Mel and I interrupt each other, raise our voices, and bulldoze our way through conversations to get the last word in. We make fun of each other and constantly share our opinions, mostly unsolicited. Mel likes to tell stories, and I like to ask questions, which means we never get to the end of our conversations.

During our reporting days, we both were dogged, and rarely cut corners. One more quote, one more photograph—we understood each other's quests. One of my interviews took seven hours, and since it was out of town, and we had driven together, Mel was stuck in the living room with me and a grieving mother. He fell asleep, and still complains to this day, but he has never questioned why I needed all that time. Yes, our manners are rotten, but our relationship is rich.

For a decade (1982–1992), we worked together at *The Post*. I was a features reporter, then I moved into news. Most often, reporters and photographers are randomly matched up for assignments depending on availability. When Mel and I discovered we shared a similar journalistic approach, we began to concoct assignments of mutual interest.

Like Parris Island, South Carolina. I am not from a military family and had no idea what boot camp was like but trusted that when Mel said following a group of local Marine recruits would be full of drama, as in good quotes and photos, it would be.

The U.S. Marine assigned to drive us to the base picked us up at the hotel around midnight. We arrived as the exhausted recruits were getting off the bus. The next 12 hours were a blur—drill sergeants yelling and cursing, boys holding back tears as their heads were shaved and their belongings were scattered. Throughout the mayhem, Mel and I would look at each other, shake our heads, and smile. This was journalism at its best.

Honduras was another trip we concocted. Mel had already been to El Salvador and Sudan, and, as he wrote in this memoir, was always looking for the local connection to take him overseas. We hooked up with a local U.S. Army reserve unit that was helping to build a road through mountainous terrain, spent a week living out of tents and shuttling to assignments via helicopter.

In 1987, the Post sent Molly and Melvin to Honduras.

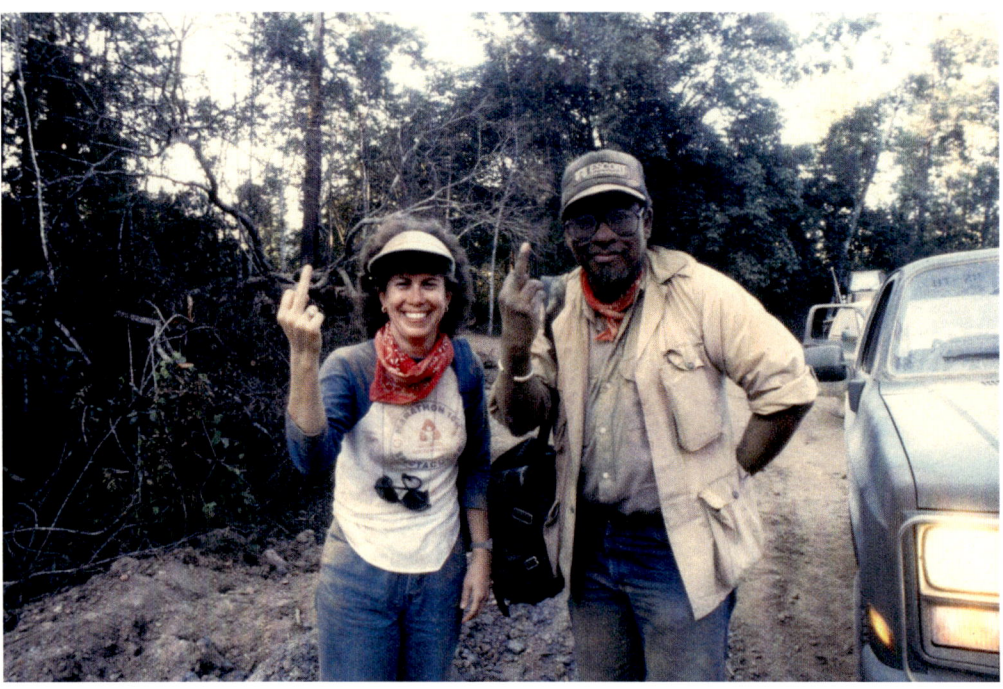

Speaking of which, did I mention that Mel is a prankster? I told him about my fear of flying, especially in helicopters, *especially* in ones with passenger doors removed. We were flying back from a mountaintop village with a group of locals, and the crew assigned our seats. Mel was directed to a seat behind the copilot, I was strapped into a seat on the side facing out, doorless. As we careened down the mountain, the pilot banked the chopper, so my side was parallel to the ground. When I opened my eyes, I turned around to look for Mel and saw him and the crew pointing at me laughing. Back home, when we were assigned to cover flooding along the Ohio River marinas, I made sure everyone knew that Mel couldn't swim and was afraid of falling in.

We also came up with local concoctions. I was a cop reporter for a spell and suggested we spend a 12-hour shift at Cincinnati Fire Department - Station 5 in Over-the-Rhine, then one of the busiest fire stations in the country. Often, when reporters show up to cover the predictable, the opposite happens, which was the case the night Mel and I spent at Station 5. But even non-eventful, boring assignments with Mel were fodder for laughter and storytelling, like a certain firefighter who was always rushing to the station phone (this was pre-cell phone) to get the latest sports results.

Another yawn was the outdoor R.V. show in Lexington. Rumor had it that the managing editor was shopping for an R.V. and decided—on the hottest day of the summer—that *The Post* needed to send a photographer (Mel) and a reporter (me) to get the scoop on the R.V. market. Sweat dripping down our faces, Mel and I could barely keep a straight face as we toured R.V. after R.V.

In 1989, Scripps Howard, which owned *The Post*, provided financial support for a new communication-professions high school housed at Hughes High School in Clifton. Mel and I approached Bill Burleigh, former *Post* editor, then a top executive at Scripps, about working at Hughes. He agreed to loan us to the high school part-time for six months. Same thing. While interacting with high-school students was not as dynamic as we had imagined, we often left the school laughing about some absurdity of the school day—each clock had a different time, more tater tots for lunch, the stairwell once again smelled of pot.

Our friendship also grew. Mel was happily married to Brenda and grew tired of hearing sob stories about my boyfriends, often over a beer at a hole-in-the-wall bar called Ogden's Place. One day, Mel invited me to tag along for a baseball game he was shooting, hang out on the sidelines with other media types, and eat free food. He introduced me to another single journalist, Frank Wiewandt, a videographer at Channel 12.

Frank and I did not start dating immediately, but when we did, I kept it a secret for a while from Mel, who prides himself about always being in the know. We were married in 1986, on June 21, which, unbeknownst to me when we set the date, was also Mel and Brenda's anniversary.

Three years later, I was pregnant and waited for Mel to figure it out. On the drive to Georgia to cover a Civil War reenactment, I munched on saltine crackers and sipped water waiting for Mel to ask why. At dinner, when I didn't order my usual Dewar's and water, I admonished him, "What kind of journalist are you? I can't believe you didn't figure it out."

Mel introduced me to jazz, and to this day, whenever I listen to Miles Davis's "Kind of Blue," I think of him. My love is poetry, and while Mel knew about poet Langston Hughes, my favorite Hughes poem "Dreams," which begins with the line "Hold fast to dreams . . ." is now also his.

Like Mel, I was born and raised in Cincinnati, but unlike Mel, I was eager to move away as soon as I could. In 1974, I graduated from Ohio University with a journalism degree. After fits and starts, my first real newspaper job was in Syracuse, and after winning a couple of awards, I figured I was ready for the big time. I moved to Boston, my dream destination, but the area was overflowing with much more qualified reporters, and I turned my sights homeward.

When I arrived at *The Post* in 1982, afternoon papers were struggling, and *The Post*'s lifeline with *The Enquirer* was set to expire in 2007. But our newsroom was robust, competitive, and full of many young, talented reporters and photographers eager to make their marks, and move on. (After I won my first award a year or so after I arrived at *The Post,* I excitedly shared the news with Mel, who replied, "What took you so long?") Farewell parties were frequent, and I had mine 10 years later, when I headed north to Cleveland to *The Plain Dealer* with Frank and our three-year-old son Cody in tow.

I often badgered Mel that he should seek employment with a newspaper in a bigger market, i.e., one with more readers and money, but he insisted "it was about the work," which he could do quite respectably in Cincinnati. End of conversation.

Mel and I continued to stay in touch, but our lives—professionally and personally—were busy, and my visits home were sporadic. I turned to emails as an easy way to correspond, but Mel complained, saying he preferred a handwritten letter "because your handwriting is so damn hard to decipher that it takes me all week to read it, which I like."

In the aftermath of the 2001 riots in Cincinnati, *The Enquirer* urged readers to get involved in its neighbor-to-neighbor initiative to bring white and Black residents together. Mel knew about my mother Jeanne, who lived in Anderson Township and was always calling *The Post* with "news tips" (on occasion, Mel was assigned to track down her news tip, begrudgingly, I might add).

Jeanne decided to start a neighbor-to-neighbor group and asked Mel and Brenda to participate. Mel moaned that he wasn't interested but became an avid—dare I say robust?—attendee. Friendships grew, which was the whole idea for the initiative. My mom and her friends would show up at Mel's exhibits, and they'd all go out for dinner. "The posse," Mel called this group of white-haired women.

In 2019, when Frank and I retired and decided to move back to Cincinnati, Mel told me about his desire to write a memoir. My response was, "You like to tell stories, and I like to ask questions. How about we work together?"

And here we are, Mel and I, 40 years and counting, still concocting . . .

UNFINISHED LIVES

KATHY Y. WILSON

Author of *Your Negro Tour Guide*

Reprinted with permission from *Cincinnati Magazine* May 2008

Melvin Grier lives in Avondale with his wife, Brenda, and from the back of their house he can almost see the stop on Forest Avenue where 48-year-old Angela Grayson caught the bus that took her to her job at Drake Hospital. She was waiting there at 11:20 a.m. on Tuesday, April 24, 2006, when 19-year-old Bryant Keese pulled up and, taking shoddy aim at his intended target standing nearby, shot Grayson instead.

Grayson died, a victim of random street violence. The public shrine to her accidental death remains today, one of numerous flower-strewn utility poles and teddy bear-laden patches of concrete throughout town. You've seen them, even if you puzzled at them, these tributes to the victims of gun violence and drunk drivers. Gaudy, garish, disintegrating monuments to lives snuffed out, they spring up like self-help street therapy assembled by friends, family, sometimes even witnesses to the tragedies who feel the need to do something immediately to remember the dead.

In early February, Grayson's memorial was marked with a semicircle of white plastic edging, the kind you see in tiny, neat front yards. Behind it were strewn pink and purple plastic flowers. One lone filthy stuffed bear was hunched in the lowest branch of a nearby barren tree; depleted i-wireless phone cards were scattered about among beer bottles, cigarette butts, and a purple rubber glove.

For Grier, the grizzled, 66-year-old veteran photojournalist who put in 34 years at *The Cincinnati Post* before it folded, public memorials like Grayson's are discordant visual poetry—heartbreaking works he knows so well he can recite the genealogy of a memorial from its inception to the day it, like the victim it was made to honor, disappears. "I think people initially have some need to show some expression of their grief," Grier explains in a growling voice that makes him sound more gruff than he is. "And they have a need to recognize that person that's nontraditional, so they tend to do it right where it happened."

Grier cares. He is connected. He sees. So he takes pictures of the memorials. He's been shooting them and compiling the details behind them—day and time of the crime, reasons behind the flash of violence, whether an arrest has been made—since 2003. He's working on a project he calls "Unfinished Lives," which includes videotaped interviews with survivors of violence. Grier intends to turn it into a gallery-caliber, multimedia exhibition. It will be a place where survivors and victims' families can connect, and where casual viewers can see the high price of violence.

On an unseasonably warm early February day, he picks me up in his Subaru to tour some of the spots he's immortalized. We're looking to see how well they've survived the winter.

Together we try to make sense of these public memorials and how they reflect the neighborhoods in which they spring up. It is an exercise in cultural anthropology.

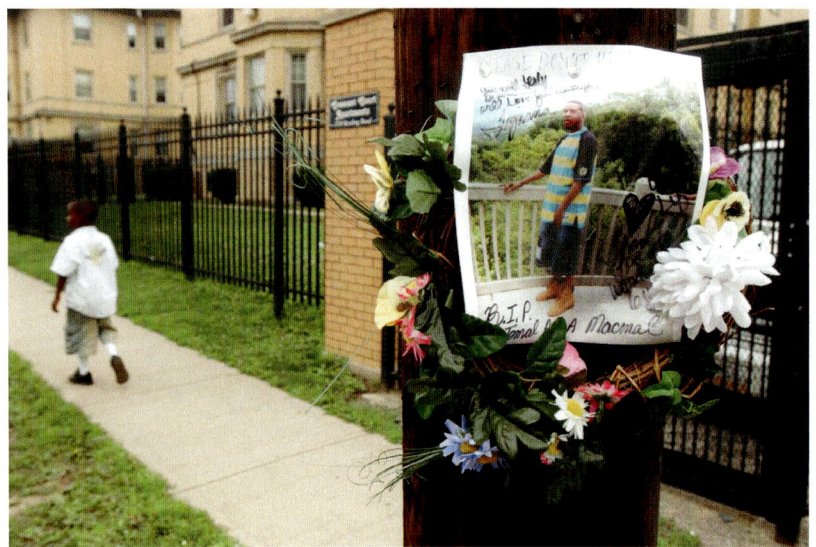

Memorial for a deceased gunshot victim on Reading Road in South Avondale.

Such missions need a soundtrack. We ease north through Vine Street traffic, to the new playground on Findlay Street in Over-the-Rhine, to check the memorial to a woman named Teresa Renee Hill. As we do, Jill Scott's booming contralto comes through Grier's speakers. "Tell me how you feel if I was, if I was gone? Tell me how you feel?" Scott sings. "What if I was gone forever? No more chocolate kisses, no mama, no daughter, no sister, no sister/friend. Tell me my brotha, what would become of you then?"

Considering our mission, the song's timing is ironic, its lyrics chilling. On June 11, 2005, Hill was shot by Jason Baker—who was aiming at someone else—while she sat in the playground with her mother, cousin, and various children. Baker, 28, pleaded guilty and got a life sentence. Like Angela Grayson, Hill was an accidental victim. Collateral damage in Baker's war with other people.

As we turn onto Findlay Street, Jill Scott fades into another song and Grier and I both crane to see the memorial he photographed less than one month after the fatal shooting—a bulge of plush bears, flowers, spent candles and large handwritten signs affixed to the fence. It is gone.

"The hardest thing about this is, when I shoot it, sometimes I don't know what it was about," Grier says, "There might be a name on [the memorial] but it might be their street name." A veteran journalist, Grier searches newspaper databases with the dates to pinpoint news accounts of the deaths. This helps him build a narrative. From there, he goes to the Cincinnati police for copies of homicide keybooks, which list the date, time, victim's vitals, incident location, suspect's vitals, and weapons used. "The upside of digital [camera-work] is it puts a date and a time [on the photograph] when you shot it and I can put two and two together," he says. Through his own research, Grier is able to fill in the blanks of who and what the memorials eulogize.

But two things still puzzle Grier, a former Air Force medic and the father of two adult children. He needs to put order to the senselessness of such acts. "Out of all the solutions," he asks, "why do you have to kill 'em?" He does not expect or wait for an answer because he knows there is none. The other thing nagging at Grier is the origin of public memorials themselves. "I wanna know when was the first time it was done. And who did it?"

Maybe these final frames will help the ones who come after us answer Grier's questions. Until then, his work will at least help us to remember these unfinished lives. The sad thing is, as long as there is violent death, he will always have work to do.

ACKNOWLEDGMENTS

John Fox at *Cincinnati Magazine* for permission to publish "Unfinished Lives" and Kathy Y. Wilson for writing it

Steve Marine for connecting me with University of Cincinnati Press

Frank Wiewandt for helping with his photo-tech expertise

Samantha Grier for shooting the authors' portrait

University of Cincinnati Press for publishing my memories

Randy Cochran for helping my creative side to take flight

Arabeth Balasko for permission to use photographs from the Cincinnati Museum Center

DONORS

A special thanks to our donors for making this publication possible:

    Kate and Bill Baumann

    Randle and Cristina Egbert

    George & Margaret McLane Foundation

    Thomas R. Schiff

Melvin and Molly thank you for your purchase of this book. Part of the proceeds will be donated to The Melvin and Brenda T. Grier Urologic Cancer Research Fund. Community support in the form of donations can be directed to the University of Cincinnati Foundation. For more information and to contact the foundation, go to foundation.uc.edu.

IMAGE LOG

Anything not noted is personal imagery provided courtesy of the author, Melvin Grier.

Page 3. "*Tremont*;" SC#115 Kenyon-Barr Collection; Provided courtesy of the Cincinnati Museum Center.

Page 4. "*Jackson School*;" SC#115 Kenyon-Barr Collection; Provided courtesy of the Cincinnati Museum Center.

Page 5. "*Cotton Club*;" SC#115 Kenyon-Barr Collection; Provided courtesy of the Cincinnati Museum Center.

Page 6. "*Cotton Club*;" SC#115 Kenyon-Barr Collection; Provided courtesy of the Cincinnati Museum Center.

Page 7. "*Holy Trinity School*;" SC#115 Kenyon-Barr Collection; Provided courtesy of the Cincinnati Museum Center.

Page 8. "*Holy Trinity Church*;" SC#115 Kenyon-Barr Collection; Provided courtesy of the Cincinnati Museum Center.

Page 12. "*DePorres High School*;" SC#115 Kenyon-Barr Collection; Provided courtesy of the Cincinnati Museum Center.

Page 19. Provided courtesy of the Cincinnati Enquirer.

Page 19. Provided courtesy of the Cincinnati Enquirer.

Page 25. "*Guy Painting*;" The Cincinnati Post Collection – Photograph by Melvin Grier; Provided courtesy of the Cincinnati Museum Center.

Page 26. "*One by One*;" The Cincinnati Post Collection – Photograph by Melvin Grier; Provided courtesy of the Cincinnati Museum Center.

Page 27. "*Man Detained*;" The Cincinnati Post Collection – Photograph by Melvin Grier; Provided courtesy of the Cincinnati Museum Center.

Page 28. "*Body Removed, 1975*;" The Cincinnati Post Collection – Photograph by Melvin Grier; Provided courtesy of the Cincinnati Museum Center.

Page 29. "*Ruppert to Court, 1975*;" The Cincinnati Post Collection – Photograph by Melvin Grier; Provided courtesy of the Cincinnati Museum Center.

Page 30. "*Frosty Horses*;" The Cincinnati Post Collection – Photograph by Melvin Grier; Provided courtesy of the Cincinnati Museum Center

Page 31. "*Coverup in Rain*;" The Cincinnati Post Collection – Photograph by Melvin Grier; Provided courtesy of the Cincinnati Museum Center.

Page 32. "*Dater Pool*;" The Cincinnati Post Collection – Photograph by Melvin Grier; Provided courtesy of the Cincinnati Museum Center.

Page 33. "*Norwood Crash*;" The Cincinnati Post Collection – Photograph by Melvin Grier; Provided courtesy of the Cincinnati Museum Center.

Page 34. "*Jymi*;" The Cincinnati Post Collection – Photograph by Melvin Grier; Provided courtesy of the Cincinnati Museum Center.

Page 35. "*Parris Island #1*;" The Cincinnati Post Collection – Photograph by Melvin Grier; Provided courtesy of the Cincinnati Museum Center.

Page 35. "*Parris Island #2*;" The Cincinnati Post Collection – Photograph by Melvin Grier; Provided courtesy of the Cincinnati Museum Center.

Page 36. "*Parris Island #3*;" The Cincinnati Post Collection – Photograph by Melvin Grier; Provided courtesy of the Cincinnati Museum Center.

Page 37. "*Laurel Homes Garden*;" The Cincinnati Post Collection – Photograph by Melvin Grier; Provided courtesy of the Cincinnati Museum Center.

Page 38. "*Horses with Tractor*;" The Cincinnati Post Collection – Photograph by Melvin Grier; Provided courtesy of the Cincinnati Museum Center.

Page 39. "*L'Burg Barrels*;" The Cincinnati Post Collection – Photograph by Melvin Grier; Provided courtesy of the Cincinnati Museum Center.

Page 40. "*Rescue*;" The Cincinnati Post Collection – Photograph by Melvin Grier; Provided courtesy of the Cincinnati Museum Center.

Page 41. "*Dunaway*;" The Cincinnati Post Collection – Photograph by Melvin Grier; Provided courtesy of the Cincinnati Museum Center.

Page 43. "*Cop Stop*;" The Cincinnati Post Collection – Photograph by Melvin Grier; Provided courtesy of the Cincinnati Museum Center.

Page 45, frontispiece, back cover. "*Welcome Home;*" The Cincinnati Post Collection – Photograph by Melvin Grier; Provided courtesy of the Cincinnati Museum Center.

Page 48. "*Man in Tree;*" The Cincinnati Post Collection – Photograph by Melvin Grier; Provided courtesy of the Cincinnati Museum Center.

Page 49. "*Commute;*" The Cincinnati Post Collection – Photograph by Melvin Grier; Provided courtesy of the Cincinnati Museum Center.

Page 50, spine. "*Port Sudan;*" The Cincinnati Post Collection – Photograph by Melvin Grier; Provided courtesy of the Cincinnati Museum Center.

Page 51. "*Bodyguard;*" The Cincinnati Post Collection – Photograph by Melvin Grier; Provided courtesy of the Cincinnati Museum Center.

Page 52. "*Saved;*" The Cincinnati Post Collection – Photograph by Melvin Grier; Provided courtesy of the Cincinnati Museum Center.

Page 53. "*Eritrean Washerwomen;*" The Cincinnati Post Collection – Photograph by Melvin Grier; Provided courtesy of the Cincinnati Museum Center.

Page 54. "*Cheetah Fashion;*" The Cincinnati Post Collection – Photograph by Melvin Grier; Provided courtesy of the Cincinnati Museum Center.

Page 55, frontispiece, back cover. "*Clothes Encounter;*" The Cincinnati Post Collection – Photograph by Melvin Grier; Provided courtesy of the Cincinnati Museum Center.

Page 56. "*Culottes;*" The Cincinnati Post Collection – Photograph by Melvin Grier; Provided courtesy of the Cincinnati Museum Center.

Page 58. "*Plaid;*" The Cincinnati Post Collection – Photograph by Melvin Grier; Provided courtesy of the Cincinnati Museum Center.

Page 59. "*Browns in Fur;*" The Cincinnati Post Collection – Photograph by Melvin Grier; Provided courtesy of the Cincinnati Museum Center.

Page 60. "*Pete Rose Press Conference;*" The Cincinnati Post Collection – Photograph by Melvin Grier; Provided courtesy of the Cincinnati Museum Center.

Page 61. "*Headset Toss;*" The Cincinnati Post Collection – Photograph by Melvin Grier; Provided courtesy of the Cincinnati Museum Center.

Page 61. "*Super Bowl XVI;*" The Cincinnati Post Collection – Photograph by Melvin Grier; Provided courtesy of the Cincinnati Museum Center.

Page 62. "*Marge With Schottzie;*" The Cincinnati Post Collection – Photograph by Melvin Grier; Provided courtesy of the Cincinnati Museum Center.

Page 62. "*Connors;*" The Cincinnati Post Collection – Photograph by Melvin Grier; Provided courtesy of the Cincinnati Museum Center.

Page 62. "*Tony Perez;*" The Cincinnati Post Collection – Photograph by Melvin Grier; Provided courtesy of the Cincinnati Museum Center.

Page 63. "*Griffey Jr.;*" The Cincinnati Post Collection – Photograph by Melvin Grier; Provided courtesy of the Cincinnati Museum Center.

Page 65, frontispiece, back cover. "*Lomax;*" The Cincinnati Post Collection – Photograph by Melvin Grier; Provided courtesy of the Cincinnati Museum Center.

Page 66. "*Ninja;*" The Cincinnati Post Collection – Photograph by Melvin Grier; Provided courtesy of the Cincinnati Museum Center.

Page 69. "*Gardener Resting;*" The Cincinnati Post Collection – Photograph by Melvin Grier; Provided courtesy of the Cincinnati Museum Center.

Page 71. "*Feeding Station;*" The Cincinnati Post Collection – Photograph by Melvin Grier; Provided courtesy of the Cincinnati Museum Center.

Page 77. "*Virginia Dancing;*" The Cincinnati Post Collection – Photograph by Melvin Grier; Provided courtesy of the Cincinnati Museum Center.

Page 78. "*Yankee Doodle Donkey;*" The Cincinnati Post Collection – Photograph by Melvin Grier; Provided courtesy of the Cincinnati Museum Center.

Page 79. "*Couple in Over-the-Rhine;*" The Cincinnati Post Collection – Photograph by Melvin Grier; Provided courtesy of the Cincinnati Museum Center.

Page 80. "*Snake;*" The Cincinnati Post Collection – Photograph by Melvin Grier; Provided courtesy of the Cincinnati Museum Center.

Page 81. "*Rosary;*" The Cincinnati Post Collection – Photograph by Melvin Grier; Provided courtesy of the Cincinnati Museum Center.

Page 94. "*Reading Road Memorial;*" The Cincinnati Post Collection – Photograph by Melvin Grier; Provided courtesy of the Cincinnati Museum Center.

Dust jacket. Authors photograph by Samantha Grier.